Clear, engaging, well crafted. And
book is going to be life changing fc

Bob Lepine
Cohost, FamilyLife Today

It was the Greeks who said great communicators embodied logos (content),
ethos (ethics or integrity), and pathos (passion). Well, if that be the case,
then Robert Wolgemuth has checked all three boxes in this much-needed
volume, *Lies Men Believe*. I found my heart greatly stirred as I read these in-
spiring words all from a man who has built a lifetime walking with Jesus
and living in authentic manhood. You will be a better man after drinking in
these words.

Bryan Loritts
Lead Pastor, Abundant Life
Author of *Insider, Outsider*

It took a long time and some unexpected circumstances for there to be a
companion volume to *Lies Women Believe*, but in God's good and mysterious
providence it is here at last. I'm thankful for Robert's efforts in writing a
book that so wonderfully complements Nancy's. This book will prove to be
both a challenge and a blessing to you.

Tim Challies
Blogger

When presented with the opportunity, I didn't immediately read Robert's
manuscript. Not seeing myself as a "lie believer," I felt no urgency. Now, I
stand corrected—and grateful! Those of us who know Robert regard him
as accomplished, gifted, and wise. He's ready for anything and gracious in
everything. As you will discover in this volume, he's also candid in exploring
the challenges men face. Learning from him was like a workout for the soul,
leaving me convicted and inspired. There were moments when I flushed with
emotion, and others that left me galvanized with resolve. *Lies Men Believe* is
personally relevant to every man and will prompt you to do business with
God—as I did. I highly recommend it.

Paul Santhouse
Publisher, Moody Publishers

The most dangerous lies are always the most alluring. They come to us in the guise of the good, the delightful, and the wise (Gen. 3:6). Thankfully, in this insightful and practical book, Robert Wolgemuth not only unmasks those lies, he teaches us how to recognize them for what they are. If only I'd had this book forty years ago!

George Grant
Pastor of Parish Presbyterian Church

Even though the most prominent word on the cover of this book is "Lies," I know from experience that the most important word can be found in the subtitle. It's "Truth." This is a book about truth . . . the power of truth. Truth that sets a man free. And this truth can be found in the absolute reliability of God's Word, the Bible.

Patrick Morley
Bestselling author and founder, *Man in the Mirror*

For many years, I have had the privilege of preaching the gospel . . . the good news of Jesus Christ who is, Himself, the Truth. This book, *Lies Men Believe*, identifies some of the awful things Satan whispers in our ears . . . lies that are shattered because of freedom that God's grace and His truth provide. I'm thankful to Robert Wolgemuth for putting this in writing and I enthusiastically recommend this book to you.

Jack Graham
Host of PowerPoint, author, and pastor, Prestonwood Baptist Church

You'll find that reading *Lies Men Believe*, with its warm, relatable style, is like having a conversation with a good friend. Be prepared, in the process, to grapple with some tough issues. And be prepared to experience the liberating power of the Truth—in your own life, and in the lives of those you influence.

Nancy DeMoss Wolgemuth
Revive Our Hearts teacher and host
Lies books series editor

LIES MEN BELIEVE

BELIEVE

AND THE TRUTH THAT SETS THEM FREE

ROBERT WOLGEMUTH

MOODY PUBLISHERS

CHICAGO

Some details have been changed to protect the privacy of individuals.

Published in association with the literary agency of Wolgemuth & Associates.

Edited by Connor Sterchi
Author Photo: Katie Bollinger Photography
Interior design: Puckett Smartt
Cover design: Erik M. Peterson
Front cover photo of apple with bite copyright © 2014 by eli_asenova/iStock (475190475). All rights reserved.

Library of Congress Cataloging-in-Publication Data

Names: Wolgemuth, Robert D., author.
Title: Lies men believe : and the truth that sets them free / Robert
  Wolgemuth.
Description: Chicago : Moody Publishers, 2018. | Includes bibliographical
  references.
Identifiers: LCCN 2018025691 (print) | LCCN 2018032641 (ebook) | ISBN
  9780802495082 (ebook) | ISBN 9780802414892
Subjects: LCSH: Christian men--Religious life. | Truthfulness and
  falsehood--Religious aspects--Christianity.
Classification: LCC BV4528.2 (ebook) | LCC BV4528.2 .W65 2018 (print) | DDC
  248.8/42--dc23
LC record available at https://lccn.loc.gov/2018025691

Paperback Edition ISBN: 978-0-8024-2532-4

We hope you enjoy this book from Moody Publishers. Our goal is to provide high-quality, thought-provoking books and products that connect truth to your real needs and challenges. For more information on other books and products written and produced from a biblical perspective, go to www.moodypublishers.com or write to:

Moody Publishers
820 N. LaSalle Boulevard
Chicago, IL 60610

1 3 5 7 9 10 8 6 4 2

Printed in the United States of America

TO DAVID SWANSON

D
r. David Swanson was my pastor for over twelve years. In 2003, I had the joy of chairing the pastor nominating committee that invited David, along with his wife, Leigh, and their three kids, J. D., Alex, and Kaylee, to come to our Orlando church. They said yes.

In 2015, I married Nancy Leigh DeMoss and moved from Florida to Michigan. Lots of adjustments to be sure, but the most challenging was saying goodbye to David. Yes, he was my pastor and a brilliant and passionate expositor of God's Word. Yes, he faithfully and courageously led the flock that was the congregation of that church.

But what I appreciated most about David was his willingness to be my friend, to come alongside—he called himself my "wingman"—during my late wife's valiant battle with Stage IV ovarian cancer. David was available 24/7—literally—as I dealt with the challenges of facing my wife's imminent death, the exhaustion of being her primary caregiver (a task I was privileged to assume), then releasing Bobbie, who stepped into heaven after almost forty-five years of marriage and thirty months of a valiant battle.

This is a book about truth. David is a truth-teller. Time and again he proved this standing in the pulpit or across from cups of steaming coffee. He proved this when truth was what needed to be said whether convenient or not. I love this about him.

So my deepest gratitude goes to David Swanson . . . pastor, precious brother, confidant, and, yes, wingman.

This book is dedicated to him.

CONTENTS

SECTION THREE: **WALKING IN TRUTH**

FOREWORD

When Robert Wolgemuth asked me to write the foreword for *Lies Men Believe* it was, for me, a foregone conclusion. I said "yes."

Decades ago, Robert's (then) publishing company gave me a start, when I had never written a book. They took a chance on publishing *The Man in the Mirror*, which has sold four million copies to date. I will be eternally grateful for Robert's confidence in me. If it weren't for him, I would still be developing real estate and building buildings for which, let's be honest, nobody really wants to pay fair market value!

So since the late '80s, Robert and I have been friends. We've had the joy of watching each other grow and mature in our love for Christ. He is a man of 100 percent integrity, complete humility, and has as much emotional and social intelligence as any man I've ever known. He's the real deal. If I were you, the reader of this book, I would want to know that about the author.

But after combing through the manuscript, there's another and, for you, much more important and relevant reason. It's a really, really good read.

If there ever was such a thing as a "shortcut" to the wisdom of the ages, it's this book. Here is the kind of wisdom that can only be earned over a lifetime of trial and error, trial and error, and, finally, trial and success. I doubt there are ten men on the planet who could have written such a book.

So, not only do I have the honor of enthusiastically endorsing this book, but to vouch for Robert as well. It would take more space than space here affords me, but suffice it to say, I have enormous respect for this man. He has been an adviser, encourager, prayer partner, colleague, and mentor to me for over thirty years.

Second, this book deals with a subject for which I have given my life and ministry. Even though the most *prominent* word on the cover is "Lies," I know from experience that the most *important* word can be found in the subtitle. It's "Truth." This is a book about truth . . . the power of truth. Truth that sets a man free. And this truth can be found in the absolute reliability of God's Word, the Bible.

As I mentioned, I trafficked in commercial real estate for many years. Many times I found myself haggling deal points having to do with a property I was buying or selling. Often these negotiations ended in a handshake and then were forever consummated by a contract. A written agreement that literally dotted all the "i's" and crossed every "t." This piece of paper, including executing signatures, sealed the deal.

The Bible is the written and sealed agreement between a sovereign God and me. And you. It's eminently reliable and trustworthy. *Lies Men Believe* is a book that lifts high the veracity of God's Word.

Years ago, in the first few pages of *The Man in the Mirror*, I wrote:

This dichotomy between God's order and the order of this world produces a strain on the Christian man trying to sort out his thinking. Are there absolutes? Do biblical principles really address the [twenty-first]-century, day-to-day problems we men have? Is it possible for us to sort through our problems and build a workable model for us to live by?

If I may answer the question I posed when I wrote these words, "Yes, biblical principles found in God's Word *do* address our problems." And I know this, not only a Christian author or a seminary graduate who you'd expect to speak this way, but also from personal experience as a businessman, husband, and father who has faced life in the crucible of trouble and pain, and emerged thoroughly convinced that God's Word is truth.

Again, in my first book, I wrote:

Biblical Christians don't live by their own ideas, but by penetrating, understanding, and applying the Word of God.

The book you now hold in your hand unpacks that clear understanding of what it means to absorb and apply the Bible's truth in the relentless hearing of Satan's whispers. His lies.

A year and a half before its publication, when Robert first identified the forty lies he was going to address in *Lies Men Believe*, he sent them to me for my review. Here's how I responded: "You are approved for takeoff on any runway you choose. Seriously, as I suspected, you most certainly don't need any help. This looks awesome. Love you buddy, Pat."

So the list of "lies" was finalized, the associated "truths" from God's Word were crafted and completed, and now the book is finished. This book. The lies and their companion explanations have been fleshed out.

And with this foreword, I have been given the chance to give the propeller a spin and send this wonderful news on its way. I'm so glad you have chosen to get on board. You will not regret it.

God bless you on this journey.

PATRICK MORLEY, PHD
Orlando, Florida
September 2018

INTRODUCTION

"Liar, liar, pants on fire!"

W hen I was a young boy, I sometimes heard this incendiary rhyme in the neighborhood or at school. Kids would taunt each other on the playground, attempting to reduce their enemy to tears.

Of course, the image of someone with his pants engulfed in flames is somewhat humorous. (Unless, of course, that someone is you.)

It seems that a young country boy was enamored with his father's cigar humidor. Even though he had been ordered to never go near the thing, one day while his father was in another part of the house, the lad undid the latch and seized a single stogie from his old man's collection.

There was a toolshed on the edge of their property and the boy headed out to the small structure to do what he had seen his father do so many times. With the strike of a wooden match, the lad started puffing away, thankfully not daring to actually suck the blue smoke deep into his lungs. Or he'd still be coughing.

Wondering, as parents do, what his son might be up to, the father called out to his boy. Receiving no response, the father strode to the lean-to, continuing to call out to his young offspring. Hearing his father's steps, the boy quickly tried to snuff out the cigar, shoving it into the back pocket of his jeans.

Of course, the smoke seeped through his britches and caught the attention of his father. Or maybe it was the terror on the boy's face that his father noticed as the lit cigar began to make a searing impression on his derriere.

In any case, the boy was found out. His deception turned to ashes. Literally.

NO HARMLESS LIES

In her bestselling book *Lies Women Believe*, my wife, Nancy, wrote:

"There are no harmless lies."[1]

Although her book was intended for women, this statement is not gender specific. It's true for everyone and it's the reason why I agreed to write this book as a sequel to Nancy's. This one is for men. For me. For you.

Really? Seriously? Isn't it interesting how frequently we hear or speak these words? Perhaps after someone says something outrageous or doubtful.

> Lying in every shape and form and size has consequences. And this is not a new concept. It's been around for a long time.

But these words would be completely unnecessary if everyone only spoke truth. Every time. All the time.

Lies come in many shapes and sizes. "Little" ones could include the way we answer a policeman who has just pulled us over for *allegedly* speeding. "No, sir, I had no idea I was going faster than the speed limit."

Or they could be whoppers like lying about an affair.

But lying in every shape and form and size has consequences. And this is not a new concept. It's been around for a long time.

It will likely come as no surprise to you that the backbone and foundation of this book is the Bible. You will find biblical accounts and insights included from front to back. The Bible tells us about lies men believed long ago—lies men still believe today. We will do our best to identify some of those lies, address them, and take them out.

WHAT ARE SOME OF THE FIRST LIES FOUND IN THE BIBLE?

Which lies spoken of in the Holy Scripture are the most egregious? The most damaging for those who believe them?

Here's one for starters:

> "You will not surely die. For God knows that when you eat of it your eyes will be opened, and you will be like God." (Gen. 3:4–5)

This was the lie that began the downward spiral of sin and death. These words were spoken by Satan, appearing to Adam and Eve, disguised as a serpent.

History's first couple was situated in a sin-free setting: the garden of Eden. And this place of perfection included a "no" directed to the man.

> The LORD God commanded the man, saying, "You may surely eat of every tree of the garden, but of the tree of the knowledge of good and evil you shall not eat, for in the day that you eat of it you shall surely die." (Gen. 2:16–17)

It was as though the Lord was saying to Adam, "This place is yours. Enjoy all of it . . . except for that tree over there. It's lovely to look at and its fruit is tasty, but stay away from it. If you disobey Me, it will be the end of you."

The first heinous lie is that we have the capacity to be like God.

And here's another one:

> Then they said, "Come, let us build ourselves a city and a tower with its top in the heavens, and let us make a name for ourselves." (Gen. 11:4)

From the first time I poured concrete into a foundation, I've been infected by the construction bug. The small company I started working for at age seventeen had just begun the process of building a house in Glen Ellyn, Illinois. I remember the delight I experienced that summer watching the house take form. Because I was the only full-time employee, not counting its founder, I learned every trade, falling in love with most of them.[2]

In fact, throughout the summer I brought my parents back to the site on the weekends just to show them the progress . . . and what their son had personally accomplished. I was proud.

The story of a group of men getting together to build something isn't unusual. But the purpose of those who came together to erect the Tower of Babel was truly unique. And awful.

The first lie is that you and I can presumptuously take the place of God and do life on our own—without Him. The second lie is that our highest goal—the ultimate source of our greatest satisfaction—is to glorify ourselves. To make ourselves great by our own remarkable accomplishments. Sounds like the second stanza of the same song, doesn't it?

WHAT'S THE TRUTH?

So what is the truth that counters these lies? I'm glad you asked.

The prophet Isaiah had something to say about the first lie from Satan about becoming like God if he and Eve would taste the forbidden fruit: "I am the LORD, and there is no other, besides me there is no God" (Isa. 45:5).

And Jesus summed up His response to the second lie about earning our way to glory and perfection in two short sentences: "The thief comes only to steal and kill and destroy. I came that they may have life and have it abundantly" (John 10:10).

So even though the word "Lies" is the most prominent word on the cover of this book, it's not the most important word. That would be a word in the subtitle: "Truth."

Are you as glad as I am there is truth that is completely reliable? A powerful antidote to the fabrications that surround us? I bet you are.

One more thing. If you haven't already, I encourage you to find a friend or two—or more—to go through the book with you. This will encourage you, keep you accountable along the journey, and enable you to be a blessing to others.

And, to help jump-start that experience, just for the fun of it, I've added a few simple questions and comments after the "truth statements" that summarize. As my dad used to say, these may help as you "double-check" your thinking about the lie and the personal application of this truth.

Good? Good.

My prayer is that this book will be challenging and redemptive, convicting, and grace-filled. It's so good to have you along. Welcome.

ROBERT WOLGEMUTH
September 2018

SECTION ONE

FOUNDATIONS

CHAPTER ONE

CROSSING THE BRIDGE

WHEN WE GET THERE

W hen Satan whispers in a man's ear, encouraging him to do something foolish (at best) or sinful (at worst), the man sometimes goes ahead against his better judgment, figuring he'll be able to work it out.

As Nancy and I fell in love and started our journey toward marriage, there were many questions to be answered. Most of them came from her.

Here was a fifty-seven-year-old woman who had never been married. It wasn't that she wasn't "marriage material." Nancy was beautiful, highly relational, intelligent, and gifted. But early in her life she had sensed the call of God to give her life to vocational ministry, which she had joyfully done for all those years as a single woman.

"And then"—if you'll forgive me for borrowing from an old rock lyric made popular in the sixties by a group called The Association—"along came Robert."

So back to those questions Nancy asked. Many of them were practical considerations, such as, where would we live? And how would we reconfigure one of our homes to accommodate both of us? There were more: Nancy is a night person, and I'm up long before dawn; how would that work if we were married? Where would we go to church? And what would happen to the ministry she founded and leads?

More often than not, my answer was a simple, "We'll work it out," because I truly believed that we would. And, for the most part, we have done exactly that. We've worked it out. But many times it seemed that "we'll work it out" was not an entirely satisfying answer to Nancy. Now I know why.

You may have never thought of it this way, but often, when a man is faced with a problem that has no immediate or obvious solution, his heart and his words may find themselves at odds. His situation could be a stalemate; in his heart he truly is not sure what to do, but his lips express confidence in the outcome. His shameless *panache* emboldens him. So he steps out and acts on the information he has.

LIES MEN BELIEVE

In 2001, Nancy authored her bestselling book, *Lies Women Believe*.[1] Now, at her request and my enthusiastic "yes," I am taking up the mantle to create a matching book, exploring some of the lies we as men tend to believe. Because men and women are both human, there is some overlap in the lies. But, because men and women *aren't* the same, there are some differences in the lies that lure us in. More important still, there is a difference in the *how* and *why* we believe these lies. As men, it seems that we are less likely to be blindly deceived and more likely to embrace lies with our eyes wide open.

As I did when faced with Nancy's questions about what married life would look like for us, sometimes you and I, in the face of uncertainty, simply push confidently ahead, as though we know what we're doing. As for the fallout? "I'll cross that bridge when I get to it."

Taking a page from the Old Testament book of Genesis, the whole idea of

> *Adam was not deceived. Adam had no such excuse. He knew what he was doing. When he took the bite, his eyes were wide open.*

"we'll work this out" makes its first appearance in the garden of Eden. Eve was deceived. But Adam wasn't. He knew exactly what he was doing. How do we know this? The apostle Paul gives us a snapshot of the man's experience:

> For Adam was formed first, then Eve; and Adam was not deceived, but the woman was deceived and became a transgressor. (1 Tim. 2:13–14)

There are two puzzling notions in this text from Paul's letter to Timothy. First, what does it mean that Eve was deceived? Second, what does it mean that Adam was not deceived? And why does any of this matter?

The serpent didn't attack Eve head-on. His approach was subtle and nuanced. He used sleight of hand. Deception. Pure trickery. "Did God actually say . . . ?" (Gen. 3:1). Eve was guilty to be sure, but her guilt was mitigated by the deception.

Adam was not deceived. Adam had no such excuse. He knew what he was doing. When he took the bite, his eyes were wide open.

TRUTH WE CAN COUNT ON

The Bible contains accurate history of ancient times. But the Bible is also enigmatic at times, as it describes various scenes that are outside our experience—floating ax-heads, chariots of fire, a talking serpent. So it's easy for some to read biblical history like they're reading Mother Goose or the Brothers Grimm. But the Bible tells us what actually happened in space and time. In the beginning there truly was a man, shaped by God's own hand from the dust. And there truly was a woman, also shaped by God's own hand, though from the man's rib. And these two lived in the middle of perfection.

In Eden there was no conflict between the lion and the lamb; there were no biting mosquitos; there was no discord between Adam and Eve. Eve never needed to ask Adam to pick up his socks (oh, wait . . . they were still naked). No shame or sickness, no death or disease, all because there was no sin. Yes, there was a time in human history when misery did not

> *I wonder if Adam determined he would rather live with his wife's approval under God's curse than to be without her affirmation under God's blessing.*

exist, guilt was unknown, nothing and no one died, and peace reigned.

Yes, all was right with the world.

And then along came Satan.

Many Bible scholars believe Adam was present for the whole conversation between his wife and the serpent. If that is the case, as it appears to be, Adam failed to stand up to Satan or embrace his calling to protect his wife. He stood there doing nothing until she offered him the fruit. And as his wife had done, he ate it. Over the centuries, theologians have speculated over Adam's motives. Looking at this encounter through my own somewhat romantic lens, I wonder if Adam determined he would rather live with his wife's approval under God's curse than to be without her affirmation under God's blessing.

Of course, you and I can't be sure of what motivated Adam. But we do know that he walked into the fateful event with his eyes open. There was no pulling a rabbit out of a hat. No trickery. He was not hoodwinked. He took the fruit with the knowledge that it was the wrong thing to do.

The difference between Adam and Eve at this watershed moment in human history may give us an insight into some of the differences between men and women—how we think and how we make choices. And what kinds of lies we are charmed into believing.

In this book, as I identify some of the lies we are tempted to believe, I will be painting with a broad brush. In doing this I'm not suggesting that all men are the same or that all women are the same. I am merely speaking of tendencies, peculiar temptations that men tend to face versus those that women may more typically encounter.

THINKING AND FEELING

All human beings, like the Maker whose image we bear, both think and feel.

> When the woman *saw* that the tree was good for food, and that it was a *delight* to the eyes, and that the tree was to be *desired* to make one wise, she took of its fruit and ate. (Gen. 3:6)

Saw. Delight. Desired. These words explain a lot about Eve's willingness to make a giant, disobedient decision.

Men, as a rule, are more prone to separate their beliefs and their feelings. You and I seek to maintain the rule of our minds over our hearts. That's one reason we, at times, tend to be less compassionate.

As I was writing this book, I had a conversation with a couple who had been married just a year. Because I was a veteran married guy and she thought I could help, the young wife said to me: "When I'm struggling with something, my husband is eager to figure out how he can fix the problem. I've explained to him that at the moment, I just want him to care, to hold me, to sympathize with what I'm experiencing."

You and I understand this, don't we?

For us, there can be another danger that first reared its ugly head in Eden. When a man operates with his head and his heart—his thinking and his feeling—in separate realms, he often moves forward with an overinflated confidence, because his mind is making his decisions. He assumes that acting out whatever he *thinks* will result in acting in a way that is right.

And even when we know the right thing to do, we often chose to do the wrong thing anyway. What follows is the folly of rationalization.

And even when we *know* the right thing to do, we often choose to do the wrong thing anyway, whether out of expediency, convenience or, just sheer laziness. What follows is the folly of rationalization. We engage our minds to come up with excuses for why we did the wrong thing.

Wrestling with this very issue, the apostle Paul described his frustration with knowing what was right, but doing what was wrong.

> I want to do what is good, but I don't. I don't want to do what is
> wrong, but I do it anyway. (Rom. 7:19 NLT)

Even when he *knew* the right thing to do, and even when he *wanted* to
do the right thing, Paul found himself impotent to *do* what was right. He
was helpless, apart from the power of the gospel and the enabling Spirit
of Christ. So are you and I.

PAYING THE PRICE (LITERALLY)

As a college junior, I was presented with "an opportunity of a lifetime . . .
a money-making chance too good to be true."

Sure enough.

I bumped into "Jenny," a high school classmate at my home church
during the short Thanksgiving break. Her dad was a church leader and
a highly respected CPA in town. Standing near the church entrance after
worship, Jenny filled me in.

The "opportunity" involved buying and
selling US Savings Bonds and circulating a
"chain" letter. "Is this legal?" I asked. "Yes,"
she assured me, "since the actual letter
doesn't use the US Postal Service. My dad
says it's totally legit."

Sounds shady, I remember thinking. *But if
Jenny's dad says it's okay, it must be okay.*

Pushing past my better judgment—my
eager mind ignoring my hesitant heart—I
plunked down $37.50 to buy the letter and
went to the bank and bought two US Savings

> Walking into the
> dorm room, I filled
> my roommate in on
> what I had done.
> His face was a
> blend of skepticism
> and wonder.

bonds for $18.75 each—made out to the guy at the top of the list on the let-
ter—another $37.50. Now I'm into this thing to the tune of $75. Not a lot of
money today, but for a college student in the late 1960s . . . a lot of money.

The next afternoon, I drove back to my college. Walking into the
dorm room, I filled my roommate in on what I had done. His face was a

blend of skepticism and wonder.

"Is this legal?" Steve asked. "Sure," I said, borrowing some of Jenny's confidence.

A few days later, I sold my chain letter and savings bond to two equally gullible classmates.

The scheme swept our campus like a tsunami. In a matter of less than a week, more than a hundred wide-eyed, eager—and equally broke—college men had jumped in. In a few more days, men from other universities within driving distance of my school learned of the opportunity (scheme) and got involved.

A week later, after two stern warnings from our Dean of Students, including a threat to expel me, I went from door to door in each men's residence hall and begged guys to stop the chain letter. Some, including my cautious roommate, had gotten caught with a financial loss.

"How much did you lose?" I'd ask each man who had swallowed the scheme. "I have been asked—ordered—by the dean to tell you not to try to sell your letter."

These men were not happy. And so, recording each of these losses in a small spiral notebook, I promised to reimburse them. Working in construction the next summer, I sent thousands of hard-earned dollars to these men to help them recover from my foolishness.

Like Adam, I knew—at least strongly suspected—in my heart that what I was doing was wrong. No one had deceived me. My eyes were wide open. *I'll work this out later*, I naively figured.

Sure enough.

THINKING CONSCIOUSLY, PLANNING CARELESSLY, ACTING FOOLISHLY

Eve's husband knew that he was not to eat of the tree. If we could have taken him aside in that dramatic moment and given him a quiz on the ethics of eating the fruit, he would have passed. But when Eve offered him that first bite, he failed.

You and I often pride ourselves on the clarity of our thinking. We seem to make dispassionate analyses, to construct carefully crafted scenarios like puzzle pieces. This affirmation leads to that affirmation, which leads us to the next affirmation. And the next.

On the surface, this looks like a good thing. The trouble comes when decisions must be made in the moment, and our carelessness pushes us to override what we, in our hearts, know to be right. And true.

ACT NOW, LISTEN LATER

When David saw Bathsheba bathing, he didn't forget God's prohibition against adultery (more about David and Bathsheba later). Thinking that his kingly position would afford him whatever he would need to "work this out later," he pushed past the law of God and the prodding of his conscience and slept with her.

Do you wonder how well David was able to put this horrible travesty behind him in the ensuing weeks? Actually, I'm guessing that, given David's willingness to use his power to abuse his neighbor's wife, and then to cover it up by having her husband murdered, he did just fine. The easily distracted and proud king got busy with his kingly duties. Busy, busy, busy. Then, one day, Nathan the prophet rained on his parade, busting him with the truth.

Once David knew he had been found out, emotions (that should have shouted in the first place) overwhelmed him. A reading of Psalm 51 paints a life-size mural of David's profound regret for making a bad decision (actually, two bad decisions).

When you and I fall prey to lies, the reason is more likely to be pride and less likely

> *When you and I fall prey to lies, the cause is more likely to be pride and less likely to be gullibility. In the moment, we think we know better than God. We know in our heart and our conscience what is right, but we choose what is wrong.*

to be gullibility. In the moment, we think we know better than God. We know in our heart and our conscience what is right, but we choose what is wrong.

Sometimes we believe the lie that God will not notice. Sometimes we believe the lie that God will not care. Invariably we believe the lie that somehow it will work out and so we go ahead and do what we want to do.

Back in the garden, Adam knew that God would not be pleased with his actions. Adam knew he and God disagreed; perhaps in that moment he was foolish enough to think that his way was right and God's way was wrong . . . or at least, that he could go ahead with this disobedient choice, he could talk his way out of a corner, and God would understand and forgive.

In the chapters that follow, you and I will consider the kinds of lies that men believe. As you read, please don't lose sight of the reason why we are susceptible to believing them. The root of the issue is pride. We think of ourselves as thoughtful and in control. We think of ourselves as wiser than the God who planned all things from beginning to end. We think we can see the future, disbelieving God and believing ourselves.

> *Jesus, who is Himself truth, has promised not just to reveal truth to you and me, but to give us the strength to obey.*

But we are called to be obedient soldiers in God's kingdom. We are called to walk with Him as loving husband-shepherds seeking to reflect our Good Shepherd, as fathers seeking to reflect the character of our great Father, or just as men, who simply want to live a holy life. We must take every thought and every emotion captive to the obedience of Christ (2 Cor. 10:5).

ORTHOPRAXY ROCKS!

We should be compelled to put aside the lies of our natural father, the devil, and to embrace the life-giving truth and the heart of our adoptive Father, God Himself. To do so we need to learn to both *think* and *feel* in accordance with God's Word and ways.

> Teach me your way, O LORD,
>> that I may walk in your truth;
>> unite my heart to fear your name. (Ps. 86:11)

There it is . . . "walk in your truth; unite my heart" . . . correctly feathering together our minds and hearts.

Theologians sometimes have a clever way of putting concepts into single words. They would say that it's not good enough to just embrace *orthodoxy*—right beliefs—but we also need to cultivate *orthopathos*—right feelings. This leads us to exactly what we're pulling for: *orthopraxy*—right behavior. So Adam *knew* what God had told him (orthodoxy). In the moment when Eve handed him the fruit from which she had already taken a bite, he probably felt conflicted. That's when a big dose of *orthopathos*—right feelings integrated with right thinking—would have enabled him to put on the brakes, to stop his wife from revising what God had told him, and to tell the serpent where to go. Literally. *Orthopraxy!* Class dismissed.

Jesus, who is Himself truth, has promised not just to reveal truth to you and me, but to give us the strength to obey, and in so doing, to set us free (John 8:32). To be this kind of a man is to be a free man, to be anchored by the truth, to build our lives on the solid Rock. This is a lifelong struggle; the devil is relentless. Persistent. But we, by God's leading, move from grace to grace, from faith to faith, from truth to truth . . . from glory to glory (2 Cor. 3:18).

As you read further, my prayer is that the Spirit of God will fill you with wisdom, sound thinking, clear emotions, and the strength to tear down the devil's strongholds. To be a man of truth. Of strength. Of orthopraxy.

So here are forty lies. My hope is that, once identified, these lies can be banished to the pit where they belong and replaced by rock-solid truth and the pure freedom it promises to you.

LIES MEN BELIEVE

CHAPTER TWO

LIES MEN BELIEVE ABOUT
GOD

"What comes into our minds when we think about God
is the most important thing about us." —A. W. Tozer

R oy had just finished two full days of working on our sprinkler system. This included simple things like replacing a few broken spray heads, and more complicated things like digging two large holes in our backyard to replace broken solenoid valves. He worked alone.

I greeted him when he started working and asked his name. A few times throughout the two days of work, I walked over to give Roy a bottle of water or to ask him how it was going. Country music blared from his smartphone and a cigarette hung from his lips constantly. We didn't actually talk at any length until Roy was about to leave.

He and I were standing in the driveway and he was reviewing all the work he had done. I was thanking him.

As I sometimes do in situations like this, I asked Roy about his family. At first he seemed hesitant to go there but soon was telling me about his divorce, the challenges of his second marriage and blended family. He acknowledged some struggles he was having with a stepson. By the look on his face, I could tell that Roy was troubled by this situation.

Then there was silence. I could tell he was ready to leave.

I reached out to shake his hand and his return grip let me know that he appreciated my interest in his life.

"How can I pray for you, Roy?" I asked.

> *"I have always believed in God . . . but I need to get serious about Him again," he confessed.*

He hesitated. He looked squarely at me and squeezed out a thin smile. "I haven't been to church for a long time," Roy began. "My first wife was a strong Christian, but since I left her and our divorce was finalized . . ."

A wave of thoughtfulness swept across his face. Then his eyes began to well up with tears.

"I have always believed in God . . . but I need to get serious about Him again," he confessed.

"That's a good idea," I returned. "Can I pray for you?"

He nodded.

Reaching over, I put my hand on his shoulder. Roy took off his baseball cap.

"Dear Lord," I began. "Thank you for Roy. Thank you for his good work here at our house. Thank you for these few minutes of getting acquainted. I pray for Roy's heart. And I pray for Roy's family. And for his son. And I pray that you will draw Roy back to You . . . nothing is more important than this."

When I finished the short prayer, Roy reset his baseball cap and reached both of his arms toward me for a hug. His eyes swimming in tears.

What a striking scene . . . two grown men on a hot summer day spontaneously embracing after a brief driveway worship service.

GETTING SERIOUS ABOUT GOD

This book is starting with a chapter addressing lies men believe about God because I believe that the struggles we face with all the rest of the lies in the pages that follow flow out of these lies.

Most men will say they "believe *in* God." That is, they are willing to acknowledge His existence. They may think that's good enough.

> *What you and I believe about God will ultimately determine what we believe—or don't believe—about everything else.*

It's not. There's more.

What you and I believe *about* God will ultimately determine what we believe—or don't believe—about everything else.

If we think the lies we believe about God are less important than the lies we believe about sex or money or marriage or our careers, we are believing the most egregious lie of all. In short, we are saying that what we believe about the God who created us can take a back seat to other more pressing, immediate things. We are saying that we can separate our convictions about temporal things and our convictions about Him. But we cannot.

FOLLOW GOD? SURE, WHY NOT?

This reminds me of a story I first heard as a youngster. It's about a guy who wanted to include God in his life. But put Him first? Not so much.

A man approached Jesus with a question. We're not told his name; we know him simply as "the rich young man."

The man asked a thoughtful question to the right person. So far, so good. But this story does not turn out well.

> And behold, a man came up to [Jesus], saying, "Teacher, what good deed must I do to have eternal life?" (Matt. 19:16)

At least this young man was thinking about eternity. This is admirable. He had accumulated a great store of wealth, but he also realized what many forget: hearses are not outfitted with trailer hitches.

But Jesus quickly discerned that for all the wisdom in the question, there was something wrong with it. The questioner didn't really understand what "good" even meant. Jesus began His reply, "Why do you ask me about what is good? There is only one who is good" (19:17). From the start, Jesus reminded the man of something extremely important: we're not good enough and we never will be. The only thing you and I bring to the table is our sin. We fall short; we miss the mark. Every time.

> At least this young man was thinking about eternity. This is admirable.

Jesus then directed the young man to God's own standards. "If you would enter life, keep the commandments" (v. 17). Of course, the Ten Commandments are a high mark to which many aspire but no one can measure up (Rom. 5:20). This, we might think, would have caused a blush from the proud man, that he would quickly grasp that he could by no means be sufficiently obedient to earn eternal life.

But instead of repenting or pleading for mercy, he doubled down. First, he looked for a technicality. "Which ones?" he asked, as if breaking just a few God's commandments would not disqualify him from entering heaven. When Jesus began to rattle off the commandments, the young man affirmed that he had kept God's law from his youth. Wow, what presumption to say that he had not broken a single law! He was good to go.

You and I may even smile at this. Not a single law? This is silliness. Of course, if a man has broken just one law, he can rightly be considered a "law-breaker."

For example, let's say I snuck into your house, stole your electronics, ransacked everything else with a baseball bat, and then I was arrested. My high-paid attorney appealed to the judge. "Sure, your honor. Wolgemuth did what he's been accused of doing; but he didn't burn the place down or steal the car or harm the children."

It's true. I didn't do these other awful things, but would I still go to the big house for what I had actually done? Absolutely.

If you were to ask the average person why he or she should be allowed into heaven, more often than not you'd get some variation of this answer: "The good I've done outweighs the bad." But God doesn't see things that way.

What Jesus did next with the eager seeker is often misunderstood. He told the rich young man to sell all that he owned, give it to the poor, and follow Him.

It's as if Jesus was saying to him, "You say you've kept the commandments of God. Let's just check and see. We'll start with the first one. Do you have any other gods? Is there anything you value and cherish more than God Himself? Your wealth, perhaps?"

The rich young fellow failed the test. Matthew tells us, "When the young man heard this he went away sorrowful, for he had great possessions" (19:22). A guilty conscience? Probably.

> *If you were to ask the average person why he or she should be allowed into heaven, more often than not you'd get some variation of this answer: "The good I've done outweighs the bad." But God doesn't see things that way.*

WE MUST LOVE GOD SUPREMELY

This story should help us see ourselves. Apart from the grace of God, we too would have a sorrowful ending, unable to part with the stuff we love and separated from the God who loves us.

Because you and I worship what we love most, there is a good reason that the first commandment is first: "You shall have no other gods before me." But before we get to that, let's check out the word "before." Have you ever read it the way I used to, thinking God is actually granting us permission to have other gods alongside Him on the condition that those gods were not as important to us as God Himself? You may have taken "before" to mean "ahead in the queue."

Be very careful. God is not content for us to have other rivals, even so long as we love Him most. "Before" means in His presence, as in "no other gods—things or people whom we 'worship'—at all."

The ultimate truth, the antidote to lies we might believe—is that God deserves the unrivaled place in our hearts. Anything short of that consigns Him to a place in the shadows. A place where He never belongs.

> *This story should help us see ourselves. Apart from the grace of God, we too would have a sorrowful ending, unable to part with the stuff we love, and separated from the God who loves us.*

Lesson one every man must learn is simple: God is God, and we are not. He is the end, not a means. Our purpose is not to use Him to secure our own desires. Our goal is not to acquire possessions, power, or prestige. Our goal is not to add Him to our list of "loves," but to love Him most.

Several months after Nancy and I began dating, I found myself falling deeply in love with her. In fact, truth be known, I had foolishly let myself put her at the top of my list of affections. This was something I knew was wrong about and, on a long video call with her and through plenty of tears, I confessed what I had done. She received my contrition with understanding and plenty of grace.

In fact, as smart and discerning as she is, Nancy was relieved. No one but God can possibly live up to this kind of worship.

Apparently Simon Peter shared this tendency to let his loves get out of alignment. One of the most important moments in the earthly ministry of Jesus happened shortly after His resurrection. He and Peter, who had three times flatly denied that he even knew Jesus, were having breakfast on the beach. It seems that, to balance the scales, Jesus asked Peter essentially the same question . . . three times in a row.

"Simon, son of John, do you love me more than these?" (John 21:15)

So there you have it. A question of great and ultimate importance.

If we are to love God at all, we must love Him exclusively, more than anything—or anyone—else.

God is a jealous God and, for our own good, He will not share the throne of our heart with a rival. That place must be reserved for Him.

> *Lesson one every man must learn is simple: God is God, and we are not. He is the end, not a means.*

1 *"God is not a whole lot different from me."*

According to Greek mythology, a handsome young man named Narcissus was traipsing through the woods one day, feeling a strange fusion of thirstiness and insecurity. He had just rejected the love of a nymph named Echo, a philandering creature, eager to sexually ensnare the man. He was not interested in commiserating with a lecherous snake. Now there's a familiar refrain.

Presently, Narcissus happened upon a small pool of water. "Ah, here is the answer to my yearning for something to drink," the man whispered to himself.

Crouching beside the pool, he leaned over, cupped his hand, and prepared to lift some of its crystalline coolness to his dry lips. But before he touched the water, its stillness lay there, flawlessly reflecting his image back to his uncertain eyes.

Narcissus froze, studying each detail of his own dazzling face. Having been unwilling to receive the advances of the nymph, Narcissus discovered a more compelling suitor. A dashing and debonair lover. Someone more delightful than anyone else he had ever seen. In that moment, the young man drifted into a slight trance. An air of worship surrounded him. His heart raced, helplessly falling in love. With himself.

Yuck!

But before we consign this girly-man to the furthest reaches of sissyland, let's lean over and look into the same still pond.

We may be looking for satisfaction of our deepest desires, our thirsts that crave to be assuaged. Answers to hard questions that plague us. Someone or something to bring us wholeness and joy. And when we see our own reflection—trying to satisfy our longings with what we're able to muster on our own—we realize that, try as we might, our own weak image does not satisfy. In fact, incessant navel-gazing nauseates us.

> *The prophet, though endowed with natural gifts and entrusted with unusual responsibility, was spellbound and speechless in the presence of pristine holiness.*

Many centuries ago, a prophet of Israel entered the Jerusalem temple. Prior to this moment, he had been assigned to declare judgment on God's chosen and sinful children. A grand appointment to be sure. One that could stir up in even the soberest of men a sense of inflated self-worth. But not this man. Not this time.

Instead, as the man approached the altar, a sound arose from the nave, a sound such as he had never heard before. His heady processional came to an end. In that moment, the prophet Isaiah saw the Lord God, high and lifted up. Isaiah's body now frozen and still, felt the shaking of the structure. Loud voices of unearthly creatures penetrated the still air.

"Holy, holy, holy is the LORD of hosts;
the whole earth is full of his glory!" (Isa. 6:3)

The prophet, though endowed with natural gifts and entrusted with unusual responsibility, was spellbound and speechless in the presence of pristine holiness. In that moment, the first words from Isaiah's mouth summed up who he really was in the face of perfection.

"Woe is me!" Isaiah said.

No kidding.

What happened to Isaiah that day would forever mark him. No longer would he be enamored of his own worth, his acclaim, his influence, his skills, his countenance, or his wardrobe. Not anymore.

Isaiah had peered into the still pond but had come face-to-face with the holiness of God. And for the remainder of his life, that experience would be enough.

IN HIS PRESENCE

When my children were small, my late wife, Bobbie, and I discussed how best to shape their conduct. What could we do to encourage their obedience, their ability to recognize their own sinfulness and be broken by it? How could we teach them the ways of God so they could embrace them as their own? And how could we engender a sense of respect for us, their parents?

We wondered aloud, "What would it be like to stand in the presence of a holy and altogether righteous God? And what would it be like to bring our children along with us?"

The answers to these pressing questions came with the power of the story of Isaiah in the temple.

We wondered aloud, "What would it be like to stand in the presence of a holy and altogether righteous God? And what would it be like to bring our children along with us? How would this experience shape their thinking and their conduct? And how would it shape ours as grown-ups, called to love and follow God and to lead these children?"

Here's an example: Something that was important to Bobbie and me was for our girls to learn good table manners. But we didn't want them to think of this as some kind of nasty boarding-school discipline. So we turned it into a game. Every once in a while, we would announce, "Tonight we're going to use White House Manners."

Even if we were eating at the kitchen table, everyone would help set it with a tablecloth, along with our best china, crystal, and sterling flatware. Even pretty linen napkins neatly folded next to the dinner plates.

And then we'd pretend that this was a state dinner. Of course, world dignitaries were present. Our manners were impeccable. Even our conversation was formal . . . in a fun sort of way. Sometimes we'd even use our best British accents. Through the portal of our imagination, we were in the presence of beauty and greatness, and this impacted the way we acted.

Isaiah's personal encounter with the living God changed his life. And this was no ordinary White House state dinner experience. It was something far grander. Even though the prophet knew about God—he was, after all, a career God-talking expert—from now on Isaiah would be aware of the One in whose presence he lived . . . day and night. Can you imagine?

The first lie about God—that He is more or less like you and me—may be the most perilous of all. He cannot be compared to us. He is . . . God. The high, exalted Creator. Securely nail this down and you're on your way to being squared away.

THE TRUTH	God is holy. His brilliant "otherness" cannot adequately be described. Once we have fully embraced this, nothing is ever the same.

THINK ABOUT IT . . . *Who is your greatest living hero? How would you act in his presence? What are some things that set God apart from everything and everyone else?*

2 *"God isn't actually involved in or concerned with the details of my life."*

Several summers ago, I visited the Grand Teton National Park for the first time. Nothing could have prepared me for the mighty size, splendor, and beauty of what I saw.

The next week, back in Michigan, I spotted a little chipmunk scampering across our deck, his tail was straight in the air. He stopped. He ran again. Then he stopped, sat up on his haunches, and nibbled on his little front paws. You may hate chipmunks. You may consider them rats with stripes. I think they're cute.

Question: Which of these—the grandeur of the mountains or the sprightly movements of a chipmunk—best characterizes our Creator God? That's right. They both do.

If we know anything about God, we realize that *He is big*. We tend to see His role as akin to a four-star general. He assesses the battlefields, counts His battalions, considers His supply lines, and plots how to win. It's the war that's His concern, the big picture, not every little skirmish or detail of the battle.

> **If we know anything about God, we realize that** He is big.

With an entire universe to create, uphold, and rule over, we may surmise that God surely doesn't have the time or inclination to attend to the petty details that make up our days. That stuff is on autopilot, like a wound-up clock moving according to its own design.

AND HE IS SMALL

The Bible moves swiftly through the mighty accounts of the patriarchs: Adam and the creation, Noah and the flood, Abraham to the grand sweep of the exodus and the conquest of the promised land. But then the Bible gently tells the small story of a single godly woman, Ruth, and the man who would redeem her and make her his bride.

Ruth had been a widow, poverty stricken, surviving by the charity of a wealthy man named Boaz. The biblical account of her story opens with these words:

Now it came to pass . . . (1:1 NKJV)

Applying these words to each scene of the drama, the death of Ruth's first husband *came to pass*. Boaz catching sight of Ruth *came to pass*. Boaz waking to find Ruth at his feet *came to pass*. And out of this, eventually *came to pass* the birth of King David, and finally, the birth of Jesus Himself.

There is much to learn from the story of Ruth and Boaz, but one thing we should not miss is the principle found in the saying that goes like this:

> *There are no small, free-standing details in life, only carefully intertwined events and circumstances that create one grand tapestry called history.*

For want of a nail the shoe was lost.
For want of a shoe the horse was lost.
For want of the horse the rider was lost.
For want of the rider the battle was lost.
For want of the battle the war was lost.[1]

The loss of a single nail, in the end, made the difference in the outcome of the war. In other words, there are no small, free-standing details in life, only carefully intertwined events and circumstances that create one grand tapestry called history.

God is big; God is small.

Sometimes we divide our lives into large moments of great import and small moments of ordinariness. However, when God gave us the Great Commandment—that we must love Him with all our heart, mind, soul, and strength—He was telling us that He wants all of us, and that means all of our moments, great ones and little ones alike.

> *God's "bigness" isn't the kind of bigness that overlooks smallness. Rather it is a bigness that encompasses smallness.*

God's "bigness" isn't the kind of bigness that overlooks smallness. Rather it is a bigness that encompasses smallness. He does not farm out the management of the details to underlings while He looks after the big stuff. He is all-knowing, His power is inexhaustible, and His control is absolute.

Sometimes this truth sounds scary; sometimes it's comforting. Knowing that God sees everything can be frightening when we want the freedom to sin outside His gaze. But it's comforting to know that there's no shadowed place He does not see. When we feel alone and insignificant, when we find ourselves consumed with our worries, it helps to remember that He has numbered the hairs on our head (Luke 12:7).[2]

He reminds us that since He provides for the lilies of the field, we can be assured that He will meet our needs (Matt. 6:28). He promises us that since He knows when even a sparrow falls to the ground, we can know He cares about us (Matt. 10:29).

We rightly ought to be scared when we are tempted to think we can safely disobey, so long as our infraction is a small one. And we ought to be comforted in knowing that every moment of our lives matters. Everything we do has meaning and significance; our faithful Father directs our every step.

Coram Deo is a Latin phrase meaning "in the presence of God" or "before the face of God." This is how we are called to live our lives. Every moment, every word, every decision, every act, every thought counts. No matter how insignificant they may seem, they are done before the face and in the presence of the living God.

And not only are we to live in fellowship with Him, we are to actually be connected to Him. In recounting the story of the final dinner the Savior hosted with His disciples before His mock trial and crucifixion, the apostle John, one of Jesus' closest friends, quotes Him:

> "Abide in me, and I in you. As the branch cannot bear fruit by itself, unless it abides in the vine, neither can you, unless you abide in me." (John 15:4)

When a tree branch is connected to the trunk, it draws life from the sap that flows into it. There is never a time when the branch doesn't need this life-giving substance. If it's disconnected, the branch dies. Should this fruit-bearing limb ever decide that it no longer needs to be connected, it becomes kindling. An ordinary stick.

Or another way to say this is that I am never *not* Nancy's husband.

No activity, no word I speak, or even random thought I may entertain can afford to be in isolation. She and I belong to each other. All day. Every day.

> When a tree branch is connected to the trunk, it draws life from the sap that flows into it.

My life should reflect this truth. People should be able to quickly tell that I am a delightfully married man.

When you and I abide in God, it should be obvious. Again, everything we do, say, or think should make this obvious to everyone.

THE TRUTH | Nothing is too grand or too insignificant for God's care. He made us and is involved in every detail of our lives, large and small.

THINK ABOUT IT . . . *The word "love" is sometimes thrown around like cheap candy. What does God's kind of love look like?*

 ## "*I can earn God's favor.*"

Have you ever noticed how "real" the Bible is? You won't find many heroes looking like stock characters from central casting. Instead you find that even the "best" men, apart from Jesus, had plenty of flaws.

If there ever were such a brigade, it would have to be the Pharisees. To the Jews of their day, they were model citizens. Since they knew of their pristine standing, they were also stuffy and self-important. They oozed pride. Unapologetic arrogance. And in the end, they turned out to be avowed enemies of the Messiah.

But hold on a second. These were men who were deeply immersed in God's law. Their unsurpassed commitment was used by Jesus Himself in giving a warning in His Sermon on the Mount: "For I tell you, unless your righteousness exceeds that of the scribes and Pharisees, you will never enter the kingdom of heaven" (Matt. 5:20). Then the gospel of John tells us about a Pharisee named Nicodemus, who came to see Jesus, one-on-One. The conversation started off well enough: "Rabbi, we know that you are a teacher come from God, for no one can do these signs that you do unless God is with him" (John 3:2).

> *If there ever were such a brigade, it would have to be the Pharisees. To the Jews of their day, they were model citizens.*

Jesus, however, didn't just receive the compliment and repay Nicodemus in kind; instead, as He so often did, He cut right to the heart of the issue.

> **Jesus answered him, "Truly, truly, I say to you, unless one is born again he cannot see the kingdom of God." (v. 3)**

Having just confessed that Jesus was a teacher sent from God, Nicodemus began to argue. Not smart. "How," Nicodemus wondered, "can a man be born again? He can't crawl back into his mother's womb" (see v. 4).

"Gentle Jesus, meek and mild" rebuked Nicodemus for not knowing this mysterious truth already. How could Nicodemus be a teacher, one of the smartest scholars in Israel, and not grasp this most basic truth?

But you and I can relate. We *should* know truth about our inborn sin nature and our need for rebirth, and too often we don't. Our pride pushes us to believe, at least subconsciously, that we can somehow earn God's favor, that if we are just good enough, God will be pleased with us and accept us. This is the heart of all counterfeit religion and the very opposite of the truth.

God is holy; He cannot abide sin. This is the precise reason why we can't earn His favor.

All of the scrupulousness of Nicodemus, all of his studies, every effort he made to earn God's favor carried with it the stain of sin. As "good" as he tried to be, he would never be "good enough."

> *This is not something we do, but something done to us. Something done for us.*

The only way to see the kingdom of God is to be born again. Just as with our first birth, this is not something we do but something done *to* us. Something done *for* us. We need His righteousness—ours is no righteousness at all. And His alone exceeds the piety of the Pharisees.

The trouble is that even though we confess our unworthiness, have been born again, and cling to the cross, we so often return to this folly. "Yes," we reason, "I am saved by the blood of Christ. But how God really feels about me on any given day depends on how well I am doing in obeying Him."

No, our standing before the Father is not determined by how we are doing, but by what the Son has done. Pride and discouragement over our sin are things we will fight until we enter eternity.

But right now, today, tomorrow, and always, if we are abiding in Christ, we rest in what He has done. When our Father looks at us, He sees Jesus. And He is well pleased. His forgiveness is real and complete. His adoption of us is irrevocable. His love for us is infinite, neither increasing nor diminishing.

So, we are to celebrate and give thanks, putting aside our pride, forsaking any confidence in our good works, for Jesus is all we will ever need.

THE TRUTH

We cannot earn God's approval. We can only receive His undeserved favor.

THINK ABOUT IT . . . *What does the expression "with strings attached" mean? What are the strings attached to God's love for you? Are there any?*

"*There are many ways to God.*"

His name was Ed, but I didn't learn this until our airplane touched down at its destination. In fact, even though he was sitting next to me on the long flight, I don't think we even turned toward each other and made eye contact until the very end of our voyage.

We only had a few minutes left before deplaning, so Ed wasted no time, cutting right to what was on his mind.

When I had first found my assigned row, secured my carry-on in the overhead bin, and settled down into my aisle seat, Ed had his nose in a book and didn't look up from his window seat. I may have said "hello," but I don't remember.

But now our airplane had safely landed and we were taxiing to our gate. Ed had closed his book, and my laptop was stowed. I turned and spoke.

"Hello," I said with a smile. "I'm Robert."

"I'm Ed," he returned (without a smile).

It seems that during our flight, Ed had glanced in my direction, visually eavesdropping on some of my email correspondence. Or maybe I was reviewing a book proposal from an author client, and he had caught some of it. In any case and without my knowing, Ed had checked me out.

We only had a few minutes left before deplaning, so Ed wasted no time, cutting right to what was on his mind.

"I'll bet you're one of those Christians who says that Jesus is the only way to God," he bristled, making no attempt to mask his disdain for surely what must have been a religious nut sharing his row.

"Actually, no," I said, intentionally trying not to match Ed's combative tone. Ed blanched, thinking he might have misjudged me.

There was a lengthy moment of quiet and then I spoke again, this time turning in Ed's direction and still smiling. "I don't need to say this," I said. "The Lord Jesus is the One who said it, and I believe Him."

Remarkably, it was though the ice crust enshrouding my seatmate's face began to soften.

"Actually," he began, trying to squeeze out a smile of his own, "I'm an elder in what you'd probably call a 'liberal' church. My fellow elders, even my minister, mock people like you as close-minded bigots. You know, fundamentalists."

Our airplane nosed itself into the open slot at our assigned gate, the engines whined their way down, the seatbelt light was turned off, and Ed and I began to gather our belongings. But he had one more thing to say. Somehow, I could tell.

"You know," Ed said. "I wish I could believe that."

The conversation reminds me of Thomas, known as the doubting disciple. As Ed might have done, Thomas certainly agreed that Jesus was a good man, an exemplary prophet, and capable teacher. Maybe He was even *a* way to get to God.

But the Savior quickly ruled out this "big tent" approach.

Jesus said to [Thomas], "I am the way, and the truth, and the life. No one comes to the Father except through me." (John 14:6)

A LIE THAT CAN MAKE A MAN MISERABLE

If you attempt to share your faith with others, you will surely run into this way of thinking, that there are many ways to God. Or you will encounter the claim that Jesus was just a good man.

In his classic book *Mere Christianity*, C. S. Lewis famously wrote,

> If you attempt to share your faith with others, you will surely run into this way of thinking, that there are many ways to God.

A man who was merely a man and said the sort of things Jesus said would not be a great moral teacher. He would either be a lunatic—on the level with a man who says he is a poached egg—or he would be the devil of hell. You must take your choice. Either this was, and is, the Son of God, or else a madman or *something worse. You can shut him up for a fool or you can fall at his feet and call him Lord and God. But let us not come with any patronizing nonsense about his being a great human teacher. He has not left that open to us.*[3]

The gospel you and I embrace is truth. The historical fact of Jesus' life, death, and resurrection brings every man hope. Even the exclusive claims of Jesus regarding Himself (which make some squirm) are "good news." In fact, our unequivocal belief that He alone grants a sinful yet contrite person forgiveness, redemption, and direct access into the presence of a holy God by way of Christ's righteousness freely imputed to us brings with it a true sense of hope. Of security and wholeness.

In the minutes that followed my brief exchange with Ed, I felt a sadness. I followed him up the jet bridge into the terminal. Knowing I was right behind him, once inside, he stopped, set down his suitcase, turned, and put out his hand.

I shook it, thanking Ed for the chance to connect. Even though he was trying to smile, the look on his face was also sad. Even miserable—the word the apostle Paul used to describe people who didn't embrace the whole gospel (1 Cor. 15:17–19 KJV).

In saying goodbye to Ed, I told him I would pray for him to someday be able to see Jesus through the eyes of faith. Without any apparent response, Ed reached down, grasped the handle of his suitcase, lifted it with a click, turned, and disappeared into the crowd headed down the concourse.

Now truth be known, I'm a diplomat. A salesman. Ask my daughters. And my wife. They'll agree that my preference is always to try to give both sides a chance. However, in this case, I do strangers and friends no favors by cutting corners on the facts.

Jesus Christ is God and He has no rival.

By His own declaration, Jesus is the great Reconciler. The only one. He takes sinful men like you and me and, by His grace, welcomes us as His sons. His brothers. Forgiven. New. Whole.

THE TRUTH

Jesus Christ is our only way to God.

THINK ABOUT IT . . . *When is the word "exclusive" an ugly word? Why is "exclusive" good news here?*

"Church? I can take it or leave it."

Sometimes popular songs take on a meaning that the writer never intended. In 1984, Bruce Springsteen wrote "Born in the USA" as an indictment on our nation, only to see it become used as an anthem of patriotism. The year before Springsteen wrote his lyric, *The Police* sang "Every Breath You Take" as a warning about stalkers. But the song strangely became a favorite love song.

So it was with the classic Paul Simon's lyric, "I Am a Rock."

Some have taken this song, with its brief and haunting refrain, as a celebration, a repetition of the bold declaration of Frank Sinatra's "I did it my way." However, the rest of the lyric tells a different story. The song is not a celebration but a lament.

> The fellowship we are born into when we are born again is the church, the bride of Christ.

In the garden of Eden, even before the fall, even before the serpent strode[4] in, God saw that there was something wrong. He said, "It is not good that the man should be alone" (Gen. 2:18). The context of this statement is the creation of Eve, but the principle clearly has broader application. It's also about community.

Just as the three persons of the holy

Trinity—God the Father, God the Son, and God the Holy Spirit—are one, we who are made in His image were not made to be alone. God's purpose for you and me is to live our lives with others. And the fellowship we are born into when we are born again is the church, the bride of Christ.

> *The church is that place where we are painfully reminded of our failures. And it is that place where we are assured of the grace of God.*

The church is the people of God, with all their warts and wrinkles, their haughtiness and hypocrisy, their scandal and their sin. The church is made up of people—people who have been declared righteous by Christ, but who still struggle with the presence and power of indwelling sin.

Remarkably, the church is actually an "exclusive" club, the one institution you cannot join unless you confess you're no good! That's our qualification. We are a gathering of failures, a congregation of rebels.

Of course, it's a common refrain that the church should be avoided because it is so full of hypocrites. But the good news for you and me is that there's always room for one more. It is precisely because we are sinners that we sometimes see sin as something "out there" rather than something "in here." Our pride leads us to see ourselves as superior, as victims who have been mistreated rather than perpetrators who mistreat.

What unites the church though is the stunning truth that our sins have been covered by the blood of Christ. It's not just a congregation of sinners, but a congregation of sinners who know the grace of God, a congregation that has been commanded to forgive as we have been forgiven.

The church is that place where we are painfully reminded of our failures. And it is that place where we are assured of the grace of God, an undeserved gift that assuages our pain and moves us to joy. To try to function apart from the local church is to miss out on the opening of God's Word and the preaching of the gospel, the good news. It is to cut ourselves off from the thing we need most—the chance to walk together in pursuing Christ and celebrating victory over sin.

And attending church needs to be more than window shopping. A mere, casual weekly visit doesn't cut it any more than going into a restaurant without sitting down and enjoying the luxury of a great dinner would satisfy you.

Nearly every week you'll hear of opportunities for service and involvement. You'll be given a chance to invest in the work of His kingdom. Not doing these things keeps you in the stands as a spectator rather than on the field as a full-fledged player.

> To leave the church is to leave Him. To cling to the church is to cling to Him.

This reminds me of my first visit to the dog track somewhere in Florida when I was in my early twenties. I watched the greyhounds race around at breakneck speeds, chasing a rag on a stick named "Rusty." This was interesting. And then I went to the window and put twenty dollars on one of the dogs. To say that watching the next race with some "skin in the game" was an entirely different experience would be the understatement of the day.

When you invest your time and treasure in a local church, you've just suited up, you've put your money where your mouth is and are in the game. This is a good thing.

One more thing: you and I have heard folks say, "Who needs the church? I just need Jesus." Sounds pious enough, right? But that's like saying, "I love Jesus, but I'm not into His bride." The church is a place for those for whom Jesus laid down His life. The church is those who are beloved of the Father. The church is those who are filled with the Holy Spirit. It is not just the bride of Christ, but the body of Christ. It's that place where we can see Jesus being formed and reflected in the lives of His people. To leave the church is to leave Him. To cling to the church is to cling to Him.

Many years ago, my late wife, Bobbie, and I met a new family who had moved into our Florida neighborhood . . . mom, dad, young daughter, and toddler. Bobbie and Judy peeled off to talk. There was sweet chemistry. I could tell right away. I approached Rick and put out my hand to shake his. I liked him right away. Confident but not strident. Warm but not wimpy.

Soon our conversation turned to faith. "Rick" told me a remarkable story about campaigning for state government several years before, going door to door to solicit votes.

"My name is Rick Davis and I'm running for Florida Congress. I'd like for you to vote for me," he said, standing on a stranger's front porch.

The man smiled. "Sure, I'll vote for you if you let me tell you about Jesus."

> *"We don't go to church," he proudly replied. "I'm a busy guy.*

The Holy Spirit hovered over the moment, convicted Rick of his sin and his need for a Savior, and the stranger led him in "the sinner's prayer."

I remember being stunned by the man's boldness and Rick's tenderness in recounting the story.

Soon our conversation turned to church. "Where do you guys attend?" I asked.

Rick's demeanor shifted. "We don't go to church," he proudly replied. "I'm a busy guy. I own a business and work hard six days a week. Sunday's my only chance to sleep in, play with the kids, and read the newspaper. I don't do church," he added.

I didn't press. But, over the months that followed, each time I'd see Rick in the neighborhood, I'd encourage him to reconsider his decision. This was not like a visit to the principal's office. I did my best to be direct yet encouraging and understanding. Rick listened and was not hostile to my gentle exhortation.

Fast forward fifteen years. Rick is a leader in a local church. An outspoken advocate of the life-changing power of community, worshiping each week with God's people. His sons attend the Christian high school there.

Sleeping in and morning newspapers can be replaced by something far more precious. Just ask Rick.

No man is a rock. No man is an island. You and I need the body, even when it hurts to be there. Love the Lord, and love His bride with all her flaws. Bring your flaws with you. Christ will wash them all, because He loves His bride.

As you and I fellowship with others, we will find sorrow and hurt. And we will find laughter and love. When we embrace the church, we will find it is well worth it.

THE TRUTH	For the believer, church should not be optional. It's standard equipment.

THINK ABOUT IT . . . *Why is it important for us to experience intentional Christian community in the context of the local church?*

CHAPTER THREE

LIES MEN BELIEVE ABOUT

THEMSELVES

Y ou've met Rebecca and Stephen, our two older children. They're good kids," the mother beamed as she spoke to me. Then she hesitated as she nodded toward another son standing in front of us: "This is Jonathan; he's our bad boy."

I turned toward the fourteen-year-old young man whose mother's words had just been aimed at him. His eyes were focused on his shoe tops. He didn't speak.

This unforgettable exchange took place decades ago when I was living on the North Shore of Chicago and involved in full-time youth ministry. On the face of it, this was a good, churchgoing family. Mom and dad married for many years, three healthy children living in a pretty suburban home at the end of a tree-lined street.

As a novice in youth work, I had no postgraduate education in psychology or human behavior. But I knew, as you would have, that Jonathan had just been sentenced. Neither a judge nor a jury was involved, but the teenager had been branded by one of the most important people in his life.

Jonathan was a bad boy.

LIES *MEN* BELIEVE

> *"How many of you had dads who told you that someday you'd wind up in a place like this?"*

As the years went by, I did my best to befriend him. Occasional visits to a local café and glasses of frosty Coke on the table between us gave me a chance to unpack the heart of this troubled teenager.

I've lost track of Jonathan since he graduated from high school. But in the years I knew him, I would describe him by echoing his mother's words: Jonathan was a bad boy.

You're doubtless wincing at what I've just said. I'm doing the same as I write these words.

This chapter is about lies we believe about ourselves. It's a reminder that the thing we call "self-image" is not something we usually come up with on our own. Self-image is a gift we usually receive from others . . . and often, as young men, from people in authority.

The great Bill Glass, number 80 all-pro defensive end with the NFL Cleveland Browns in the late 1950s and '60s, founded a prison ministry called "Behind the Walls." Since 1972, Glass has spoken to tens of thousands of inmates, sharing with them his love for Christ and inviting them to receive Him as their Savior and Lord.

One of the questions Bill frequently asks incarcerated men when he addresses them is this: "How many of you had dads who told you that someday you'd wind up in a place like this?"

According to his own account, Bill Glass says that the vast majority of men raise their hands. As Jonathan's mother expressed to me about her son, these men are "bad boys." They know it and have grown up proving these verbal assessments to be true.

WHAT SHOULD YOU KNOW ABOUT THIS IMAGE THING?

If it's true that our "self-image" is a "gift" presented to us by folks in authority over us, then I have good news for you. It's about our "image" from the Genesis account of the creation of heaven and earth.

So God created man in his own image,
>   in the image of God he created him;
>   male and female he created them. (Gen. 1:27)

Imago Dei is a Latin theological term meaning that mankind is created in the image and likeness of God. Two important things are true about this image. First, we are distinct from animals. In fact, as image bearers, we have been given dominion over all the other creatures God made. Our dominion should include compassion and good stewardship of His creation.

Second, being made in the image of God means that we reflect something of the glory of the Lord. As the moon echoes the brightness of the sun, our lives should mirror the grandeur of our sovereign Creator.

So what does this look like?

I'm glad you asked.

THE BOY WHO WOULD BE KING

Do you know any eight-year-old boys? What does the average boy do at that age? What were you like when you were eight?

Six and a half centuries before the birth of Jesus Christ, there was an eight-year-old boy named Josiah. He lived in the land of Judah and had a wicked father and grandfather. These two men had been the kings of their nation and had completely forsaken the God of their fathers. Good excuses for Josiah to be a "bad boy" as well.

But, according to many scholars, Josiah had two secret weapons: his mother and his grandmother. Jedidiah was Josiah's mother. Her name means "the beloved of the LORD." And Jedidiah's mother, Adaiah, was also blessed with a great name meaning, "the honored of the LORD."

Why these two women were married to such scoundrels, we don't know, but Amon and Manasseh's epitaphs describe wicked despots.

[Amon] did what was evil in the sight of the LORD, as Manasseh his
father had done. He walked in all the way in which his father walked
and served the idols that his father served and worshiped them. He

abandoned the LORD, the God of his fathers, and did not walk in the way of the LORD. (2 Kings 21:20–22)

> *So instead of being raised as a rascal, Josiah could have been reminded that he had all the makings of a king.*

So back to the eight-year-old boy. It's probably not a stretch to believe that Josiah's mother and grandmother spoke truth to the boy. These women loved and honored the Lord. They likely would have been familiar with their godly Jewish heritage and the words from Genesis that they had been created in the image of God. So instead of being raised as a rascal, Josiah could have been reminded that he had all the makings of a king.

And so it was that

[Josiah the king] did what was right in the eyes of the LORD and walked in all the way of David his father, and he did not turn aside to the right or to the left. (2 Kings 22:2)

YOU ROCK

Another example of this self-image-is-a-gift comes from the New Testament account of the disciple named Simon. Here was an impetuous fisherman whom Jesus invited to join His band. At about the halfway point in Jesus' three-year ministry He took His disciples to a region called Caesarea Philippi in northern Palestine. It was at this small gathering that Jesus gave Simon a new name, a new identity.

[Jesus] said to [the disciples], "But who do you say that I am?"
Simon Peter replied, "You are the Christ, the Son of the living God."
And Jesus answered him, "Blessed are you, Simon Bar-Jonah! For flesh and blood has not revealed this to you, but my Father who is in heaven. And I tell you, you are Peter, and on this rock I will build my church, and the gates of hell shall not prevail against it." (Matt 16:15–18)

That morning Simon woke up just an ordinary man. That night he laid his head down a new man. A rock. Would it surprise you that this same man, the apostle Peter, would later write these words to the church, to men like you and me?

> As you come to [Jesus], a living stone rejected by men but in the sight of God chosen and precious, you yourselves like living stones are being built up as a spiritual house, to be a holy priesthood, to offer spiritual sacrifices acceptable to God through Jesus Christ. (1 Peter 2:4–5)

You and I may not have had a godly mother or grandmother like Josiah's, who spoke the image of a good king into our young hearts. But we do have a Good Shepherd who knows us. A heavenly Father who sent his perfect Son to reconcile sinful men with a holy God. He chooses us as His sons. He is a Savior who calls us to be kings and priests.

> *You are a man, created in the very image of the almighty God.*

There's no need to live in the shadows of what you were told as a boy. No reason to wade in self-pity and fear. Like David, Josiah's (seventeen greats) grandfather, and Joseph, his (twelve greats) grandson, the earthly father of Jesus Christ, you have been granted status as a royal.

You are a man, created in the very image of the almighty God.

This isn't veneer. It's not empty motivational pap. It's true.

6 "I'm not responsible for my actions."

You may be too young to remember the comedian Flip Wilson. He hosted his own television show in the early 1970s. One of Wilson's most famous lines, once he had been caught doing something naughty, was "The devil made me do it."

This phrase drew a laugh from the audience every time. It may be funny to some, but it's not true.

Ol' Flip was saying what many men believe about their conduct. I'm not responsible. When I sin, it's someone—or something—else's fault.

OUR NATURE

Imagine that science progressed to the point that it could pinpoint in certain people a "bank-robbing gene." Suppose you had such a gene. To make matters worse, you inherited it from your father and his father before him, both of whom were professional bank robbers. You were reared in bank robbing; the food on your table as you grew up came from larceny.

Now suppose you followed in your dad's steps when you reached adulthood and pulled off a massive bank heist of your own. Then you were caught. Would you tell the judge he must let you go because you have the bank-robbing gene, because your fathers before you were bank robbers? Of course not.

> We excuse our disobedience this way, declaring ourselves "not guilty" because of our wayward DNA.

We come by our skills at passing the buck naturally. It was Adam, our first father, who started this. Thanks, dad.

In our sophisticated age many, both inside and outside the church, are reluctant to affirm a real, historical Adam. So we substitute more scientific sounding excuses, blaming our genetics or our upbringing. Our inborn nature. We excuse our disobedience this way, declaring ourselves "not guilty" because of our wayward DNA.

OUR NURTURE

So there's also our surroundings to blame.

Consider Adam. Only moments before his fall he had been perfect, clean from all sin. He took the fruit from his bride, bit into it, and suddenly everything changed. God came into the garden of Eden and asked

Adam if he had eaten of the forbidden fruit. At least Adam admitted that he had done so.

But then the sins escalated exponentially. "It was the woman," he said, throwing his beloved under the elephant. But to make it even worse, he continued. "It was the woman *that You gave me.*"

Adam was so eager to evade responsibility for his sin that he started with his wife and then ended up blaming the God who made her. It's as if Adam was saying to the Almighty: "I was just taking a nap, minding my own business, when You had to barge in and make this creature from my rib, and now look what happened."

It's true. We are influenced by our environment, but it's a fact that we also bring something to the party . . . our own DNA.

IT'S ME, O LORD

Modern man was not the first to discover the influential power of our surroundings. Remember Isaiah's response to being brought into the very throne room of God. "I am a man of unclean lips, and I dwell in the midst of a people of unclean lips" (Isa. 6:5). However, Isaiah was confessing his sin, not trying to pass it off on someone or something else. He affirmed that he was a sinful man. That is his nature . . . who he is. He affirmed as well that he lived among sinful people (i.e., his environment or his nurture).

Neither Isaiah's nature nor his nurture excused him from his sins. The same is true of you and me. As theologians often point out, "We are not sinners because we sin. Rather, we sin because we are sinners."

> "We are not sinners because we sin. Rather, we sin because we are sinners."

The apostle Paul, in his letter to the church at Rome, echoed the wisdom of Isaiah when he answered the objection to our guilt that we are not ultimately responsible for our sin, that we can't help it because it's the way we were made or we're surrounded by bad influences.

> But who are you, O man, to answer back to God? Will what is molded
> say to its molder, "Why have you made me like this?" (Rom. 9:20)

The truth is this: you and I, precisely because we are men of unclean lips and dwell in a land of unclean lips, stand guilty before the living God. Wishing it weren't so won't make it go away. Doing better won't change a thing. Our situation is dire; we are broken clay pots headed toward the scrap heap.

> But God, being rich in mercy, because of the great love with which he
> loved us, even when we were dead in our trespasses, made us alive
> together with Christ—by grace you have been saved. (Eph. 2:4–5)

The answer to the lie that we are not responsible for our disobedience to a holy and perfect God is His sending His Son to be responsible, to receive the punishment we deserve. Our calling is not to point our fingers at our Maker, but to stand humbly before a holy God and cry out like the tax collector, "God, be merciful to me, a sinner!" (Luke 18:13).

That, and only that, is how we can be justified. The answer to the lie is the One who is the Truth.

THE TRUTH

Regardless of what kind of upbringing we may have had, what may have been done to us, or the difficult or dysfunctional circumstances we may find ourselves in, we are responsible for our own actions.

THINK ABOUT IT . . . *Making excuses takes no effort at all. What is the value of owning our own stuff?*

"Pleasure and entertainment can satisfy me."

Do you remember the story of the troll in the tale of the "Billy Goat's Gruff"?

This was an early account of a tollway . . . in this case, a toll bridge. Or let's call it a "Troll Bridge."

In the story, little goats were trying get from point A to point B but needed to cross the bridge to get there. But the nasty troll claimed the bridge to be his and threatened the goats with their very lives if they tried to traverse his structure.

Have you ever wondered how much fun it would be to own a tollway or toll bridge? Every time someone—motorcyclist or big-rig operator—wanted to drive on your road or bridge, they'd have to pay you a fee? Talk about making money while you sleep!

Of course, you would have had to pay for the construction of your road or bridge in the first place and also be responsible for all the maintenance (including snow removal in the winter).

Never mind.

Sadly, toll roads and bridges are a fact of life. Stopping to pay can be the cause of major traffic jams. Fortunately, in many states, you can drive under electronic readers that communicate with a transmitter on your windshield. You pay the toll without even slowing down. Cool, painless, but still expensive. That sucking sound is the cash being surgically extracted from your wallet.

SOLOMON: THE ORIGINAL (VERY RICH) TROLL

Jerusalem, Solomon's fortified city, was perched on top of one of the world's busiest and most profitable trade routes. The prosperous Hittites, Babylonians, Sumerians, Assyrians, Persians, and Medes traveling to or from Libya, Egypt, Ethiopia, or Turkey were continually moving and trading. Being a walled city on a narrow trade route meant every merchant, often every traveler, had to pay a toll simply for passage. This provided a lavish source of income to the local government, and the king who presided there.

From history we know that Solomon laid claim to some of these popular routes and placed a surcharge each time they were accessed. Money while he slept.

The Old Testament book of 1 Kings, chapter 10, tells us about the wealth and wisdom of King Solomon. He may have been the richest man to ever have lived. In today's dollars, he was likely worth over $2 trillion![1]

> *We know that Solomon laid claim to some of these popular routes and placed a surcharge each time they were accessed. Money while he slept.*

And stuff? Did Solomon have a lot of it? Yes. In fact, during the forty years of his reign, he was visited by perhaps the wealthiest women of her time, the Queen of Sheba. One of the purposes of her visit was to see Solomon's possessions for herself. Like a man checking out his new neighbor's garage to see the guy's power-tool collection, the queen wanted to see if the rumors of Solomon's extravagant wealth were exaggerated.

But what about smarts? Was Solomon also wise? Again, the answer is a definite "yes." The book of Proverbs was this man's personal journal!

Solomon knew no restraint when it came to merry making. He wrote: "Whatever my eyes desired I did not keep from them. I kept my heart from no pleasure, for my heart found pleasure in all my toil, and this was my reward for all my toil" (Eccl. 2:10).

So you'd think that as he approached the end of his life and looked back over his shoulder, he would feel an enormous sense of satisfaction over all he'd collected and accomplished. You'd think that nonstop cash, entertainment, and lavish possessions would leave a permanent smile on his face.

Not so.

Actually, Solomon's is one of history's most heartbreaking epitaphs. In Ecclesiastes, a book the man wrote himself, Solomon summed it all up this way:

Vanity of vanities! All is vanity. (Eccl. 1:2)

Or, as two other translations render it:

Absolute futility. Everything is futile. (CSB)

Utterly meaningless! Everything is meaningless. (NIV)

> *This outwardly prosperous man confessed to me, "I'm the loneliest man I know."*

Scan Ecclesiastes for yourself and you'll see. Solomon strikes a pathetic silhouette on the history of mankind.

Years ago I had the opportunity of meeting a man with a worldwide reputation for thinking good thoughts. His chiseled face wore a permanent grin. His words—written and spoken—were consumed by millions who paid high prices to read and hear them. His lavish home and property were surrounded by a twelve-foot rock wall, with sophisticated security cameras perched at every conceivable angle. Yet in an uncharacteristically vulnerable moment, riding to an event with me in my car, this outwardly prosperous man confessed to me, "I'm the loneliest man I know." His thin smile belied the internal reality no one would have imagined to be the case.

Like you, I am bombarded every day with the illusion that possessions and pleasure can truly satisfy me. "Beautiful people" walking red carpets wearing huge smiles—and sometimes little else—can be alluring. Maybe a little of that would spice up the mundane corners of my life, I can fantasize. Or if I could just have a home in that prestigious neighborhood or buy that amazing new car. But when I remember the vacant life of someone as fabulous as Solomon, my envy screeches to an abrupt halt.

In contrast to true riches—gold, silver, costly stones—the Bible calls this empty stuff, "wood, hay, stubble" (1 Cor. 3:12 KJV). We get this metaphor, don't we?

You and I can be tempted to invest our lives as hedonists pursuing the next big rush. Or as collectors hoping for satisfaction from having it all. Take it from Solomon or from this other guy riding shotgun. It's a waste of time, like chasing the wind.

THE TRUTH

| "He is no fool who gives what he cannot keep to gain that which he cannot lose." —Jim Elliot, martyred in cold blood on the mission field at age 29

THINK ABOUT IT . . . *What do you think would literally be worth dying for?*

 8 *"I'm the master of my own destiny."*

Whether or not we've ever played the lottery, many have at least day-dreamed about what it would be like to win the jackpot. It's difficult not to imagine what we might do with such a windfall of money: the house we would live in, the car we would drive, and, if we are even a bit pious, the causes we would support. Money, however, is just one thing most men crave. Another is power. Power protects money.

King Nebuchadnezzar had both. He was both extremely rich and the unchallenged head of the greatest empire in the world.

The Old Testament book of Daniel reveals the account of this king strolling about on the balcony of his royal palace in Babylon. He stridently lifted his head and his voice.

"Is not this great Babylon, which I have built by my mighty power as a royal residence and for the glory of my majesty?" (Dan. 4:29–30)

You and I may not speak like this because we're not kings of a great empire. However, we can face the same kind of temptation. We look at the work we do, the wealth we have accumulated, the homes we live in, and see them as merely the fruit of our own labor, a monument to our own greatness.

The trouble is, all that wealth and power can easily go to a man's head, which is exactly what happened to Nebuchadnezzar.

God, however, has assured us that He will not share His glory with another. In this case, God is quick to let the king know. These are sobering, tragic, and powerful words to an arrogant king from the Creator King who made him.

> *Nebuchadnezzar fell from the pinnacle of human standing to the status of a common animal.*

While the words were still in the king's mouth, there fell a voice from heaven, "O King Nebuchadnezzar, to you it is spoken: The kingdom has departed from you, and you shall be driven from among men, and your dwelling shall be with the beasts of the field. And you shall be made to eat grass like an ox, and seven periods of time shall pass over you, until you know that the Most High rules the kingdom of men and gives it to whom he will." Immediately the word was fulfilled against Nebuchadnezzar. He was driven from among men and ate grass like an ox, and his body was wet with the dew of heaven till his hair grew as long as eagles' feathers, and his nails were like birds' claws. (Dan. 4:31–33)

Can you imagine? This is no ordinary fall from grace. Nebuchadnezzar fell from the pinnacle of human standing to the status of a common animal. And crazy as it may sound, this was not just a fall from grace, but mercifully, a fall into grace. God will not share His glory, but it is His glory to lead us to repentance, which is just where the king ended up.

At the end of the days I, Nebuchadnezzar, lifted my eyes to heaven, and my reason returned to me, and I blessed the Most High, and praised and honored him who lives forever,

> for his dominion is an everlasting dominion,
> and his kingdom endures from generation to generation;
> all the inhabitants of the earth are accounted as nothing,
> and he does according to his will among the host of heaven
> and among the inhabitants of the earth;
> and none can stay his hand
> or say to him, "What have you done?"

(Dan. 4:34–35)

> We open our hands in a posture of generosity and wonder.

You and I did not create ourselves. Nor do we make ourselves what we are. The truth is this: we have nothing that was not first given to us. This is why we say "grace" when we sit down to eat. We are acknowledging that it is God Himself who sets the table, who provides for us our daily bread. It's our heavenly Father who turns the dead stuff we are eating into nutrition. Our times are in His hands. He is the Potter and we are the clay.

So what do we do with this truth? Actually, that's easy. We take a posture of gratitude and humility. We treat everything we own as a gift from our heavenly Father. We open our hands in a posture of generosity and wonder. We guard our thoughts and our mouths, emptying them of sinful, cynical, and critical words, filling them with praise and thanksgiving to God.

Don't make the mistake of the great King Nebuchadnezzar. You are not a self-made man. Praise Him for all that He has given you. Acknowledge His power, His glory, and His mercy, remembering that He gives grace to the humble and sometimes humiliation to the proud.

And that is a good thing.

THE TRUTH

The Master is the master of our destiny. Daily submitting ourselves to Him will bring us joy, purpose, and true riches.

THINK ABOUT IT . . . *How would you define the word "submission"? In what kinds of situations is submission a good idea? A bad idea? When is it hard for you to submit?*

"Real men don't cry."

The Old Testament records two defining moments in King David's youth. The first happened when the prophet Samuel visited the boy's home looking for the man who would someday be the king of Israel. The youngest son and least likely candidate, David, came in from tending sheep to receive the anointing and then went back to work.

The second moment was when David encountered Goliath in a contest that would determine the outcome of a battle.

It's the stuff of epic cinematography—hillsides filled with thousands of jostling soldiers, clattering armaments, and everything at stake.

Forerunners of the ancient Greeks, the Philistines were accustomed to deciding battles in an arena—gladiator style—rather than hand-to-hand combat between armies. The Philistine army surely felt confident that day with a massive warrior like Goliath in their ranks. But they didn't reckon on the young boy who believed that his God was capable of anything. Winding his way through the company of Israel's soldiers, David's innocent questions were met with shock and derision. The youth, in turn, was astounded by Israel's lack of faith.

Even the king was afraid. "Don't you know who you're fighting for?" David may have asked Saul. "Where's your trust in Him?"

The courage David had exhibited as a boy defending his father's sheep from wild animals would now defend God's people from a godless thug. And the same confidence in the God of his fathers marked his life in the years that followed.[2] David was a shepherd, a warrior, a hero, and a conquering king, a walking testimony of vigor and faith.

And he was also a poet.

THE SOFT SIDE OF A TOUGH MAN

Many of the Psalms were penned by David, written during various seasons of his life. There are psalms praising God for deliverance, extolling His majesty, celebrating His faithfulness, and confessing sin against Him.

There are also multiple Davidic psalms expressing lament and pain. With passion and tenderness, David poured forth his fears, his anguish, and his tears.

In Psalm 42 we see his dependence on God's gracious presence.

As a deer pants for flowing streams,
  so pants my soul for you, O God.
My soul thirsts for God,
  for the living God.
When shall I come and appear before God?
My tears have been my food day and night. (vv. 1-3)

This was not a man who kept his emotions in check. He was not shy, reticent, reserved. He was open before God, expressing the depth of his sorrows.

And it was not just for a brief moment that David's eyes grew a bit misty. He did not have a solo rogue tear escape down his ruddy cheek. No, his tears were his "food day and night." He wept, he wailed, he poured out his heart before God, and in composing the psalm allowed untold generations of pilgrims to enter into his journey.

> *The reality is that it's often a demonstration of our weakness that stifles our tears.*

As men, sometimes you and I think we're supposed to suppress our emotions, apologize for them, or hide them from those in our own homes whom we are called to protect. We think such sensitivity exposes out weakness. Not so. The reality is that it's often a demonstration of our weakness that stifles our tears. David, a man's man, did not have that trouble.

WHAT DID JESUS DO?

If that's not enough for you and me, consider another Man—David's greater Son, Jesus. The shortest verse in all the Bible still packs a punch.

Jesus had returned to his dear friends, Mary and Martha, who were mourning the loss of their brother, Lazarus. And John, in his gospel, tells us simply, elegantly, "Jesus wept" (John 11:35).

And this would not be the last time Jesus would openly display deep feelings.

On the night in which He was betrayed, Luke tells us,

> And being in agony he prayed more earnestly; and his sweat became like great drops of blood falling down to the ground. (Luke 22:44)

So if Jesus—a man's man, to be sure—expressed His emotions in the midst of excruciating circumstances, does that mean we are better than He when we cover ours up? No it doesn't.

We are not to let our emotions rule over us. But nor are we to suppress them, to will them away. That's not strength; it's dishonesty. We need to remember the words of the first song you may have learned at church: "We are weak, but He is strong."

THE TRUTH

Real men are free to feel and express deep emotions. When we do so, it's actually proof that we are men with a heart like God's.

THINK ABOUT IT . . . *Do you sometimes apologize for your tears? In what situations are a grown man's tears a bad idea? When are they good and appropriate?*

 10 *"I don't need close male friends."*

Remember that old playground retort? *Whenever you point a finger at me, you have four more pointing back at you.* As with many playground sayings, there's wisdom in this one.

As I've heard it said, "You are not stuck in traffic; you *are* traffic. You are the other car annoying the people in the other cars!"

Sometimes we go through life wearing blinders, forgetting what it must be like for someone else to do life with us. This is why it's so important to get perspective from others. Without knowing it, our backgrounds and biases color the way we see reality. Like a mirror, true friends can help each other objectively see what they may not be able to see on their own.

THE PERILS OF ISOLATION

Early in my business career, after having experienced a year at the helm of a prosperous company, a friend paid me a visit. He had been alerted to a problem in my business and came calling. His opening line was this: "There's something you need to know."

> Like a mirror, true friends can help each other objectively see what they may not be able to see on their own.

Even though I was sitting in my office chair, I pretended to fasten my seatbelt. Good thing I did. The news was brutal . . . and true. What he had to say about my business, my colleagues—and me—was hard to take. But it was exactly what I needed to hear. This man proved himself to be a true friend, and that conversation was a defining moment for me.

The book of Proverbs, the book of wisdom, tells us about a man without friends.

> Whoever isolates himself seeks his own desire;
> he breaks out against all sound judgment. (18:1)

At the end of this same chapter in Proverbs, separating casual acquaintances from close friends, Solomon writes,

> A man of many companions may come to ruin,
> but there is a friend who sticks closer than a brother. (18:24)

How good is this?

The first verse tells us of the peril of isolation. The last teaches us something about how to spot a real friend. Together these give us a clearer picture of why we need friends, what to look for in a friend, and how to be a good friend to other men.

No doubt from personal experience—and how else do we learn such important lessons?—Solomon is encouraging us to not succumb to the temptation of drawing back and living alone. And he's also suggesting that the solution isn't just hanging out in a sports bar with a whole bunch of guys but making sure we have a close buddy, a confidant . . . a friend who sticks closer than a brother.

WOUNDS AND KISSES

So why are we sometimes tempted to choose isolation? To live detached from authentic community? Is it pride, thinking we can manage on our own? Is it a fear of accountability?

A friend is someone who is willing to tell us the truth, even when it hurts. Another proverb explains this with a powerful word picture:

Faithful are the wounds of a friend;
profuse are the kisses of an enemy. (27:6)

Solomon turns his phrases brilliantly. We don't typically think of friends wounding us and enemies kissing us. We hate wounds and love kisses, hate enemies and love friends. But in truth, enemies can seek our favor through flattery. Friends are those who are willing to risk our friendship, temporarily hurting us by speaking truth for our well-being.

Imagine a doctor who is always smiling. Imagine every report he gives us is positive. Imagine that he encourages our unhealthy habits. When we are sick, he

> *A friend is someone who is willing to tell us the truth, even when it hurts.*

prescribes ice cream. When we are afraid heading into surgery he tells us that it's fine if we don't want to go ahead with the procedure. That's a crony, not a friend; an enabler, not a trustworthy physician.

The doctor who truly cares for us tells us about our high blood pressure. He warns us about our bad habits. And he even sticks us with needles, and if need be, cuts us open that we might be made well.

So it is with a true friend. His wounds heal. A true friend is like a brother, someone who loves us enough to speak with surgical precision and truth. A man from whom we are even willing to hear his concerns for us. The proverb is not simply saying, "Surround yourself with people who are down on you. It will do you good." Rather, it is telling us that someone who loves us speaks hard truths and offers wisdom. In response, we listen and thank our friend for loving us so well.

Men need not just casual buddies but faithful friends—men who stick closer than a brother . . . a good brother. Male friends have a better understanding of the weaknesses of other men, of our patterns of rationalization. And they can speak the kinds of words that will encourage us the most. Men need male friends who come equipped with both courage and wisdom, and a shared commitment to obediently follow in the path of our greatest friend, Jesus.

A FRIEND WHO UNDERSTANDS

Speaking of our friend, the Lord Jesus, the author of Hebrews reminds us, "For we do not have a high priest who is unable to sympathize with our weaknesses, but one who in every respect has been tempted as we are, yet without sin" (Heb. 4:15).

Jesus is our elder brother, the firstborn of the family of God. He always speaks truth to us through His Word. And His end for us, if we are His, is that we would be happy. Blessed.

He is God in the flesh. But He is also a man, just like us, except without sin. And He calls us to not only *have* friends like brothers, but to *be* friends like brothers. Life is tough. Living with integrity and purity are endless battles. And as we both know so well, it's a war out there.

You need friends. I need friends . . . friends who not only speak truth but friends who challenge us with the integrity and example of their own lives. We need to love each other well, well enough to dare to hear and speak truth.

Recently Nancy and I had a "triple date" with my two daughters and their husbands (I love these men who call me dad) . . . what a sweet time it was. As we were updating each other on our lives, my sons-in-law shared how they have regular contact with male friends for Bible study, prayer, and accountability. At one point, one of them leaned in and said, "Dad, who are the men who are speaking into your life?"

> *He calls us to not only have friends like brothers, but to be friends like brothers. Life is tough. Living with integrity and purity are endless battles. And as we both know so well, it's a war out there.*

Bam!

Truth be known, when I married Nancy and moved to Michigan, I left my accountability brothers behind. These few men stood by my side when Bobbie was diagnosed and when she stepped into heaven. One of them actually called himself "Robert's wingman."

But the admonition of my son, who loves me enough to speak honestly, got my attention.

Since that little visit to the "honest planet," I've begun meeting with a new friend—a Christian brother—on a regular basis. How good this feels. Again.

Thank you, to my sons. How blessed I am to have friends like them.

How about you? If I asked you the same question about having a trusted friend who shares your life with you, what would you say?

THE TRUTH

We need godly, male friends—faithful brothers— who love us enough to speak truth. Men whose lives are also open to us so we can speak truth to them.

THINK ABOUT IT . . . *Who are your closest male friends? Name two or three. How well do they know you? Do they speak truth? Are they a safe place for you to go?*

CHAPTER FOUR

LIES MEN BELIEVE ABOUT

SIN

S amuel Langhorne Clemens—Mark Twain—is said to have boasted of playing a practical joke. "I once sent a dozen of my friends a telegram saying, 'Flee at once - all is discovered.' They all left town immediately."[1]

In addition to being a famous author, Twain was also known as a practical joker. A humorist. But this is not funny. How many of us, upon receiving such a message, would be afraid of some embarrassing secret having been found out? For many men, guilt hangs over their heads like a dark cloud on a spring day.

Truth be known, we don't talk about guilt or shame or sin much anymore. But this does not change the fact that we feel guilty and sometimes the things we do are shameful. So whether we talk about it or not, you and I still sin. And our sin is serious.

WHAT HE DOESN'T KNOW

When my siblings and I were kids and visited our grandparents, I remember thinking that they were not only old but also old-fashioned.

A little slow to catch on. When we were with them, we avoided conversations about contemporary music or the latest movies, assuming they just wouldn't understand. Tragically, some treat our sovereign Creator the same way. He's nice and all, but He's just not up to speed with what's really going on.

The concoction of our age is a "God" who looks the other way, who just doesn't get it, or who gently pats our heads and winks at our sin. A God who was rather grumpy in the Old Testament but has now become kinder and gentler.

This may be a nice enough thought, but this narrative suffers from one fatal flaw. It's not true.

SO WHAT'S THE PROBLEM?

It is true that we cannot *earn* God's favor with our obedience. We may suppose that if we kept God's law perfectly He would be perfectly pleased with us. That may be true, but we'll never know since no one (besides Jesus) has ever done that, or ever will.

> Try as we might, our hearts were naturally drawn away from pure thoughts and obedience to God's laws.

Before you and I knew God and through confession and repentance received His salvation, our lives were like a carriage wheel helplessly dropping into a rut on a muddy lane. We could not help it. Try as we might, our hearts were naturally drawn away from pure thoughts and obedience to God's laws.

TAKING GRACE FOR GRANTED

But we know God and have been given a new nature and new affections. We don't have to sin, thanks to the power of the God's Spirit living in us. We are no longer helpless.

It's a fact that, even though you and I were born into sin, under God's judgment, we can *have* God's favor, if we rest in what Christ has done for us rather than what we do ourselves. This is called grace. It's God's favor resting on us, though what we are due is His wrath. Grace is a glorious thing, something we will give thanks for into eternity.

However, like every good gift, grace can be abused and can become for us a danger. As my daddy used to say, sometimes grace becomes "license."

The apostle Paul was well acquainted with his own dependence on God's grace and the dangers of taking grace for granted.

Prior to being knocked to the ground on his way to Damascus and meeting Jesus, Paul had been a card-carrying Pharisee. A "policeman of policemen." A "junior high principal of principals." *La crème de la crème.* He had been scrupulous in seeking to obey all that God commands. But he failed in truly knowing the God whom he thought he knew.

In fact, Paul failed to grasp God's grace to the point that he became an enemy of Christ and His followers, dragging Christians off to prison, even standing by approvingly when Stephen was brutally martyred. In His own time and way, God supernaturally overcame Paul's resistance, showed him his need, and lavished grace on him. God changed his perspective and his standing.

Having experienced the transforming power of grace, Paul came to understand that grace could be abused, a concern he confronted head-on in the New Testament churches. Following Paul's conversion and after several years of study and training, he became a church planter. As needed at times, he was a sort of "doctrinal fireman," putting out flare-ups in those churches through his letters. One of these churches received at least three epistles from him, two of which are included in our Bible.[2] The situation in this church was a mess.

The city of Corinth was renowned as a town given to vice and the pursuit of sensual pleasures. It was a wealthy city as well, one of the most prosperous in the world at the time.

Maybe this sounds like your town. God can (and does) rescue people from such corruption. His grace is more potent than any evil. But while God removes from us the guilt and shame of our sin the moment we come to faith, He does not immediately remove from us its power and influence. The believers in Corinth, like the believers where you and I live, were sinners—before and after receiving Jesus by faith. And they were practicing many of the same repulsive sins as their unbelieving neighbors did. They were prideful, given to pursuing sensual pleasures.

While God removes from us the guilt and shame of our sin the moment we come to faith, He does not immediately remove from us its power and influence.

In chapter 5 of his first letter to the Corinthian believers, Paul identifies the gravity of the people's sin . . . and these were card-carrying church members. He begins, "It is actually reported that there is sexual immorality among you, and of a kind that is not tolerated even among pagans, for a man has his father's wife. And you are arrogant! Ought you not rather to mourn? Let him who has done this be removed from among you" (1 Cor. 5:1–2).

Question: Which was Paul more outraged about: the sin itself or that the church—God's holy bride—not only felt no regret, but was actually proud? Their flagrant sexual sin was bad enough, but why in the world would they be proud of such scandal?

UNDERSTANDING GRACE

This clearly demonstrated, in their minds, their tip of the hat to grace. Like a "Get Out of Jail Free" card pulled from the "Chance" or the "Community Chest" stack in Monopoly, they figured that grace would always excuse whatever sin they embraced.

Or like doting and oblivious grandparents overlooking the wayward activities of their grandkids, these folks blindly accepted their own unruly behavior as well as the sin of others around them. They believed that grace wouldn't label anything as a sin at all. They thought of themselves as sophisticated, beyond such judgmental, pharisaical attitudes.

They proudly insisted that whether they intentionally received it or not, heinous sinners still got grace.

The trouble with this thinking is, of course, that grace does not refuse to call sin what it is. Instead, it honestly identifies and then forgives sin. In fact, if there is no such thing as sin, there is no need for grace. Insofar as grace is the forgiveness of sin, sin is necessary for grace. The people in the church at Corinth had taken the good news that Jesus had come to save sinners and turned it into something terrible—the notion that through grace, sinners actually aren't sinners at all. It certainly sounds nice, kind, inviting. But it leaves sinners in their sin and those being sinned against with no recourse.

The real scandal of grace is that it offers real forgiveness for real sins.

The real scandal of grace is that it offers real forgiveness for real sins.

In Acts 9, a man named Ananias came face-to-face with that scandal. He met a notorious sinner, a man named Saul. But this man had encountered the Lord Jesus on the road to Damascus and was sent help by Ananias, an emissary of God Himself.

As the story unfolded, the Lord spoke in an audible voice to Ananias. This was a devout follower of Christ who had known of this Saul scoundrel and his threats to the church. But the Lord instructed Ananias to visit the recently blinded Saul, lay his hands on the man so his sight could be restored.

Probably more interested in doing away with Saul, Ananias was not a big fan of this hard assignment.

It's never a wise thing to question your Maker, but Ananias has my sympathy. He knew well the reputation of Saul of Tarsus, and knew what a threat he was to believers, so he answered,

> "Lord, I have heard from many about this man, how much evil he has done to your saints at Jerusalem. And here he has authority from the chief priests to bind all who call on your name." (Acts 9:13–14)

Ananias was afraid and seemed to think that perhaps the all-knowing God had somehow forgotten who this blind man was and what he had done. Ananias was scandalized by God's grace and didn't believe it was sufficient for a scoundrel like Paul.

Of course, we understand the conundrum. As Jonah was reluctant to preach to a city as heinous as Nineveh, we can hardly believe that God's grace could forgive really bad people. But the temptation for men who have no open scandal is to forget that we stand only by God's grace. We will never be good enough. We are guilty before a holy God. We mistakenly assume that because we're pretty good guys, we are "deserving" of God's grace. Sadly, this is to deny that grace is available at all.

Some of the Pharisees thought they were too good for God's grace. Some of the tax collectors thought they were too bad for God's grace. They were both wrong.

One of the Pharisees' great complaints about Jesus was that He was a friend of sinners. Yes, Jesus reached out to and kept company with tax collectors and prostitutes. But what these "holy men" missed was that they, the Pharisees, needed to repent just as much as those whose sin was more flagrant. These "righteous" men saw their own sins as small and not worthy to be considered. They were wrong.

Some of the Pharisees thought they were too good for God's grace. Some of the tax collectors thought they were too bad for God's grace. They were both wrong.

So the dividing line between those who receive God's grace and those who do not isn't measured by the number or seriousness of the sins they have committed. Rather it is between those who have repented and those who have not. The promise of God is simple enough:

> If we confess our sins, he is faithful and just to forgive us our sins and to cleanse us from all unrighteousness. (1 John 1:9)

Every sin is serious and should make us grieve. God does not grade on the curve. A flippant attitude is the very opposite of repentance. If, however, we confess and repent, our duty is to believe the promise of God, to be thankful, and to celebrate. His grace is sufficient; our worst sins cannot outrun His kindness toward us.

It's His grace that convicts us of our sins, and it's His grace that gives us peace in our hearts, peace with Him.

> *His grace is sufficient; our worst sins cannot outrun His kindness toward us.*

11. "Who others think I am matters more than who I really am."

My brother, Dan, was a high school and college wrestler. For me, as a junior-high boy, I had enough of a brush with this sport to know two things: (1) It was the most physically strenuous and exhausting thing I had ever done, and (2) I was not meant to be a wrestler.

But Dan had the mental toughness and physical strength and flexibility to do quite well . . . well enough to make his high school and college teams.

A broken leg in Dan's freshman year at Taylor University not only cost him that season, but it also stifled any competitive interest in the sport until his senior year. Taylor was a small-college powerhouse in the sport, and that lured Dan out of retirement and back to the mat for one final season.

Early on in the fall wrestling calendar, Taylor hosted a tournament with an array of highly respected competitors. Colleges big and small made their way to Upland, Indiana, for two intense days. Matches began on Friday night with the preliminary rounds. This framed the matchups for the finals on Saturday.

Difficult early round matchups and the home crowd created a perfect storm for an unfortunate first night. A fierce and seasoned competitor from an elite wrestling program proved a formidable first opponent for Dan. Given the stature of the opponent and by all indications, his three-point loss was respectable.

But in the locker room after the final whistle sounded that first night, Dan's coach exposed the lie that had been reflected not only in his performance but in several of his teammates as well.

> *Jesus had (and still has) an uncanny ability to look beyond appearances and into the motivation of the heart.*

"Men, many of you walked onto the mat tonight with one single objective. You're good enough to beat these guys, but instead of focusing on winning, you were trying to avoid embarrassing yourself against tough competition. You resigned yourself to losing before you stepped onto the mat. All you wanted was to appear competitive. You were lookin' pretty, but gettin' beat."

As you may remember, Jesus had (and still has) an uncanny ability to look beyond appearances and into the motivation of the heart. "Lookin' pretty" wasn't high on His happy list. And He knew what was going on inside men's hearts. Every time, He knew.

WHAT'S THAT SMELL?

Late in His earthly ministry, the Messiah had a few things to say to men who were more interested in how they looked on the outside than who they really were. On the inside.

> "What sorrow awaits you teachers of religious law and you Pharisees. Hypocrites! For you are like whitewashed tombs—beautiful on the outside but filled on the inside with dead people's bones and all sorts of impurity." (Matt 23:27 NLT)

How's that for graphic?

If we think that Jesus was denouncing men who were the scum of society, we need to think again. He was addressing what would look like a church leaders' conference today. These men were elders and deacons. They were small-group leaders and committee chairmen. And they were pastors. At a glance, they looked terrific.

> *They were small-group leaders and committee chairmen. And they were pastors. At a glance, they looked terrific.*

But strip off their holy and attractive vestments, and they smelled like an open grave. An uncovered septic tank in your backyard.

"Lookin' pretty, stinkin' up the place."

Even if you and I don't have a leadership position in our church, we can't escape this same kind of judgment. What we look like on the outside may have nothing at all to do with who we really are.

Even the apostle Paul, a self-admitted "Hebrew of Hebrews," came to understand the tragic space between his appearance and his heart. He wrote:

> So you see how it is: In my mind I really want to obey God's law, but because of my sinful nature I am a slave to sin. (Rom. 7:25 NLT)

Another sobering account of sin lurking on the inside is the one about another man named Ananias[3] and his wife, Sapphira, found in Acts chapter 5. This lovely, church-attending couple put up a convincing front of generosity but inside were greedy and dishonest.

> *Our great temptation is to be more concerned with how things look than the way they truly are.*

But this isn't just a story about a couple with funny names. It's about the conundrum you and I face all the time. Our great temptation is to be more concerned with how things look than the way they truly are.

We are only one revelation away from the truth being exposed, and potentially, from total ruin. We live our lives precariously balanced between what the apostle Paul identifies as looking good on our outside and the truth of what actually is on our inside.

CLOSING THE GAP

One of my favorite realities of God's Word is that it doesn't identify the problem without presenting the fix. In this case, the false pretense of a slick exterior and the sin that lurks inside has a solution. A fix.

God informed the Jewish nation, through the prophet Samuel, that their first king, an extremely handsome man, was a fraud. A looker on the outside but pure corruption on the inside, He sent this message about King Saul to his people.

> The LORD said to Samuel, "Do not look on his appearance or on the height of his stature, because I have rejected him. For the LORD sees not as man sees: man looks on the outward appearance, but the LORD looks on the heart." (1 Sam. 16:7)

So our self-righteousness—the pretty outside—and our unrighteousness—the ugly inside—are both counted as sin.

Since confession is good for the soul, and you and I confess that we have these two personas . . . the outside angel and the inside demon . . . I have a question: Which of these guys did Jesus die for?

Did the Lamb of God go to the cross to save the guy who's lookin' good or the one who's gettin' beat?

That's right.

Jesus died for both. Why? Because both of these guys are hopeless sinners in need of a Savior. They are two sides of the same coin . . . and when the coin gets lost, both sides are lost.

You and I do constant battle with authenticity. Who others think we are and who we really are. I was once reminded of this when a local, well-dressed television news anchorman found himself shamelessly exposed by his "loyal" production crew.

He had just finished his daily broadcast and thought the cameras were no longer rolling. Waist up, behind the desk, the guy looked like something from GQ. But as he stepped out from behind his broadcast table, he was wearing torn, baggy basketball shorts and flip flops.

This was a hilarious made-for-television moment. Even the anchorman laughed.

But living a double life is not funny at all. We know this is true.

| **THE TRUTH** | God's grace is needed for both the phony everyone sees and the scoundrel inside we know so well. |

THINK ABOUT IT . . . *How would you define the word "grace"? Why is this an important concept to understand in your relationships and in your walk with Jesus?*

 ## *"If I mean well, that's good enough."*

When my daughter Julie was a little girl, she discovered what she thought was a catchall for each time she was caught red-handed in a family infraction. She would speak these words with a tilted head and a look that was intended to melt her daddy's heart. Sometimes she was successful. Usually not.

"But I didn't mean to."

For you and me, given our natural bent toward, "I'll figure this out later," our default is often, "I'm sorry, but I meant well."

You've heard the expression, "The road to hell is paved with good intentions." The reason it's so popular is because "I meant

> *"I meant well" is our most frequently used rationalization for our own sins.*

well" is our most frequently used rationalization for our own sins. Sometimes we get bolder still, with the foolish, "God knows my heart." Of course He does. Better than we do. And He knows every bit of ugly in it. Sadly, I'm not in *less* danger because He knows my heart, but *more*.

There is a legal principle in American law that pushes us in this same direction. In order to be considered legally guilty of a crime, I must be shown to have had a *mens rea*, a guilty mind. If I shoot a man, and I can prove that at the time I thoroughly believed he was himself a murderer with immediate and threatening sinister intentions, I am not guilty.

Which means that as long as I can convince myself that I actually mean well when I sin, I have no need to fear consequences from God. After all, He accepts my intentions. Right?

Meet Nadab and Abihu. These brothers do not take up a great deal of biblical ink, but their story powerfully illustrates just how wrong we are about how seriously God takes His rules . . . and how "I meant well" doesn't count. These men were the sons of Aaron, Moses's brother. Nephews of the great liberator of Israel. They were tasked with the responsibility of bringing fire into the tabernacle in order to facilitate worship. And so they did.

Have you ever found yourself reading Old Testament books like Leviticus, only to find yourself bogged down in all the seemingly arcane rules God laid down? Perhaps that's what happened with these two young priests.

> Now Nadab and Abihu, the sons of Aaron, each took his censer and put fire in it and laid incense on it and offered unauthorized fire before the LORD, which he had not commanded them. And fire came out from before the LORD and consumed them, and they died before the LORD. (Lev. 10:1–2)

They knew they were breaking the law. They must have figured that their good intentions counted. But in a dramatic pyrotechnic display, God struck them down. Toasted them on the spot. Immediately. He did not rebuke them and encourage them to get it right next time. He didn't say, "I'm going to count to three and you better have corrected this by the time I'm done." Nor did He say, "I don't care what kind of fire you bring before Me. All I care about is that you meant well." No, He killed them instantly.

Why? Bible scholars have considered this question for centuries. Various theories have been proposed. Some have suggested the brothers used the wrong fire out of

> *But in a dramatic pyrotechnic display, God struck them down. Toasted them on the spot.*

some nefarious motive. Others have speculated they unwittingly got a hold of some explosive materials that just got away from them. There is, however, no need to puzzle over why God did this. The text tells us. Their father, Aaron, probably stunned, and perhaps angry at God's short fuse, goes to Moses to ask this question: Why?

> Then Moses said to Aaron, "This is what the LORD has said: 'Among those who are near me I will be sanctified, and before all the people I will be glorified.'" (10:3)

There's the clear answer. God treats His rules consistent with what He is: holy. The verse ends with Aaron's fitting response to this message from the Lord. "And Aaron held his peace."

God determines His law. He determines how important it is. He will judge what He will judge. And we are not free to stand in judgment over Him. You and I have no right to suggest He is too picky or that He treats as important what is unimportant.

This doesn't mean, however, that our God is cranky or capricious, given to flying off the handle. The law of God is clear. It's binding on everyone. And He requires obedience, not just for His sake, but for ours as well. God's law is always designed to help us, to bless us. It is not His way to impose onerous obligations on us. His rules are an invitation to joy. We disobey at our own peril, not just because we offend Him, but because His law reflects the best of how He made us.

If you'll forgive an illustration from a dog guy, God's rules are something like little crates we buy for our puppies. Of course, these structures keep them from running free in our homes or scampering into traffic. But they also provide a safe place, free from outside danger. So it is with God's laws.

> **True happiness in our hearts is found in obedience. In the end, this is pure joy.**

The image of the American cowboy has sometimes been seen as the ultimate icon of freedom. Now, just in case you make your living as a cowboy, let me be quick to say that some of my closest friends are cowboys. But when it comes to our souls, the open range and living an unfettered, unchallenged life is actually bondage. True happiness in our hearts is found in obedience. In the end, this is pure joy.

Jesus, God's perfect Son, submitted to His Father's rules. And as our Advocate, our perfect example, Jesus set the high mark of perfect obedience. The road to heaven is paved with His willing compliance to God's law. And His suffering was in our place for our failure to obey. God's fire took out His Son instead of us.

THE TRUTH | God cares about His rules. We must do the same, for our own good.

THINK ABOUT IT . . . *Like stripes on the football field, how are rules in life a good idea? Why are God's rules so important?*

 ## *"My sin isn't really that bad."*

It was my first new car. My college graduation gift. I will never forget the feeling of pulling away from the dealership in Arlington Heights,

Illinois. The new-car prep men had cleaned and polished every surface and cleaned every crevice. The 1969 light, metallic green Chevelle Malibu was spotless. I opened the door, slipped behind the wheel, and took a deep breath. The smell of a brand-new car was intoxicating. I looked around at the interior, took another deep breath, and slowly let it out. All was well with the world.

> *The car in front of me came to an abrupt and unexpected stop. I saw him, but it was too late.*

This was my pride. My joy. Over the next few weeks, it was even the subject of some of my dreams. At stoplights, I'd look to my left or right and see how much better my car looked than the guy idling next to me. Don't judge me. You've done the same thing.

Then one Sunday afternoon, just a few weeks later, driving along Roosevelt Road in Glen Ellyn, Illinois, not far from my parents' home, it happened. The car in front of me came to an abrupt and unexpected stop. I saw him, but it was too late.

Before I could do anything about it, I slammed into the back of his car with a dreadful thud. Both cars were still drivable, so we didn't call the police. We exchanged phone numbers and I drove away . . . with a horrible sinking feeling. The front end of my brand-new car smooshed in.

Something unforeseen swept across my mind.. It snuck up on me without warning. My broken heart over my now imperfect car began to be strangely assuaged by my careful observation of the dents and scrapes of other cars on the road. They were everywhere.

And, truth be known, my pushed-in grille wasn't as bad as most of the stuff I saw on other cars driven by . . . other losers.

I was strangely comforted by this.

You and I do the same thing with our moral lives, don't we? When we get in trouble, it's "only natural" to look at others who are in worse shape. While many people don't believe that hell is real, many of those who do think this awful place is primarily reserved for the Hitlers of history. Mass murderers. Serial killers. Incorrigible crooks. Hell is a lonely destination for only the vilest of sinners. Don't such wicked men reassure us that we're not so bad by comparison? Our dents are not nearly as bad as theirs.

> *Our hearts deceive us when we think the great sins of others will somehow make ours less significant.*

But this isn't the way it is. The Bible tells us that there are only two categories. Showroom flawless and ready for the scrap heap. Nothing in between.

It tells us that "there is none righteous, no, not one" (Rom. 3:10 NKJV), that we are "brought forth in iniquity" (Ps. 51:5) . . . sinners from the beginning, and that our hearts are "desperately wicked" (Jer. 17:9 NKJV).

Our hearts deceive us when we think the great sins of others will somehow make ours less significant.

This is not to say that we ought never to make any comparisons. We should. We ought not compare ourselves to Hitler in order to make ourselves feel better, but we ought to compare ourselves to the perfect holiness of Jesus. He is the mirror that rightly shows how filthy we actually are. We are all an infinite distance away from Jesus.

The only reason you and I think our sins are not so bad compared to others is because we have such little understanding of the seriousness of sin and the depth of our own wickedness. We flatter ourselves into thinking we're not that bad.

But tragically, every sin, even those most would consider insignificant in the big scheme of things—a "little white lie," a brief outburst of temper, a lustful thought—is actually cosmic treason. It is an affront to the living God, an attempt to wrest Him from His heavenly throne. With each sin committed, we say to the Almighty: "You shall not reign, but I."

Forgive the graphic picture, but thinking we're better than others isn't just whistling in a graveyard but whistling while dancing blindfolded on the cusp of hell. How utterly scary is that?

We *don't*, we *can't* measure up. But Jesus does. And further, when we rest in Him and receive His obedience, His perfect life of no sin, He takes upon Himself the deserved punishment for our rebellion. And we are wiped clean. The chastening due us has fallen upon Jesus.

| **THE TRUTH** | We cannot look at other, more wicked men to make us feel better. The only comparison that matters is to look the one righteous Man, the sinless Savior who alone can make us whole. |

THINK ABOUT IT . . . *Do you compare and compete? When are these good things? When are they not?*

14   *"God could never forgive me for what I've done."*

I once read something in a book that stopped me cold.[4]

The author observed that sometimes it's easier for us to forgive others who sin than it is to receive God's forgiveness for what *we* have done. Granting others grace can be a lesser challenge than embracing the same grace ourselves.

So why is this true? Why am I willing to "stoop" to forgive you for something you've done when I hesitate to receive the forgiveness that's mine through the cross of Christ? The writer suggested that it's pride. I agree.

Somehow, I'm willing to cut others slack when they fail, recognizing that they are sinners, but my arrogance keeps me from admitting the same.

Do you remember the story Jesus told in Luke 18 about the two men who went into the temple to pray? One guy was fastidiously religious. A model citizen.

The other man was a despised tax collector—an extortionist. A cheater; a dirty thief. No one needed to tell this fellow that he was despicable.

Other worshipers in the vicinity probably sneered at the thought of him setting foot in the temple.

The first man's "prayer" went something like this: "Thank you, God, that I'm not like this tax-collecting slime bag." But the second man, deeply ashamed of his own behavior, refused to even look heavenward, begging God to grant him mercy because of his sin.

The fact is, both of these men were miserable sinners, but the first was unwilling to go there. His sin was his self-righteousness, but, of course, he'd never be vulnerable enough to own up to his sinfulness. Just think of what that would do to his pristine image among his friends and colleagues.

> Somehow, I'm willing to cut others slack when they fail, recognizing that they are sinners, but my arrogance keeps me from admitting the same.

At the close of this parable, Jesus left no doubt as to the different outcomes of these two worshipers. The first guy, the one who thought he was a paragon of virtue, left the temple blinded by his self-deception and self-righteousness. The second man, the one he and everyone else knew to be a guilty sinner, went home "justified." Clean, as if he had never sinned.

The devil is not only a deceiver, but a clever and effective one at that. You and I tend to picture him tempting us toward egregious sins. Of course, these kinds of temptations are tools in his arsenal and something we should be on our guard against.

But broadside temptation is not the principal means by which he attacks us. The root of the word "Satan" (transliterated from the Hebrew *satan*) means literally "slanderer" or "accuser." His bread and butter may be less to tempt you toward new, "big" sins than to cause you to spiral down into despair over the sins you have already committed. He wants you to believe that the store of your past sins is somehow too vast for God's grace. Tragically, we are tempted to believe this lie: *God could never forgive me for the many things I have done.*

The late Dr. R. C. Sproul told the story of a student who came to him for counsel. It seems the young student had committed a terrible sin and was not feeling forgiven in spite of many attempts to repent and confess to the Lord what she had done.

"I'd suggest that you go back to your dorm room, get on your knees, and plead with God to forgive you of your sin," the wise theologian said.

"I want you to go plead that God would forgive you for failing to believe His promises."

Completely crestfallen, the student explained, "I'm afraid you haven't been listening. Repenting is all I've been doing, and it hasn't done any good."

"I heard you just fine," Dr. Sproul told her, ". . . I want you to beg God to forgive you for not believing His promises. He said, 'If we confess our sins, he is faithful and just to forgive us our sins and to cleanse us from all unrighteousness' (1 John 1:9)."[5]

God is dead serious about this forgiveness thing. His promise to wipe our slate clean is just that . . . an unqualified promise.

This covenant promise is yours and mine. Whether we experience the low-grade headache of secret sin or have fallen into more visible and shocking sin, Satan's message is that we're beyond God's ability or willingness to forgive us for what we've done. He whispers that we are just too wicked to be forgiven, that God's grace is only for people whose sins are not as glaring as our own.

It is not humility but arrogance that would say to the Lord of heaven and earth, "Surely You forgive others, but You cannot forgive me."

The good news—the gospel—is that the grace of God is sufficient to cover every sin no matter how small or great. When we succumb to the temptation to believe we have sinned beyond His ability to forgive, we belittle the grace of God and the God of all grace.

It is not humility but arrogance that would say to the Lord of heaven and earth, "Surely You forgive others, but You cannot forgive me."

Humility is evidenced in refusing to listen to the lies of the Accuser and resting in the assurances of our heavenly Father. He has promised us complete forgiveness, securing that promise through the death and resurrection of His own Son.

He calls us to believe the good news that Jesus came into the world to save sinners. Sinners like you and me.

| **THE TRUTH** | Nothing we have done puts us out of reach of God's complete forgiveness. Nothing. |

THINK ABOUT IT . . . *Who sets the example for forgiveness? In the context of God forgiving you, why is it important to forgive others?*

 ## "*I can hide my secret sin since it only hurts me.*"

Actually, in this one lie there are two untruths tucked in together.

The first lie is that you can successfully hide your secret sin. The second is that your secret sin doesn't hurt anyone else.

As it relates to hiding our sin, there's a Bible story that has haunted me since I read it as a kid. It's even more sobering to me now as a husband, dad, and granddad.

A TRUE STORY ABOUT A MAN WHO TRIED TO HIDE

As the sun rose over Jericho, Achan, of the tribe of Judah, joined the rest of Israel's army, falling in line behind the priests, who marched before the ark. On this morning, the soldiers proceeded around the city, not once, but seven times. Achan must have looked up at faces that had now grown familiar—Jericho's guards standing duty on the city walls. *All of them*, he thought, *will be dead by sunset.*

Earlier, Joshua had instructed the Israelites, telling them that God would destroy the city of Jericho and, because it would be His strength and His power that accomplished this, there was to be no taking of the spoils of war. He warned the army of Israel that disobeying His command would bring destruction on their own nation (see Joshua 6).

Suddenly Achan heard the sound of a trumpet blast followed by Joshua's urgent command: "Shout! For the LORD has given you the city" (v. 16). A loud cry went up from all the people, and the walls of Jericho crumbled like a Saltine cracker in a man's hand.

After a time, once the chaos had diminished, I can picture Achan alone in a house. Stepping over the dead bodies, he stumbled onto a scene that arrested his attention—spoils from the new land—a beautiful robe draped across a chair, a mound of silver, a wedge of gold. Perhaps the people who lived here had hoped to escape with their treasures.

Achan remembered Joshua's warning that the spoils belonged to the Lord. Any man who acted otherwise would bring trouble on himself, on his family, and on all of Israel. *But what trouble could come from merely touching the robe and feeling the heft of the silver and the gold*, Achan may have rationalized?

Surely the garment was the finest he had ever seen.

Did God really say that something as marvelous as this robe was to be destroyed? *Why*, thought Achan, *should I deprive my family of the good things my own hands have won?* Glancing around furtively to be sure he wasn't being watched, he wrapped the gold and silver carefully inside the robe's folds, tucking the precious package beneath his tunic, and fled.

Of course, I'm supplying some imagination here—Scripture doesn't tell us what was going through Achan's mind at the moment. But we know that his secret sin would not remain hidden. Its effects would extend far beyond Achan. His transgression was exposed by way of a stunning victory by the soldiers of Ai, a little nuisance city that Israel's army should have easily defeated. As a result, Israelite lives were needlessly lost.

As I mentioned, the second part of this lie is that your secret sin doesn't hurt anyone else.

Standing before a large company of Israelites, Achan confessed his disobedience. Then Joshua, together with all Israel, took Achan; the silver; the robe; the gold wedge; his sons and daughters; his cattle, donkeys, and sheep; his tent and all that he had to the valley of Achor. And Joshua said, "Why have you brought this trouble on us? The LORD will bring trouble on you today" (Josh. 7:25 NIV).

It's sin's nature to hide.

Then in a public way of executing those convicted of treason before God, the people of Israel picked up large rocks and threw them at Achan, his family, and his possessions. Can you imagine the awful scene? When they were all dead, crushed under the rocks, the Israelites burned them. Over Achan they heaped a large pile of rocks, which remained for many years. His sin not only led to his own death but also to the deaths of his family members and the soldiers at Ai.

Achan may not have been a bad man, at least to begin with. Growing up during the years of the Israelites' wilderness wanderings, he may even have fed himself on dreams of what life would be like in the promised land where he could build a life for his family. He may have rushed into Jericho fully intending to follow the Lord's commands. But then came an opportunity to do otherwise. And that's when his resolve faded.

Achan's disobedience was compounded when he attempted to cover up what he had done, burying the stolen goods beneath his tent. How could he think he could hide from the God who had made him, the God who had parted the Red Sea and the Jordan River, the God who had just caused the walls of a fortified city to crumble without a weapon being raised against it? Why was Achan foolish enough to think that God would be unable to see through his little deception?

It's sin's nature to hide. Consider your own experience. Do you find it hard to admit your sins to others? Is it sometimes even difficult to admit them to yourself? You and I can come up with ingenious ways to hide the ugliness of sin from ourselves and others, by rationalizing, excusing, and even forgetting things we've done wrong. But Achan's story tells us that God is never fooled by such foolishness.[6]

Many years ago, a friend of my wife asked me to visit their home. It was an evening I will never forget. The woman's husband had been caught in an illicit affair and had decided that his paramour was more desirable than the faithful mother of his children. Now he was going to inform his two sons that he was leaving home.

After he pathetically tried to explain his rationale for this tragic decision and promised to "stay in touch with them," the younger of the boys began to softly cry.

"What's the matter, Kyle?" his daddy said with no more emotion than he would have displayed had he asked his boy why he was wearing a blue shirt rather than a green one.

The boy's lip quivered as he replied softly: "I'm very sad."

Clearly guarding his own emotions, the father responded with a steely glaze. He said nothing.

Simple obedience to the Word of God and the keeping power of His grace are the best defense against sin. But knowing that others whom we love will be (often deeply) impacted by what we choose to do ought to be an added deterrent.

TRYING TO COMPARTMENTALIZE SIN

As men, you and I can be experts at compartmentalizing. Women often tend to be more global. Relational, practical, and balanced. Here's an example.

I'm a builder at heart. When Nancy and I were dating, she casually mentioned that, because she loves to host friends for dinner (and does a lot of it), she'd like to have the deck on the back of the house expanded. That's all I needed to hear. In fact, I had to concentrate like a surgeon on the rest of our conversation because all I could see was this brand-new deck. "Robert the focused carpenter" took over.

A year later we were married and the deck became an obsession. In fact, expanding this structure from five hundred to a thousand square feet, including drilling sixteen post holes in the backyard, dozens of two-by-eights and two-by-tens, and installing brand-new deck boards on the whole thing only took me three weeks . . . while working a full-time job completely unrelated to construction.

> **Until I finish, I'm a builder. Eating and sleeping will come later.**

So how did I do this? I didn't eat. And I hardly slept. When I'm building something with my own hands, I get so obsessive, I consider eating and sleeping a complete waste of time. Until I finish, I'm a builder. Eating and sleeping will come later.

This can work to our advantage. But it can also be a huge liability.

Because I traffic in word pictures, I have been fond of the title of a book published in 2007: *Men Are Like Waffles—Women Are Like Spaghetti.*[7] I'm sure this is a terrific book, but I've not read it. I don't need to. The title is good enough for now.

Can you see it? You and I tend to have little compartments in order to organize stuff—work, fathering, church, husbanding, hobbies, and so forth. Our wives tend to be connectors—relationships, emotions, knowledge, past experiences. Get the picture?

When my friend in the story above was breaking his covenant vows that ultimately destroyed his family, he was thinking waffles. Not spaghetti. He was living in a small compartment of his own making, but this was wrong. His actions were inseparably intertwined with his family.

So even though he had put his little affair in a confined space, hoping it wouldn't slosh over into anything else, he failed to realize how truly connected everything really is. Spaghetti, not boxes or waffles.

When you and I try to hide our sin, or fail to do the right thing, we only compound the problem by attempting to put it in a container. We cover our sin by forgetting its certain consequences on many others beside ourselves.

What do we do with this? We must go directly to God, admit the truth of our selfish waywardness and confess our sin, expressing our sorrow and asking His forgiveness, certain that He will give it.

Then, we can go to those whom we have wronged, seeking restitution and restoration. If this is you, now you know what to do.

The landscape of history is littered with the wives and children of men who flippantly refused to do these things . . . men who have paid a costly price. But this does not need to be.

> *When you and I try to hide our sin, or fail to do the right thing, we only compound the problem by attempting to put it in a container. We cover our sin by forgetting its certain consequences on many others beside ourselves.*

Whoever conceals his transgressions will not prosper,
but he who confesses and forsakes them will obtain mercy.
(Prov. 28:13)

THE TRUTH | Our secret sins cannot be hidden indefinitely. They will one day be brought into the light. We live in community. Our marriage, our children, our neighborhood, our church, our workplace . . . what we do—good and not so good—impacts those around us.

THINK ABOUT IT . . . *How do your sins impact other people?*

"Holiness is boring."

From the time I was a young boy, I remember hearing the word "holiness" used as an adjective. For example, it modified the word "camp," as in "Holiness Camp." This place located in Lancaster County was filled with plain women sporting unflattering, baggy dresses, eyes looking heavenward as they glided from one meeting to the next, squeezing thin smiles through their tightly pursed lips.

When boys like me attempted anything resembling play or levity, we were scolded with a cleared throat, a sideward glance, and furrowed brow.

I did not select "holiness camp" among other summer options. Fact is, I had no choice. From my eight-year-old perspective back then, it came close to "cruel and unusual punishment."

> **There was no doubt. This holiness thing was serious business.**

My hosts were my paternal grandparents. My grandmother never would have been caught wearing anything colorful. Black and gray—or navy blue when she was feeling wild and crazy—were the only hues we ever saw on her. Her husband, whom she called "Papa," dutifully followed her everywhere. She may have tried to force an occasional smile. He? Never.

There was no doubt. This holiness thing was serious business.

Of course, I was also accustomed to the word "holy" paired with "Bible," "Communion," and the night that is Christmas. But using the word to describe people like you and me? That sounded anything but scintillating. I'd seen these people. Lots of them. No, thank you.

SO THIS IS HOLINESS?

With the sense of humor that God clearly has, I married a woman in 2015 who had written a book titled *Holiness: The Heart God Purifies*. So not only is holiness a word that describes a cloistered, boring campground;

now it's the title of one of Nancy's bestselling books! Oh, my.

In the first chapter, Nancy tells of her early experiences with the concept.

> *I was blessed to grow up in a home where holiness was emphasized and taken seriously. . . . From earliest childhood, I remember thinking that holiness and joy were inseparably bound to each other.*[8]

Holiness and joy? Blessed? Seriously? I don't know about you, but I want some of that.

In fact, in the book Nancy describes her dad, Art DeMoss, a man whom I never met but a man who left an indelible mark on his daughter, his wife and children, and tens of thousands of others.

> *Prior to his conversion in his mid-twenties, he had been a free-wheeling gambler in mad pursuit of happiness and thrills. When God reached down and redeemed him, his lifestyle changed dramatically—he no longer desired the earthly "treasures" with which he had been trying to fill the empty places of his heart. Now he had found "the pearl of great price" he had been lacking for so many years. He loved God's law and never considered holiness burdensome—he knew that sin was the* real *burden, and he never got over the wonder that God had mercifully relieved him of that burden through Christ.*[9]

A lost man, now found and new . . . and seeking holiness. Isn't this amazing?

ABOUT ANOTHER DAD

When Missy was born in September 1971, I had the privilege of becoming a father. Three years later it happened again when Julie was born. I know what it is to love my children more than life itself. And as they grew, I had the privilege of shepherding their hearts. Every Christmas I would write a letter to my daughters, affirming my love for them and assuring them of my prayers on their behalf. I did my best to write truth and wanted them to know what mattered to me and to be reminded of things I trusted would matter to them. A letter like this written to those you love is a priceless thing.

In his later years, the apostle Peter wrote a letter in which he challenged his friends with remarkable honesty and persuasion.

> As obedient children, do not be conformed to the passions of your former ignorance, but as he who called you is holy, you also be holy in all your conduct, since it is written, "You shall be holy, for I am holy." And if you call on him as Father who judges impartially according to each one's deeds, conduct yourselves with fear. (1 Peter 1:14–17)

So did Peter write this letter as punishment to these people, or was it written from the heart of a man who loved them deeply and longed for God's best for them? Yes, to the latter.

And did he candidly admonish them, for their own good, to pursue holiness before a holy God, with deepest reverence and respect? Again, yes.

In his book *A Hole in Our Holiness*, Kevin DeYoung sums up the reason we should long to be holy:

> *God is our heavenly Father. He has adopted us by his grace. He will always love his true children. But if we are his true children we will also love to please him. It will be our delight to delight in him and know that he is delighting in us.*[10]

THE TRUTH

Living a holy life, in dependence on the power of the Holy Spirit, is a wonderful thing . . . it is the pathway to happiness and pure joy.

THINK ABOUT IT . . . *What does the word "holiness" mean to you? Can you think of reasons why personal holiness matters?*

CHAPTER FIVE

LIES MEN BELIEVE ABOUT

SEXUALITY

In the spring of the year, the time when kings go out to battle, David sent Joab, and his servants with him, and all Israel. And they ravaged the Ammonites and besieged Rabbah. But David remained at Jerusalem. (2 Sam. 11:1)

The king drew in a long breath of fresh air and looked slowly around the city. The sun was beginning its descent in the west, casting long shadows across the city he loved. The city over which he reigned. Except for an occasional chirp of a bird and the shuffle of the footsteps of a passerby on the cobblestones below, all was quiet. Oh how he relished these late afternoon visits to the palace balcony.

"This is all mine," David whispered to himself. "Mine," he repeated.

Light from a lamp flickered in a window below. His eye scanned past the casement and then returned to it.

Was there someone there? Yes, a woman.

Was she bathing? Again, yes.

David summoned an aide who arrived quickly.

"Who is that woman?" the king inquired.

"Is not this Bathsheba, the daughter of Eliam, the wife of Uriah the Hittite?" the servant replied (2 Sam. 11:3).

David's pulse quickened. *I have not been with a woman in too long*, he may have thought to himself. *But she is someone's daughter. And someone's wife. I cannot.*

But I am the king, he must have rationalized. *No one has the right to stop me from this pleasure. I must. I will.*

For a moment, the conflict raged. And then it subsided. Immediate pleasure and the need for the king to prove his own power and importance prevailed.

Just like this city, she can be mine as well.

"Go," David ordered his servant. "Bring her to me."

In the moments that passed between his order and the arrival of the women in his private chamber, the king's mind was in a swirl. He knew what he was doing was a violation of God's commands. He would surely regret it. But in this moment, it did not matter. Passion prevailed.

The woman was escorted into his chamber; her glance met the king's eyes; the servant bowed low and made his exit.

His decision had been made. David knew the law. He was well-versed on what the consequences could be. But in this moment, logic did not matter. Intense desire shrouded sound thinking. The king would figure this out. He always did.

And with David in the place of ultimate power and authority, Bathsheba hardly had a choice in the matter.

ADULTERY'S AFTERMATH

The following morning, Bathsheba returned to her home. David returned to his kingly assignments. Within a few weeks days, the rendezvous may have been a faded memory.

For the king, work had to be done, wars needed his undivided attention and strategy. The tryst found a quiet enclave in his memory.

And then word arrived: the woman was pregnant.

David's mind raced. His options formed a single-filed queue like obedient servants. And as he had always done in battle, a plan was birthed.

> So David sent word to Joab, "Send me Uriah the Hittite." And Joab sent Uriah to David. (2 Sam. 11:6)

But the king's scheme ended in tragedy. A loyal soldier fell cold on the battlefield. A child lay dead. The king's heart was ruined.

Like a boiling thunderstorm building low in the western sky, this historic sequence had been predicted.

Back in Eden, when Eve took and ate the forbidden fruit and when Adam, consumed by his ability to rationalize, joined her, the consequence was death.

Like a boiling thunderstorm building low in the western sky, this historic sequence had been predicted.

> And the woman said to the serpent, "We may eat of the fruit of the trees in the garden, but God said, 'You shall not eat of the fruit of the tree that is in the midst of the garden, neither shall you touch it, lest you die.'" But the serpent said to the woman, "You will not surely die." (Gen. 3:2–4)

Tragically, in spite of the liar's promise, die they did. Spiritually they died. In that instant, sin separated them from God.

Their bodies? Not in this moment, of course. But for the first time since their creation, their bodies began to age . . . to wrinkle, to grow weary and sick. And then, to perish.

ADULTERY IS EVERYWHERE

There's little doubt that you know at least one man who has had a sexual affair. A husband who has violated his marriage covenant and slept with a woman who was not his wife.

Or maybe you've been a covenant-breaker yourself. If so, you know the battle that rages in your soul. The panic that sets in during moments of quiet. Moments you do your best to avoid.

Like Adam, like David, you stepped into this with your eyes open. You rationalized. You built a case. You caved. You suffered. Something died.

Even men who claim no biblical moorings experience this pain. A piece on the internet quoted married men explaining what it's like to have an affair. A thirty-two-year-old attorney reflected candidly on his regrets:

> I'll never do it again. But it's not like I've had some ethical reawakening. All that sneaking around will drive a man crazy after a while. Even if you're in a bad place in your marriage, the deceit will weigh on you and it's just not worth it in the end. My exploits will probably send me to the grave a decade earlier than scheduled. And for what? Some cheap thrills . . . ?[1]

The stats are easy to pull up. But we don't need these numbers to know. Adultery is everywhere, virtually and for real.

The stats are easy to pull up. But we don't need these numbers to know. Adultery is everywhere, virtually and for real.

As men, you and I understand this relentless pull toward infidelity and unfaithfulness. In fact, as though He needed to make it worse, Jesus adds a layer of impossible in His most famous sermon:

"I tell you," Jesus prefaces a left hook directly at the noses of every man everywhere, "that anyone who looks at a woman lustfully has already committed adultery with her in his heart" (Matt. 5:28 NIV).

Seriously? Just lusting and not actually doing anything? Guilty as charged.

But why would God place in our bodies a drive so insatiable that must be held in check? An appetite so pervasive and strong with the capability to send even the world's most admired men—even Christian men—down to sniveling defeat and public shame. Why would He do this?

Is this a cruel joke? It may seem as though He hands us a grenade with the pin removed and tells us to carry on.

Early in my career, I had the privilege—some days, the sentence—of serving in youth ministry. Each summer we would sponsor a camp experience for hundreds of teenagers. These featured the usual horseback riding, boating, campfire s'mores . . . and breakout sessions. For many years I taught the one on sexuality. And can you guess how well it was attended? Right. It was full every time.

As a newlywed, I had all the information I needed to talk about this with some credibility. The teenage girls who were there loved the session. They "ooed" and "ahhed" when I talked about romance and sex and babies and the joy of becoming a dad.

The boys looked like pressure cookers, sitting there with placid looks on their faces but steam rising from their necks. These are the kids—years ago, before the advent of the internet and instant access to everything a boy would like to know about the plumbing—who hurried to the reproduction chapter in their biology textbook. Don't judge them. You did this, too. In fact, you may have hurried to the sexuality chapter in this book, "just to be more informed."

But, again, I ask, "Why? Why would God place this almost irrepressible drive inside us?"

There must be a good reason. In fact, I think I may have a metaphor that works.

The internal combustion engine.

Because it's so common, we can forget how explosive and dangerous gasoline is. In fact, just a few days prior to writing these words, the driver of a tanker truck in Karachi, Pakistan, lost control of his rig and rolled it into a ditch.

People quickly assembled. Using makeshift containers, they began capturing some of the valuable fuel that was leaking out of the capsized truck. Eyewitnesses reported that one of the bystanders lit a cigarette. And in a flash (literally) the entire scene mercilessly erupted in a fireball. Over 150 people perished. Instantly incinerated. Many more, standing at a significant distance, were severely burned.

Incredibly, the very same thing happens when you and I twist the ignition key—or touch the ignition button—in our cars. But thankfully, this explosion happens under controlled and safe circumstances, inside the confines of almost six hundred pounds of steel in our engine block.

> But thankfully, this explosion happens under controlled and safe circumstances, inside the confines of almost six hundred pounds of steel in our engine block.

Without this explosion, we would sit quietly and unproductively in our garages.

With divine purpose in mind, God has placed in you and me this almost unquenchable drive.[2]

Down through the centuries, men have taken this potentially lethal power and claimed uncharted territories. They have scaled mountains, traversed perilous trails, conquered vicious foes, standing victorious over them. Men have wooed reluctant virgins to their embraces . . . and to marriage altars.

Using this God-ordained passion and drive, this energy, the Creator has placed in your heart and mind a boiling potential for service, leadership, greatness, integrity, discipline . . . and yes, humility.

This chapter will unpack that sexual strength, that surge of energy, which, when expressed under His control, can empower you and me for great things in His name. And which, when misused or abused or done in secret, will explode in lethal carnage.

This God-given power can—and will—dethrone men of every stripe, including preachers and kings, or galvanize them to historic greatness.

 ## "*A little porn is harmless.*"

When my sister, Ruth, was a toddler, her parents (mine, too) decided that she didn't need to taste candy. "Why get her started on sugar?" they must have determined. Ruth never knew what she was missing. Until a nice lady at church—where our dad was the pastor—slipped her a LifeSaver. Little Ruthie carried the candy around in her tiny fist like it was a toy. But the sticky got the best of her and she licked her hand.

The look on Ruth's face must have been one of astonishment. And joy. And don't you know she was not a little upset at her parents for keeping the delight of candy from her. My siblings and I laughed when our mother told us this story.

My first look at pornography happened a few doors down from my dormitory room in college. Several men were huddled around a magazine, opened to photographs of naked women. One even featured a couple in a sex act.

> *And like my sister and the LifeSaver, one taste is never enough. Never. It always leads to an appetite for more. Always.*

This was in 1965, over a half century ago, and I can still "see" these images.

Maybe you have a story about your "first time." That unforgettable taste.

And like my sister and the LifeSaver, one taste is never enough. Never. It always leads to an appetite for more. Always.

And, thanks to the internet, the story of my going a few doors down to see pornography has changed. Consider these facts:

- Americans spend over three hours on their smartphone each day.[3]
- A variety of apps are used to facilitate sexual encounters between strangers.
- Pastor and author Levi Lusko says: "Pornography has become such a problem that boys as young as twelve are sent to live-in porn detox camps—some lasting as long as nine months—to kick the porn habit. One teenager enrolled at one such organization said he had been watching pornography for up to nine hours a day on his Nintendo DS."[4]

Pornography use is pandemic. And it's not just a problem "out there" in the world. In fact, about two-thirds of Christian men watch pornography at least monthly, the same rate as men who do not claim to be Christian.[5]

So what would we say about the temptation toward pornography? How's this strong admonition from the apostle Paul:

> Fix your thoughts on what is true, and honorable, and right, and pure, and lovely, and admirable. Think about things that are excellent and worthy of praise. (Phil. 4:8 NLT)

SELF-GRATIFICATION

Back in the garden of Eden, when Adam took a bite of the forbidden fruit, he knew exactly what he was doing. His rationale may likely have been that he'd figure this out later. Someday he'd hike up his self-control and get past it. Someday.

Tragically, you and I still live with this empty someday fantasy. "Someday" has never arrived.

Before moving to Michigan in 2015, I lived in Orlando for almost sixteen years. During that time, my late wife and I visited Walt Disney World and Universal Studios many times. These popular theme parks promise experiences of delight and wonder. And for most of the millions who visit them every year, the promises are kept, thus the repeat customers.

In those years there was something I never saw. Not once. I never saw anyone—young or old—visiting one of these parks, or the hundreds of other remarkable "attractions" that central Florida features, *alone*. No one—at least that I witnessed—went to these places by themselves. Nor did I ever go there by myself. Why is this true? You know the answer, don't you? Ecstasy you experience by yourself is really no fun at all.

For example, the intense euphoria men experience during masturbation is short-lived. Yes, it can be gratifying. And by definition, masturbation is something men do alone. But, compared to sharing intercourse with a wife whom you love, the ecstasy you experience by yourself is empty. In fact, your mind can take you to horrible places in the moment. An erection has no conscience.

Right now, as you read this chapter and, presumably, have "your wits about you," do you think it might be good time to make a decision regarding what you watch and what you do with what you watch? You may need a seasoned pastor or professional counselor to help you get there. But even the simple decision to get help is your first step to healing from this powerful addiction.[6] This courageous move will begin to help you deal with your insatiable draw to pornography.

Terminating our attraction to pornography isn't simply a dusty experience of choosing cloistered monastic living. We're not digging our fingernails into our gums in an act of self-mortification and feeling a sense of pride because we've conquered a treacherous foe.

> *"Saving yourself" for your wife is worth the investment.*

No, we are not walking away from something perilous with nothing worthwhile to take its place. "Saving yourself" for your wife is worth the investment. When a man walks away from pornography, there's no sinking regret here over losing something wonderful.

Pornography, and the deed it forces on us, is a synthetic substitute for something far more wonderful. For a married man, God gives a joy that makes self-gratification as exciting as the twenty-five-cent plastic pony ride at Walmart compared to riding "Kingda Ka" at Six Flags in New Jersey.[7]

Shared sexual expression in the context of a Christ-centered, monogamous marriage is fantastic. Euphoric. Better than anything we could ever do alone. Why? Because intercourse is a gift you are giving to your wife. It's not primarily about you. This is real. It's true. It's worth trading in self-gratification for something better.[8]

And for an unmarried man, intimacy in a relationship with Christ that focuses energy toward pleasing Him and serving others fills the vacuum of unexpressed sexual intimacy in a sweet and powerful way.

I have a Christian friend who, as a result of a challenge from a speaker at a marriage conference, confessed a pornography addiction to his wife.

The years that ensued were painful for this couple. Many sessions with a godly counselor, and coming to terms with both the sin and the gift of God's grace, slowly released this husband and wife from the ravages and consequences of this awful stuff.

> For an unmarried man, intimacy in a relationship with Christ that focuses energy toward pleasing Him and serving others fills the vacuum of unexpressed sexual intimacy in a sweet and powerful way.

Today this couple has a powerful under-the-radar ministry to couples facing the same terror. Their story is a testament to all we've talked about in this chapter. If this is your story, the same can be true for you and your wife.

For a married man, whether it's visiting pornography and masturbating, or living in an adulterous relationship, these are accurately described as sexual immorality. And "sexual immorality cuts off the wings that lift us toward the highest, richest, most durable joy."[9]

This is raw, unvarnished reality. Straight talk from a friend. I promise. Like poison, all kinds of pornography are devastating to your heart.

| **THE TRUTH** | Pornography is deadly. For a married man, it is virtual adultery. Intimacy with Christ and sexual expression in the context of monogamous marriage offer far greater satisfaction. |

THINK ABOUT IT . . . *Do you know someone who is caught in the awful web of porn? Are you? What is this doing to him? To you? Can you think of any good reason why this guy— or you—should not stop this right now?*

18   *"What my wife doesn't know won't hurt her."*

"Can we have lunch?" My friend had just called me without notice. "It's been too long," he added.

A few days later we met at our favorite Mexican restaurant. Lunch with this guy was always fun. But sadly, not this time.

"Patrick" had a hugely successful computer software business. And he had recently opened a men's clothing store in our town ("just for kicks"). I was eager to hear how it was going—especially his new venture.

But Patrick didn't want to talk about suits and ties and dress shirts. Something was clearly heavy on his mind.

"I don't want to talk clothing," he said. And after a few silent moments, he cut to the chase. "I'm having an affair," he said, his eyes glazing with tears.

> *"I'm having an affair," he said, his eyes glazing with tears.*

"Does 'Sandra' know?" I asked.

"She has no idea," he replied.

Slowly Patrick unpacked the story. The woman was a colleague at work. Bright, articulate, beautiful, and in an unhappy marriage. But Patrick still loved his wife and his kids. And, in his heart, he really wanted to do the right thing.

Patrick knew he had no choice but to tell his wife. I encouraged him in this decision to confess the affair to Sandra. And I offered to go with him. He agreed.

GUARDING YOUR HEART

The core issue here regarding sexual temptation is the condition of our hearts.

"Guard your heart above all else," a concerned dad warned his young adult son, "for it determines the course of your life" (Prov. 4:23 NLT).

Many years ago I had a close friend who made a bad decision to hang out in a hotel bar and stay there until late into the night. This man had never been unfaithful to his wife. But after a few extra drinks, he began a conversation with a woman that continued into the early hours of the next morning.

Before going to their separate rooms, they exchanged cell numbers. When he returned home from the trip, my friend told me all about the woman. "Nothing bad happened," he said, cautiously defending himself. "But we did share phone numbers," he added.

I remember this conversation as though it happened last week. My friend and I were in his office. He was behind his desk; I was standing in front of him. And I spoke to him as lovingly and directly as I could.

"Guard your heart," I pleaded with him. "Guard your heart."

"Guard your heart," I pleaded with him. "Guard your heart."

FOR BETTER OR FOR WORSE

You and your wife may have written your own wedding vows. Or you may have taken them from a contemporary source. But you'll remember that the traditional wedding vows included "for better or for worse."

When you are hiding a secret from your wife, this qualifies as "for worse." You feel this in your gut. It keeps you awake at night. Or it impacts your eating—some guys overindulge, others starve themselves. Some buy a membership to a local health club and become obsessed with getting buff. One guy I knew, with a body resembling a beached manatee, signed up for a triathlon while he was cheating on his wife. Crazy. What's for certain, however, is that the situation you're putting yourself in is going to have an impact on you. It's inescapable.

Keeping secrets is like standing chest-deep in water, trying to hold a beach ball down. It takes both hands and lots of energy. But eventually, physics will win out. You'll run out of energy and the ball will explode through the surface. You will be found out.

Jesus talked about hidden things in no uncertain terms:

"Nothing is covered up that will not be revealed, or hidden that will not be known. Therefore whatever you have said in the dark shall be heard in the light, and what you have whispered in private rooms shall be proclaimed on the housetops." (Luke 12:2-3)

In the context of hiding secrets from my wife, this passage sends chills down my back. What I am hiding will become common knowledge, not only to her but also to everyone. Eventually. One day these secret things will be headlines for all to read. My good choices are either to not push the beach ball down in the first place—not to harbor the secret—or if I do have something to tell her, let it gently surface under controlled conditions as soon as possible.

Keeping secrets is like standing chest-deep in water, trying to hold a beach ball down. It takes both hands and lots of energy. But eventually, physics will win out. You'll run out of energy and the ball will explode through the surface. You will be found out.

"Honey, can we talk tonight?" you can say to her. "There's something really important that I need to share with you."

And then you sit down and unpack what's on your heart. You assure her that you have taken this up with the Lord. You've repented and He has granted forgiveness. And now you'd like to tell her about it and you're willing to deal with the consequences, whatever they may be.

The situation with Patrick and Sandra started with that tough conversation between them . . . the one I witnessed. In fact, Sandra was so crushed by the betrayal of trust that she asked Patrick to move out. He complied with her request, promising her that he would do everything in his power to restore her confidence in him. He promised to end any contact, even in business, with the woman.

After several weeks had passed, when Sandra saw Patrick's resolve, she invited him to return home. The three of us met weekly for several months to talk about how to restore Patrick and Sandra's marriage, especially her trust in him.

The last time I was with them was over dinner. I asked how they were doing. They joined hands on top of the table, looked lovingly toward each other, smiled, and said they were doing great. I believed them.

| **THE TRUTH** | An honest, open, and transparent relationship with our wives will be sweet . . . worth whatever it takes to get there. |

THINK ABOUT IT . . . *Are you hiding something from your wife? When are you going to open your heart to her?*

 ## 19 *"If I experience same-sex attraction, I should pursue a same-sex relationship."*

The sexual revolution of the last fifty years or so has gathered steam and swept through the Western world with tsunami-like force. Moorings we once assumed to be immovable have shifted and virtually vanished from sight at a dizzying speed. Nowhere is this truer than in regard to the matter of homosexuality.

The result is a deeply embedded cultural expectation, and increasingly, a mandate enforced by the state, that homosexual practice must be embraced across the board as normative and acceptable. To suggest that such behavior is unnatural, not in the best interest of human flourishing, and runs contrary to God's good design is to expose oneself as the worst sort of knuckle-dragging bigot.

Even a growing number of those who profess to know Christ now accept, celebrate, and advocate for same-sex relationships, asserting this position to be in line with the Word of God—and on the "right side of history."

This shift is driven by a confusing pair of affirmations. First, that sexuality is fluid, changing, amorphous, and second, that it is iron-clad, unchangeable, hard-wired. Some insist, "I can be whatever I want to be," while others insist, "I have to be what I am." In both instances, the conclusion is: "I have nothing to feel guilty about."

> Some insist, "I can be whatever I want to be," while others insist, "I have to be what I am." In both instances, the conclusion is: "I have nothing to feel guilty about."

And these are not just theoretical or hypothetical issues that *others* have to deal with. You almost certainly know individuals within your circle of family and friends who identify as gay or lesbian—perhaps boldly and brazenly, or conversely, feeling trapped and too ashamed to ask for help. You may know others who sincerely love Christ but struggle with same-sex attraction while choosing sexual abstinence.

Or . . . you may be one of these individuals yourself. You may be in a same-sex relationship; or you may feel helplessly trapped and deeply ashamed of choices you've made that you know deep down to be wrong; or you may be struggling to live out a biblical morality that doesn't feel natural or possible.

Regardless, in some way or another, every man is faced with questions and confusion that abound in this arena. For sure, the Enemy has succeeded in deceiving many in our generation about the nature of same-sex passions, sexual engagement, and marriage. He has sold the lie that our sexual practice is a matter of personal choice or of innate, inborn orientation over which we have no choice.

It is not within the scope of this book to address or unravel the many different threads and issues related to this topic.

But as a starting place in the heat and swirl of the cultural debate, those of us who know Christ and trust His Word can anchor our hearts in two affirmations we know to be true:

- God's ways are not only right; they are also good. And He desires and has made provision for the very highest good—*summa bonum*—for all of His creatures.
- God is God, and we are not. As the Creator and Designer of the human race, He is the only one who can write the operator's manual for how we are to function. He is the Potter, and we are the clay. It is not our place to tell Him how we wish to be formed or to resent or resist His ways when they do not conform to ours.

BORN THIS WAY

We may never be able to unravel the mystery of whether same-sex attraction comes from nature or nurture, or some combination of the two. The fact is, we live in a fallen, broken world in which we are *all* prone to disordered attractions and affections. There are things we would like to be and do and have that run contrary to what He has created us to be and do and have.

> *We live in a fallen, broken world in which we are* all *prone to disordered attractions and affections.*

Further, we were all born with an innate bent to go our own way and to live our lives independently of our Maker's direction. Another way of saying that is that we were born into sin.

But our propensity to any kind of sin is not an excuse for sinning. You and I are responsible for what we do. God holds us accountable for the choices we make.

The opening, foundational chapter of God's Word reveals that He created the human race, in His own image, with two distinct genders: "male and female he created them" (Gen. 1:27). In every way, the two were suitable for each other, one made to fit with the other.

> And God saw everything that he had made, and behold, it was very good. (Gen. 1:31)

The whole of Scripture makes clear that He designed men and women to function in ways that are complementary and that reflect the diversity and intimacy within the Trinity.

True freedom is not the absence of boundaries or the autonomy to gratify and act out of our basest appetites, desires, and bents. Instead, true freedom is the fruit of humbly submitting ourselves to His plan.

Our enemy deceitfully promises hedonistic abandon and pleasure to those who choose his word over God's. But the pathway to blessing—peace, joy, satisfaction, well-being, and fulfillment—is to say *yes* to our Creator. His grace will enable us to be and do and desire and have all that He has ordained as holy and good.

> **True freedom is not the absence of boundaries or the autonomy to gratify and act out of our basest appetites, desires, and bents. Instead, true freedom is the fruit of humbly submitting ourselves to His plan.**

This does not mean there will be no more struggle. Christopher Yuan was an agnostic gay man and now teaches the Bible to college students. He explains:

> *So the question is, if I continue to have these feelings I neither asked for nor chose, will I still be willing to follow Christ no matter what? Is my obedience to Christ dependent on whether he answered my prayers my way? God's faithfulness is proved not by the elimination of hardships but by carrying us through them. Change is not the absence of struggles; change is the freedom to choose holiness in the midst of our struggles. I realized that the ultimate issue has to be that I yearn after God in total surrender and complete obedience.*[10]

Our world and all of humanity is fallen and broken. That includes you and me. Things do not always work as they were intended to function. Our natural desires and inclinations do not always align with God's good, created order. But our Creator God is redeeming this prodigal planet and making all things new—including you and me.

Rosaria Butterfield grew up in a family of "committed unbelievers" and became a tenured English professor living with her lesbian partner. Then in a profoundly transformational way, her life was invaded by the gospel and person of Christ. She writes:

> My hands let go of the wheel of self-invention. I came to Jesus alone, open-handed and naked. I had no dignity upon which to stand. As an advocate for peace and social justice, I thought that I was on the side of kindness, integrity, and care. It was thus a crushing revelation to discover: it was Jesus I had been persecuting the whole time—not just some historical figure named Jesus, but my Jesus, my prophet, my priest, my king, my savior, my redeemer, my friend. That Jesus.[11]

> *Our Creator God is redeeming this prodigal planet and making all things new—including you and me.*

And this must be our longing for those caught (whether willfully or reluctantly) in the sinful behavior of homosexuality, or any other kind of sexual sin: that they will "let go of the wheel of self-invention" and find freedom and fullness through an encounter with Christ.

Whatever sin you or I may be struggling with, when we acknowledge, repent, and turn from it, we can be made new through the power of the gospel.

> Do not be deceived: neither the sexually immoral, nor idolaters, nor adulterers, nor men who practice homosexuality, nor thieves, nor the greedy, nor drunkards, nor revilers, nor swindlers will inherit the kingdom of God. And such were some of you. But you were washed, you were sanctified, you were justified in the name of the Lord Jesus Christ and by the Spirit of our God. (1 Cor. 6:9–11)

If you or someone you love is caught up in the net of homosexuality, there is hope. We will not be cleansed by denying our sin, nor justifying our sin, but by confessing our sin and turning from it.

| **THE TRUTH** | **God's created order for men, women, and human sexuality is right and good. When we accept His way, repent of going our own way, and rest in Christ, we find forgiveness and the power to live in accord with His plan.** |

THINK ABOUT IT . . . *God's order regarding sexuality is meant for our good. Are you willing to lovingly and gracefully stand for this truth?*

20 *"I have sexual needs my wife can't fulfill."*

Though people have believed this lie through the ages, it has been given a megaphone in our Madison Avenue/internet era.

For example, on the home page of my favorite news outlet, I've just been invited to view a video featuring the brand-new Bentley SUV. It's called the Bentayga and it retails for a cool $231,000. The video shows this car and a few of its perfectly clean sisters and brothers off-roading in shin-deep mud. I don't think so.

Anyway, thanks to this promotion, I'm now being tempted to believe that "I have automotive needs that the vehicle currently in my garage can't fulfill."

Here's another. In April 2017, Kenyan-born Geoffrey Kirui won the Boston Marathon in 2 hours, 9 minutes and 37 seconds. The footage of the final few hundred yards shows Kirui smiling and waving to the crowd as though he's standing on a float in the Rose Parade. This after clicking off twenty-two consecutive sub-six-minute miles.

If I had no access to this news, I wouldn't know about it. But I do.

> *The internet and the general media fuel comparison and discontent and increase our sense of needing something we don't have.*

Ergo, the temptation to believe: "I have athletic needs my current legs, stamina, and condition can't fulfill."

So back to the current lie: "I have sexual needs my wife can't fulfill."

And how do we know about these "needs"? Once again, the internet and the general media fuel comparison and discontent and increase our sense of needing something we don't have. Because you and I have access to this, we can routinely see women with more alluring, glamorous bodies than our wife's body, women draped in less-than-adequate coverage.

And whether or not we have seen them actually do anything sexual, that doesn't matter. Our minds have wandered in this direction once the impression has been seared into our brains.

An article in *Psychology Today* reveals this fact. "It's essential to note that the literature specifically studying men's arousal patterns . . . has repeatedly emphasized their sensitivity to visual cues. As soon as the lust-inspiring image registers in their brain, they become turned-on—not only physically but psychologically, too."[12]

So there you have it. You and I can be completely stimulated by our eyes and our imaginations. But, truthfully, this isn't something we needed to read about to believe. Right?

GROWN-UP SEXUALITY

You may be married or you may be single. You may have children or not. But, since I am married and have children and grandchildren, I'm going to use an example from my own life as an illustration of something important about our sexual desires.

When my daughters were born, it became immediately clear to my late wife, Bobbie, and me that these little critters were inordinately selfish.

The fact that their parents were bone-tired and sleep-deprived made no difference to them. If they were hungry or hot or cold or had a poopy or wet diaper, they wanted immediate relief.

As they grew, Missy and Julie learned that not everything in the cosmos was about them. They even began to experience the joy—even the fun—of serving others. As their dad, when I'd catch them doing something kind or helpful, I did my best to praise them for it.

So for these women, "growing up" meant learning to experience pleasure, as Jesus said, to serve and not be served.

Like every groom, the anticipation of my first wedding night was palpable. This would be my first sexual experience. And, candidly, it was pretty much about me. My wife meeting my needs.

Bobbie and I were married for more than forty-four years. And I would say that our sexual relationship was sweet. But, from our first night together in a hotel room and over the next four decades, my sexual needs gradually changed. Let's say they grew up.

Like a newborn baby, my early experience was quite selfish. And it was primarily about my own pleasure . . . physical *and* visual. But during those decades we—Bobbie, essentially—went through two pregnancies. She had two back surgeries and suffered from endometriosis, limiting the number of children she could bear. Although she was intentional and vigilant

> *The most glaring error in this lie about your wife meeting your physical needs is the assumption that the purpose of sexual intercourse is to meet your desires.*

about eating right and exercising regularly, the body I slept with in 1970 changed over the years.

So, my view of my sexual fulfillment grew up. It became more than the act itself. Tenderness, sweet words, gentleness were added to the dance card. Intimacy was as much about *us* as it was about *me*.

The most glaring error in this lie about your wife meeting your physical needs is the assumption that the purpose of sexual intercourse is to meet your desires. But what if we were to shift the focus from *your* needs and desires to meeting *her* needs and desires?

Doing this right can take a great deal of time. And perhaps one of the great ironies about successful lovemaking is that it generally takes far less time for you to be "ready" than your wife. Your climax can happen in a matter of minutes. Not so much with her.

God's design for your wife is that it takes time for her to be prepared to receive you.

And this preparation is not only physiological—though it *is* that—but her readiness must be fully encircled. It's psychological. Emotional. Spiritual. Physiological.

Although you could try to persuade your wife to have sex with you any time, this will not turn out well for her. And, ultimately, not for you either.

Lovemaking that is satisfying to your wife requires two things of you: patience and tenderness. Granted, there may be an appropriate and delightful time for a "quickie," but gently leading your wife to an exciting sexual experience is going to take time. This is why occasional getaways with just you and your wife are a great investment. No distractions. No interruptions. No kids standing outside your locked bedroom door, trying to get you to respond to them. One hundred percent focus on each other . . . with time to spare. This is a good idea.

> *Your goal is that your intimacy with her makes your wife feel secure.*

And if you're not sure about her satisfaction with your performance, ask her. And don't do this "in the moment." Find some other place besides your bed to tell your wife that you're eager that your lovemaking be a wonderful experience. For her. Invite her to tell you what works. And what doesn't.

Then, when she tells you, listen carefully. Your goal is that your intimacy with her makes your wife feel secure.

Safe. Loved.

YOU'RE NOT FINISHED
WHEN YOU THINK YOU'RE FINISHED

In a book I wrote for husbands a few years ago, I challenged husbands with this important reminder about physical intimacy:

In lovemaking, you are likely to reach climax before—maybe long before—your wife does. And, physiologically, your body is telling you that you're finished. You wooed. You prevailed. You conquered. You're done.

Not so fast.

Even though your body has reached its euphoric pinnacle, your wife may still want your tenderness. Your touching. Your caress.[13]

You may not be good with words, but when you read these penned by King Solomon, who must have been some kind of lover, you are reminded of the whole notion that physical intimacy is a lovely, pleasurable adventure, not simply a moment in time.

Drink water from your own cistern,
  flowing water from your own well.
Should your springs be scattered abroad,
  streams of water in the streets?
Let them be for yourself alone,
  and not for strangers with you.
Let your fountain be blessed,
  and rejoice in the wife of your youth,
  a lovely deer, a graceful doe.
Let her breasts fill you at all times with delight;
  be intoxicated always in her love.
(Prov. 5:15–19)

THE TRUTH | Because we love our wife, her sexual fulfillment should be more important than ours. And when it's really good for her, it will be really good for us.

THINK ABOUT IT . . . *If you're a married man, do you think your wife enjoys sex with you? Can you think of ways to improve the quality of your lovemaking with your wife? What are they?*

CHAPTER SIX

LIES MEN BELIEVE ABOUT

MARRIAGE
AND FAMILY

Y ou may be married. You may not. If you're not married, you may
have plans. You may not. In any case, my hope is this chapter will
be helpful for you or other men you know who are married.

HOW IT HAPPENS . . .

Boy sees girl. Girl meets boy. The two start dating, fall in love, and make
plans for the wedding. You get the idea. If you're married, you have your
own story.

But this sequence is a modern construct.
Back in biblical times, marriages were primarily arranged. Boy's parents meet girl's parents.
Arrangements are made. The groom meets
his bride. No lazy walks in the park or late-
night kissing in the shadows.

Grown-ups who knew more about their
children than the children knew about themselves made the plans. Boys and girls fell in

> *Grown-ups who
> knew more about
> their children than
> the children knew
> about themselves
> made the plans.*

love after the wedding. Sometimes.

In the past several hundred years, marriage in the West has taken a different approach.

THE NEW-FASHIONED WAY

I've been married twice. The first was in 1970. The second in 2015.

Both of these weddings were special, God-honoring events. In each case, I married a woman who loved the Lord. And me.

My first marriage was to Bobbie Gardner. She had grown up in the Washington, D.C., area in a home where the local country club was the weekend sanctuary of choice. But because of the faithful witness of a Christian neighbor named Libby, Bobbie and her family came to faith in Jesus Christ.

From the time she was a little girl, Bobbie dreamed of getting married. As a young woman, she participated as the soloist (she had a beautiful singing voice) or bridesmaid—or both—in many weddings. Each of these confirmed her desire to one day wear the white dress. She was called to be married and she knew it.

My second marriage was to Nancy Leigh DeMoss. She had grown up in a family where God and His Word were honored. Her parents had a passion for ministry and literally thousands of people came to faith in Christ through various outreaches her parents hosted in their home.

Nancy developed the same love for Christ as Bobbie did and, as a child, sensed a strong call to serve Him vocationally. As a young adult, she increasingly sensed she would do so as a single woman, without the distractions of marriage and family. It's not that she was unattractive or lacked relational skills or the opportunity to marry. Not at all. Nancy simply wanted to serve the Lord, her Bridegroom, with "an undivided devotion" (see 1 Cor. 7:34–35).

TURNING A PAGE: STARTING OVER, STARTING NEW

Bobbie and I were blessed with nearly forty-five years of marriage. Then, in early 2012, she was diagnosed with Stage IV ovarian cancer. Thirty-two months later, her battle with this disease ended and she gently stepped into heaven. The final marriage chapter was finished. That book was closed.

In the months that followed Bobbie's death, my heart was drawn to a woman whom I had known professionally. I had met Nancy a dozen years earlier and served as her literary agent for a brief period.

I had deep respect for her heart for God and His Word and her skills in ministry, writing, and speaking. Now I began to sense a desire to pursue a friendship with her. Although Nancy was beautiful at fifty-seven, my attraction to her—in addition to her physical beauty and charm—was rooted in something even more compelling. Presumptuous as this may appear, I believe it was a call from the Lord.

> *In the months that followed Bobbie's death, my heart was drawn to a woman whom I had known professionally.*

I reached out to Nancy, first, in a few brief email exchanges, then in a ninety-minute conversation in a friend's office. In the weeks that followed, as she describes it, "love was awakened" in her heart.

This woman who had never prayed for a husband or dreamed of a wedding began to sense that the Lord might be calling her into a new season of serving Him. A season of marriage.

This chapter speaks to some of the lies men believe about marriage and family. But before you turn the pages, I would like for you to consider something that's going to sound radical.

Remember the you-saw-her-across-a-crowded-room thing? That boy meets girl thing? That of-all-the-girls-in-the-world-I-pick-you thing?

Let me suggest something else for you to consider.

A DIVINE APPOINTMENT

Even though, from an earthly perspective, it looked like I had taken the initiative to develop relationships with Bobbie and Nancy that led to marriage, the truth be known, the Lord providentially brought us together in His way, for purposes that were far greater than we could have realized at the time.

The first time I was quite oblivious to this "appointment." But the second time, it was crystal clear to me that this was His doing. And, although Nancy—not to mention her closest friends and ministry associates—was taken by complete surprise, eventually the Lord confirmed this same leading in her heart as well.

As we grew to believe we were to marry each other, Nancy and I heard another distinct call. In fact, regardless of the details of your own marriage story, this call also came to you. Gary Thomas, author the bestselling book *Sacred Marriage*, says it well:

> *God does not direct us to focus on finding the right person; He calls us to become the right person.*[1]

A BIGGER PICTURE

So, although you and I have photos of our wedding (who *were* those kids?), our heavenly Father had something far more important in mind than ring bearers and flower petals strewn down the aisle. Our wedding ceremony wasn't about dressing up and mothers sniffling and receptions and eager grooms; our weddings were birthing ceremonies.

You and I were setting aside the independence and multiple options that marked our single lives. We were submitting to something different. Something that would deny us our opportunities for turning back. Like a boy crawling through a culvert pipe under the driveway, straight ahead was our only choice. And even more important than becoming an award-winning husband, in getting married, God was calling you and me to love one woman and, if the Lord blessed you with children, to love them, too. This was a new and different kind of greatness.

SO WHAT'S THE LIE?

What are the lies in this chapter? The ones about marriage and family? I'm glad you asked. Are you ready?

The lies about marriage and family are that these have anything to do with fulfilling your wildest dreams of conquest and accomplishment. Your wife and your family (if you're married and have children) have been put in your life to be a full-length mirror. To show you yourself and to convince you that without a redeeming Savior, you're a mess, and your marriage is doomed to mediocrity at best, failure at worst. And your children will be handed a life sentence of growing up to be just like their father.

But if you dare to grasp it, the stunning truth is that you have been called to this relationship. As Jesus was called to the kind of humility we can't quite comprehend in order to love and serve His bride, we can do no less.

So if this sounds like bait and switch, it is. Precisely. What we thought was going to be a life of candlelight dinners and non-stop tossing in the sheets has turned into the kind of work we've not tackled before.

> *Your wife and your family (if you're married and have children) have been put in your life to be a full-length mirror.*

Another way of saying this is that marriage is not a DIY project. You know, do-it-yourself. Since I find myself in a full-confession mode, I'll admit that I have always been drawn to the dangers and risks of doing things on my own. I have remodeled an entire basement, including a full bath, office, and living room, using a single sheet of graph paper as my blueprint. More than once.

I've built a thousand-square-foot, curved deck with $20,000 worth of pressure-treated lumber and composite materials, with no written plan at all. Maybe you have a few pure-courage stories yourself.

But tackling a marriage without knowing where you're headed is not

> *Tackling a marriage without knowing where you're headed is not a good idea.*

a good idea. Taking on this kind of responsibility without coming to terms with some of the lies you're facing is an invitation to frustration. Maybe to tragedy.

My hope is that uncovering and exposing these lies will get you on the right foot if you're newly married, on better footing if you've been married for a while, or, if you're single, help you to be a wise, godly encourager to your married friends . . . or help you to be well-prepared if and when she appears, across that crowded room.

 ## *"Love doesn't require spoken words."*

For reasons I won't go into here, my dad, who died in 2002, had a hard time verbally expressing his love for me. Like out loud.

Not long ago, we found some postcards (I'll explain what those are some other time) he had sent from somewhere around the globe and, interestingly enough, these cards included loving words. Even though I can't put my hands on these at the moment, I can visualize his handwriting: "I love you, Bobby."

My heart jumps even as I write these words so many years later. But I rarely heard my dad actually speak these words to me.

Was this caution about expressing affection something he inherited from his parents? Of course. Did he love me? Yes. Did he want the best for my siblings and me? Absolutely. Did my dad do plenty of kind and helpful things that demonstrated that love? Again, yes.

But, as I look back over my relationship with my father, I find myself wishing I had heard these words more often. Audibly.

THE LOVE LANGUAGE EXCUSE

In 1992, the original edition of Dr. Gary Chapman's mega-bestseller, *The 5 Love Languages*,[2] was published. Maybe you know about this book. Today sales stand at 11 million, so you're likely somewhat familiar with it.

The premise is that people lean toward giving and receiving one of five "love languages." A quick refresher: Words of Affirmation, Acts of Service, Receiving Gifts, Quality Time, Physical Touch.

So what's the excuse?

Well, my dad was clearly an acts-of-service guy. When I'd come home for a weekend from college, he'd sneak out and get the oil changed in my college ride. Or get the tires rotated with new ones for the front. This was his language, and my siblings and I truly appreciated it . . . for reasons any broke college student thoroughly understands.

> *We know our wife's love language is acts of service, so we do a nice thing and we're good. One and done.*

It would be possible for someone to think that because his language is acts of service, he does not need to speak "words of affirmation" to those he loves. Or sharing gifts or investing quality time. That's the excuse, and sometimes men are caught believing it. We know our wife's love language is acts of service, so we do a nice thing and we're good. One and done.

"You know I love you, honey, I unloaded the dishwasher."

Or gifts: "What do you mean, do I love you? Don't you remember the flowers I gave you for your birthday?"

Nice. Close, but no cigar.

I believe your wife is looking for both deeds *and* words. For gifts and words. For time and words. For touch and words.

I'm thinking about the old Certs breath mint television commercial. "Certs is a breath mint," one actor says. "Certs is a candy mint," the other defiantly replies. They go back and forth until the narrator, using his real announcer voice, interrupts. "Stop, you're both right."

So let's talk about loving words and loving actions.

In your relationships, you need to offer both: meaningful, tender words to back up your thoughtful actions, and loving actions to back up your tender words. "I love you," coming from a cruel or thoughtless man is hypocrisy. It falls on deaf ears. But kind deeds without verbal affirmations of love can also be less than satisfying.

> *In your relationships, you need to offer both: meaningful, tender words to back up your thoughtful actions, and loving actions to back up your tender words.*

Of course, the classic conversation in "Fiddler on the Roof" between Tevye and his wife, Golda, is Exhibit A. Their daughter is getting married because she's . . . in love.

A conversation ensues. Tevye wants to know if Golde loves him. Even after twenty-five years of washing his clothes, preparing his meals, cleaning the house, milking the cow, and mothering his children . . . he still wants to know that she loves him. Her deeds should speak for themselves, but this time they don't.

"But do you love me?" Tevye begs plaintively (for the full effect, repeat this with a heavy Russian accent). He wants to hear her *say the words.*

SHOW AND TELL

So my somewhat introverted dad was probably not all that unusual. His way of expressing affection was to do loving things, not necessarily to verbalize. As men, I suppose our tendency is to "show" first and "tell" later.

"Do I love you?" you might ask rhetorically. "Are you serious?" Then we could recite a litany of good deeds we perform for this lady: daily hard work, financial provision, protection. Given the alternative (laziness, poverty, carelessness), these deeds are a good choice.

"But do you love me?" your wife wants to know (*without having to ask*).

SO WHAT'S A GUY TO DO?

Let me suggest that you probably need to speak more than you do. Speak more than you think you should. If you have a kind thought, *say it.*

What a kind and faithful wife I have. Speak the words.

Wow, does my wife ever look lovely today. Speak the words.

> *If you have a kind thought, say it.*

I so appreciate the way she speaks encouraging words to strangers. Speak the words.

And if you have kids . . .

I'm so proud of you, son. No dad could be happier. Speak the words.

Do what King David said. "Say so."

> Oh give thanks to the LORD, for he is good,
> for his steadfast love endures forever!
> Let the redeemed of the LORD say so. (Ps. 107:1–2)

If your wife were marooned on a desert island and you were the first to show up, what would you do for this starved, thirsty woman? You'd give her something to drink. You'd feed her.

So what if she's starving for you to speak? Thirsting for encouragement and kindness? You'd feed her the good stuff. You'd treat things you say as King David's son, King Solomon, suggested.

> Gracious words are like a honeycomb,
> sweetness to the soul and health to the body. (Prov. 16:24)

When I asked my wife about the importance of good words and kind actions, she summarized it as only she could so well: "Words without works are shallow, empty, and lack credibility. Works with words speak sacrifice, tenderness, and romance."

Sign me up.

| **THE TRUTH** | In addition to doing good things for our wives, they need to hear us say kind things to them . . . especially those three magic words: "I love you." |

THINK ABOUT IT . . . *Have you told your wife you love her today? Have you texted her the same? If not . . . just do it. Right now.*

 ## "*My wife is supposed to make me happy.*"

I had been married to Bobbie for almost forty-five years, widowed after she lost her courageous battle with ovarian cancer. Then in November 2015, I married Nancy Leigh DeMoss. She was fifty-seven years old.

This marriage was a first for Nancy.

As she and I got to know each other better, I discovered something about this woman that I found deeply attractive. For almost six decades, Nancy had been single; but rather than spending these years waiting and hoping and pining for someone to come along and "complete" her, she fully embraced singleness as a gift from the Lord—a calling to serve Him and others.

One of my first clues as to what mattered to this woman met me when I first walked into her house. There, next to the kitchen table, was a high chair. A high chair! And when I walked downstairs to the finished basement, I discovered a guest room and living area, as well as a rec room with lots of comfy seating and all kinds of games and toys for young and old . . . cool games and toys like pool and Ping-Pong tables, foosball, and one of those double-basketball carnival-like hoop things with nets on either side. One that had an electronic, fully lit scoreboard!

And then as I met her friends, they told me stories about the home of this single woman . . . a home that was perpetually open to friends and strangers alike. One couple told me they had lived with Nancy for over three years. Another for almost two years. Still others for months at a time.

142

As Nancy and I talked about these people, and I observed how she had selflessly served them, I realized that this woman wasn't looking for a husband to bring her happiness. Or purpose. Or fulfillment.

> *I didn't come along to bring her joy. She already had this in full measure.*

I didn't come along to bring her joy. She already had this in full measure.

NOT GOOD TO BE ALONE?

When God created the expanse of the universe, the animals, and Adam, He assessed His work. And, even before sin reared his ugly head, God said, "It is not good that the man should be alone" (Gen. 2:18).

So here's an obvious question: Why is it not good to be alone? Wasn't Nancy's life without a husband a good thing? Yes, it was a good thing because, even though she didn't have a spouse, she wasn't alone. She intentionally filled her life, her home, and her heart with others to love and care for. This was very good.

Over the first few weeks of getting acquainted, I realized that Nancy was a woman who daily found deep satisfaction in the steadfast love of the Lord. He was her friend. Her companion. Her Lord. Her husband.

So early on, I knew that Nancy would not be looking to me to make her happy. She was not looking for her other half. In Christ, she was already complete. I knew that if she were to fall in love with me, Nancy would make an amazing wife because she wasn't desperate for someone to come along and make her life full. She was already there.

If you are single and not looking for a wife, the apostle Paul applauds you:

> I want you to be free from anxieties. The unmarried man is anxious about the things of the Lord, how to please the Lord. But the married man is anxious about worldly things, how to please his wife, and his interests are divided. (1 Cor. 7:32–34)

> *If you're single and are eager to have a wife, let me encourage you to find a woman who is busy loving God and serving others. A woman who isn't setting her hopes on a man to bring her fulfillment and happiness.*

Give yourself to ministry? Go for it.

But if you're single and are *eager* to have a wife, let me encourage you to find a woman who is busy loving God and serving others. A woman who isn't setting her hopes on a man to bring her fulfillment and happiness. If that's what she's looking for, you already know what she's going to find in you. Or not find. She is destined to be deeply disappointed.

And don't make the mistake of looking to her to make you happy. For starters, there is no woman on the face of the earth who can bring you the full measure of happiness that you long for. Not if that's what you're focused on pursuing.

And besides, your personal happiness is far too small a goal for marriage! God longs for you and your wife to experience the incredible joy of being *givers*—poured out for His sake and for others.

So back to the lie. It's something we have talked about in other chapters. At the end of the day, only a relationship with your heavenly Father will fulfill you and make you happy. No one and nothing can fill that place in your heart that was made to be occupied and filled by Him.

> *The pursuit of our own pleasure and happiness will always be, in the end, chasing after the wind.*

God operates His world in ways that are the polar opposite of the way we naturally think. He tells us that the first will be last (Matt. 20:16), that if we would lead we must serve (Mark 10:45). He tells us that if we would gain our lives we must lay them down (Matt. 16:25). The pursuit of our own pleasure and happiness will always be, in the end, chasing after the wind (Eccl. 2:11). And seeking the glory of God, whether in marriage or singleness, will always lead us to the deepest kind of joy and satisfaction.

God did not give you your wife first and foremost to make you happy. He gave you your wife to make you holy. And He gave you your wife so that you might partner in glorifying His Son and making His name known wherever He places you.

THE TRUTH	Whether we are single or married, God alone can give us ultimate happiness and fulfillment. As we seek *Him*, we will find the truest joy.

THINK ABOUT IT . . . *Are you a loved man? How do you know? What does this mean?*

23 *"I don't have what it takes to be the CEO of my home. I can leave that role to my wife."*

A few years ago I put together a proposal to send to publishers for a new book I was planning to write. The title was: *Like the Shepherd: Leading Your Marriage with Love and Grace.*

Because I have been in publishing industry for over forty years, many of my closest friends are in the business. One of these friends called me after his company received the proposal. I could tell right away that he was not about to give me good news. The halting tone in his voice was my clue.

His publication committee had met. They liked my proposal. That's the good news.

But the bad news was that they would like to change the first word of the subtitle. He didn't give me an alternate word but let me know that "leading" wasn't going to work. At least, not with his team.

At many levels, I understand the concern. I really do. In fact, as I was composing the manuscript for the book, I read another book that may have been one of the reasons for the committee's concern. This book, published by a prominent Christian publisher, was the first-person account of a woman who was severely and repeatedly abused—verbally, emotionally, physically—by a husband (a pastor) who shouted "Wives, submit to your husbands" as he was mauling her. It's been a few years now since the book was published, and I've heard nothing about this woman's former husband suing for libel. My assumption is that the story is true.

> *The whole idea of biblical leadership is a lot different than many people understand.*

As it turned out, I did find a publisher for my book who embraced my perspective, which, contrary to the horrible account I just told you about, encourages husbands to "lead like a shepherd."

And I believe "lead" is the right word to use.

Why? Because the whole idea of biblical leadership is a lot different than many people understand.

THE TOWEL AND THE BASIN

If you're familiar with the story of Jesus and His disciples on the night He was betrayed, you will remember that the Messiah—the Creator and Lord of the universe—gave us an unforgettable picture of what this leadership is supposed to look like.

> Jesus, knowing that the Father had given all things into his hands, and that he had come from God and was going back to God, rose from supper. He laid aside his outer garments, and taking a towel, tied it around his waist. Then he poured water into a basin and began to wash the disciples' feet and to wipe them with the towel that was wrapped around him. (John 13:3–5)

Take a moment and consider this incredible account. Here is the

Son of God, sharing a simple dinner with His closest friends. Unlike the da Vinci painting of the Last Supper, these men were not sitting on one side of a cloth-covered table. They were more likely reclining on the floor. They were with their Friend, their Lord, their Savior, the One who had created them.

So what did this Man—this Leader—do as a symbol of this role? How did He act? What did He do to "prove" His leadership? How did He treat them?

He lovingly and gently served them. Then He died for them, reconciling each one with His Father. And, except for one, they loved and served Him in return.

When the apostle Paul tells wives to "submit" to their husbands, this is the kind of leader he had in mind that she should submit to (see Phil. 2:3–11). And leaving nothing to chance, this is exactly what Paul tells us to do:

> Husbands, love your wives, as Christ loved the church and gave
> himself up for her. (Eph. 5:25)

BACK TO THE LIE . . .

The interesting thing about this lie ("I don't have what it takes to be the CEO of my home. I can leave that role to my wife.") is that the first part is actually not a lie. It's the truth. We *don't* have what it takes to provide Christlike, servant-hearted leadership in our homes.

Even though I have written a book on the subject and have done everything in my power to be this kind of leader, the truth is, I don't have what it takes to be the spiritual leader in my home. I really don't.

And just between us, you probably don't either.

Let me say that the kind of leadership I believe Scripture calls us to assumes a gentle humility. A kind of grace that honors her, protects her, affirms her, defends her, and loves her.

The fact is, you and I are by nature too proud, selfish, lazy, and demanding to be the kind of shepherd that our wives and children long

> *You and I are by nature too proud, selfish, lazy, and demanding to be the kind of shepherd that our wives and children long for and need.*

for and need. We do *not*, in fact, have what it takes to do this well . . . day after day after day.

That's right. We don't have what it takes . . . but we still must do what we have been called to do.

In this situation, our best go-to promise is this one. You and I cannot. God can. And He will, as we acknowledge our inability and ask Him to fill us with Himself.

Maybe the apostle Paul was feeling some of this kind of inadequacy when he wrote:

I can do all things through him who strengthens me. (Phil. 4:13)

THE CEO?

Having spent most of my career in business, including being a "founder and CEO" of a company, I'm personally aware of the weight of this title . . . the "leader."

Notice I didn't say monarch or potentate. Absolute authoritarians who make cruel and capricious demands of their wives and children, then sit back and expect to be worshiped and served.

To the contrary, as you probably know, the chief executive officer (CEO) is ultimately responsible for the company's overall operation and successful performance. Typically, he or she answers to the board of directors, the body that has the right to hold the CEO responsible for the success of the firm. It's the CEO's job to make sure his employees are instructed well and empowered and served in order to

> *You and I cannot. God can. And He will, as we acknowledge our inability and ask Him to fill us with Himself.*

ensure the successful accomplishment of their duties.

So you and I are the CEOs of our families. We answer to the God of the universe. He holds us responsible for our assignment to lead. And then we do our best to take this special task seriously.

What might this look like for you and me? Let's see.

The writings of King Solomon that we find in Proverbs are a cornucopia of wisdom for husbands and fathers. Here are a few big ideas to help you and me please our heavenly Father and effectively lead, serve, and provide for our families. And since we have already spent time talking about your relationship with your wife (Lies #18, 20, and 22), let's focus on your CEO role with your kids.

TEACH YOUR CHILDREN TO LOVE AND FEAR GOD

In the same way a CEO is subject to the direction of his board of directors and is to speak well of them to his troops, you and I are to model a loving respect for God and teach our children the same.

> The fear of the LORD is the beginning of knowledge;
> fools despise wisdom and instruction. (Prov. 1:7)

Foundational to our CEO role at home is teaching our children an awe of God. This does not show up in sermons preached at dinner, but in a lifestyle of constant recognition of God's greatness and splendor.

When my children were young, they often heard their dad remark about something beautiful—a wildflower, ants crossing the sidewalk in perfect single file, a deer scampering through the backyard, a mountain stream . . . I'd say, "Hey, Missy and Julie, look at that. Isn't God amazing?"

And this exclamation didn't need to be followed up with a summary of the pastor's three-point sermon from the week before. Simply recognizing something wonderful from

Foundational to our CEO role at home is teaching our children an awe of God.

creation and giving the Lord credit can be powerful in the moment.

But the fear of the Lord also includes a fear of His displeasure. Again, as fathers you and I model this. And our obedience to God's commands isn't primarily based on avoiding His punishment but loving Him so much we choose to willingly follow His instructions.

I love the apostle Paul's view of this obedience. He tells us that God's unconditional love "compels" us to honor God's unconditional instructions (2 Cor. 5:14 NIV). In other words, our behavior is a result of our love for Him, not our obligation to be good.

TEACH YOUR CHILDREN TO OBEY YOU

In addition to Solomon's directive about honoring the Lord, Proverbs is filled with his strong encouragement for his son—his children—to listen to their father . . . and mother.

> Hear, my son, your father's instruction,
> and forsake not your mother's teaching. (Prov. 1:8)[3]

From experience, the most important part of encouraging my children to obey me is modeling obedience myself. I could try to be a completely undisciplined man, demanding that my children overlook my lack of self-control and obey me anyway. I could do this, but it wouldn't go very well.

TEACH YOUR CHILDREN TO SELECT
THEIR FRIENDS CAREFULLY

As you spend time in Proverbs, you notice that Solomon usually cuts to the chase. He may not have been officially limited to 280 characters (or whatever), but he could have and still been successful!

> My son, if sinners entice you, do not consent. (Prov. 1:10)

When our parents were growing up, their parents could have a good sense of who their children were interacting with. They could bring these friends home from school to visit. Or parents could meet their kids' friends in person at church.

But no more.

Thanks to technology and social media, young people are "friends" with hundreds of people their parents don't know and will never

> **As the dad, you have the right to ask about your children's friends.**

meet. They can be influenced in so many ways by these people. Some are good people. Some are not.

Over and over Proverbs encourages parents to challenge their children regarding their relationships. As the dad, you have the right to ask about your children's friends. In fact, invite them to your home often. And follow your kids on social media. No good CEO wouldn't do this.

TEACH YOUR CHILDREN SEXUAL PURITY

It's only natural to think that temptation to sexual immorality is a contemporary phenomenon. But even a cursory reading of Proverbs makes it clear that this was a challenge thousands of years ago.

And there may be no more important encouragement for your children coming from you than an encouragement to love and choose sexual purity. The transparency of your own struggles and your journey in this area will be a powerful catalyst as you share the sweetness of God's plan.

Pray with and for your children, asking for God's strength to be poured out for yourself and for them.

"I CAN LEAVE THAT CEO ROLE TO MY WIFE."

The second part of the lie is that we can simply turn this role over to our wives, relinquishing our responsibility. *After all,* we may think, *she'll be better at this than I would be.*

In some cases, our wives may be better and more naturally gifted at leading than we are. But we still have a God-given responsibility to provide leadership for our homes while also honoring our wife's gifts and helping them to flourish, as a good coach would with a star athlete.

Now, here's something important to remember. Since your wife is probably a nurturer, if you don't assume the job of leading in your home, she'll tend to feel she has to step into that leadership role. She may not want to, but your negligence will create a vacuum, and your wife will be drawn in to fill that vacuum.

Shortly after *Like the Shepherd* was published, I met for lunch on four consecutive Thursdays with about thirty husbands who were reading the book together. As we talked, I explained to my friends that very little of this kind of leadership comes "naturally." I reminded them of the promise of God's Word:

> If any of you lacks wisdom, let him ask God, who gives generously to all without reproach, and it will be given him. (James 1:5)

Sometimes men aren't great at coming up with specific, creative things to do when it comes to building relationships. So our group came up with some practical to-dos. Here are a few:

- pray with your wife out loud before you go to sleep
- anticipate her needs, including chores around the house—before she asks
- surprise her with random "I love you" texts
- be the first to ask for forgiveness when you've done or said something unkind or foolish
- be generous with your time and money
- brag about her when you're with your friends (this report will travel back to her by way of your friends' wives)

When I asked what their mates thought about what they were getting out of our study, their response was almost unanimous. "My wife loves what I'm learning from the book . . . and from this group. Thank you!"

If leading your marriage (and family) meant dominating your wife and kids and making them toe the line against their will, these men's wives would not have responded as they did. But if the result of leading God's way is humble, confident, serving leadership that is actually attractive, a way of leading that lovingly draws them in, I think we might just be onto something . . . with the help of our Good Shepherd.

> The fruit of the Spirit is love, joy, peace, patience, kindness, goodness, faithfulness, gentleness, self-control. (Gal. 5:22–23)

THE TRUTH | God has called us to provide godly leadership for our family. We don't have what it takes to do that; but when we ask Him, He will give us all we need to do it well.

THINK ABOUT IT . . . *How would you describe "servant leadership"? Is this something your wife and your family could use more of from you?*

 ## "*I don't have to grow up.*"

In 1991, Paramount released its follow-up to the classic 1953 Disney animated film called *Peter Pan*. In this sequel, called *Hook*, Peter Pan (Robin Williams) has forgotten his past and is living an ordinary life as a mild-mannered attorney. Then he is dragged back to Neverland, rescues his children, and in the process rediscovers his inner child. It's a happy ending. But this story is fantasy, not reality. It's not true.

We live in a culture that worships youth. Billions are spent on cosmetics, surgeries, exercise equipment, all a vain attempt to hold on to our youth. It doesn't, however, stop there. And for some, it's not just that they don't want to grow *old*, but that they don't want to grow *up*.

It's called the boomerang effect: young adults leaving the nest, only to swiftly return. Sometimes it's called "failure to launch." The phenomenon has reached epidemic levels in America and around the world. Sometimes this return to home is for a short period of time, necessary for economic reasons. But too often it's clinging to adolescence after it has long passed, a refusal to grow up and take on adult responsibilities.

A Pew Research poll released in 2016 found that American men age 18 to 34 are more likely to be living with their parents than in any other living arrangement.[4]

But is this wrong? Doesn't the Bible commend in us a childlike faith, Jesus telling us we must become like children to enter the kingdom? Yes, it does. But there is a big difference between being childlike and being child-ish. The first is commendable, the second is not. Yes, there are weights, responsibilities, and hard work that come with being a grown-up. But there are also feelings of success, accomplishment, and self-respect.

But like many good things, they can evolve into something that is distracting, consuming, and diverts us away from a God-glorifying purpose.

Some have suggested that young men have a need to feel that sense of accomplishment, and that success playing video games fulfills that need, all without any real accomplishment. On one hand, as with many things, video games can be okay in moderation. On the other hand, this can get out of control and snowball into a time-wasting, all-consuming addiction. What this satisfies in men is false, empty, selfish, and misleading.

Men have God-given desires to be part of something bigger than themselves, and perhaps this is the longing that many men attempt to fulfill by obsessive commitment to a sports team. As with many things, sports and video games can be fine and good. But like many good things, they can evolve into something that is distracting, consuming, and diverts us away from a God-glorifying purpose.

What the Bible calls you and me to is perseverance, to maturity, to finishing the race.

The apostle Paul wrote:

> Until we all attain to the unity of the faith and of the knowledge of
> the Son of God, to mature manhood, to the measure of the stature
> of the fullness of Christ, so that we may no longer be children, tossed
> to and fro by the waves and carried about by every wind of doctrine,
> by human cunning, by craftiness in deceitful schemes. (Eph. 4:13–14)

The temptation is to see "mature manhood" merely in spiritual terms, as if Paul is encouraging us to become armchair theologians, blogging and texting our wisdom from our mother's basement. But the division between the spiritual and the physical is a false one. Paul also commands that we pursue maturity in our physical lives, staying away from men who refuse to grow up.

The division between the spiritual and the physical is a false one.

> Now we command you, brothers, in the name of our Lord Jesus
> Christ, that you keep away from any brother who is walking in idle-
> ness and not in accord with the tradition that you received from us.
>
> For you yourselves know how you ought to imitate us, because
> we were not idle when we were with you, nor did we eat anyone's
> bread without paying for it, but with toil and labor we worked night
> and day, that we might not be a burden to any of you.
>
> It was not because we do not have that right, but to give you in
> ourselves an example to imitate. For even when we were with you, we
> would give you this command: If anyone is not willing to work, let him
> not eat.
>
> (2 Thess. 3:6–10)

It sounds like this "failure to launch" thing isn't new. And it's pretty serious.

The thing I like about this is that Paul is direct and strong. His admonition may be for you. Or it may be for someone you know and love. Either you need to have a sit-down with yourself and admonish your own heart in no uncertain terms, or you need to have it with that other guy.

Enough is enough. It's time to get busy and be productive.

If you're in a situation where you need to confront a young man who has decided not to grow up, my counsel is pretty simple: get a job—no, it doesn't need to be your dream job . . . just get a job; work hard—whatever this job is, show your boss that he made a great decision hiring you. Regardless of how mundane the work is, this will bring you pleasure.

If this lethargic person is you, if you're the one who's mooching off his parents instead of growing up, you know what to do.

Young men refusing to step up and be men isn't just the stuff of humor or social commentary, but a serious reality that cripples men, their families, and our culture.

> *Sadly, for many men, our "system" allows for—even subsidizes—laziness.*

Sadly, for many men, our "system" allows for—even subsidizes—laziness. But if you are able-bodied, you need to find a job, and earn a living. This will result in a level of self-respect that no video game will ever provide.

> Whoever loves pleasure will be a poor man;
> he who loves wine and oil will not be rich. (Prov. 21:17)

Scripture makes clear the God-given responsibilities we have as men. Ignoring them won't make them go away. We are called to exercise dominion, to work as unto the Lord, to embrace the callings of manhood, marriage, and parenting (if called to these), and to do so joyfully. Is it scary? Yes.

Even at my age, the weight of daily responsibility still scares me. But my heavenly Father is with me, equipping me, working through me to love and serve my family. That others depend on me reminds me that I must depend on the Lord for wisdom, strength, and discipline to faithfully carry out my responsibility.

| **THE TRUTH** | God calls us to become men who love, serve, protect, and provide for ourselves and for our families, by His grace and for His glory. |

THINK ABOUT IT . . . *Why are some men afraid of growing up? Do you know anyone like this? How can you help?*

 25 *"If I discipline my kids, they'll rebel."*

Nearly every man loves motorcycles. Even if it's his wife's "strong preference" for him not to own one, it's almost impossible for him not to take a second look at one in a parking lot—especially if it's a huge, shiny Harley. Or most men will turn their heads when they see one rumbling down the highway. Of course, the great sound these massive machines make is part of the wonder.

I have only ridden a motorcycle a few times in my life (see previous paragraph about a wife's strong preference), but the feeling of raw power at the turn of the hand grip is almost indescribable. You get on the cycle, fire it up, click it into gear with your foot, and twist your wrist. It's amazing. When it's time to take off, a motorcycle is always obedient.

Not every man likes to ride horseback. I'm one of those men. A bad experience while riding a horse as a little boy at my uncle's farm sealed this for me. That horse didn't even have the courtesy of throwing me off his raring back onto something soft like the meadow. No, it was a gravel driveway that greeted my fall.

So why am I drawn to motorcycles and not horses? Lots of reasons, but the primary one is that, unlike the immediate compliance of the hunk of shiny chrome and steel, a horse does (or doesn't do) what it wants. Or what you want. It may respond with a thumbs up to your encouragement to go forward. Or it may toss you into the ditch. Or onto the road.

Raising children is more like riding a horse than riding a motorcycle. Compliance to your wishes (instructions or commands) is up to them. These kids may obey you or they may defy you . . . tossing you—or your wife—onto the street below.

TRY SWADDLING A TEENAGER

From the time they're tiny babies, these selfish little critters have a will of their own. You bring them home from the hospital (or the adoption agency), swaddled like mummies, but soon they try to take charge. The look on the sleep-deprived faces of the parents of newborns says all you need to know about this adventure.

> One of the ways our heavenly Father (the perfect model) expresses His love for us is by disciplining us.

In any case, as a hopeless claustrophobic, when I see a little kid wrapped like a burrito, I squirm, glad it's them and not me. But for parents, this helps keep the baby from actually exercising its will—at least temporarily.

But once babies are old enough to not be swaddled anymore, parents must begin to turn them loose. And that's when their wills start to be evident. Because they're no longer portable and bound tightly with a little cotton blanket, they can do what they want. They can obey you or they can choose to go their own way. (Think parents chasing their kids at Target.)

So back to the lie about your kids rebelling if you discipline them.

Not surprisingly, the Bible has something to say about parenting our kids well. These admonitions make clear that one of the ways our heavenly Father (the perfect model) expresses His love for us is by disciplining us.

> "My son, do not regard lightly the discipline of the Lord,
>   nor be weary when reproved by him.
> For the Lord disciplines the one he loves,
>   and chastises every son whom he receives."
> (Heb. 12:5–6)

And our discipline under God becomes "Exhibit A" for the way we handle our children. We learn to be obedient to His directives and then show our kids what discipline and obedience look like.

> For they [our earthly fathers] disciplined us for a short time as it seemed best to them, but he [our heavenly Father] disciplines us for our good, that we may share his holiness. For the moment all discipline seems painful rather than pleasant, but later it yields the peaceful fruit of righteousness to those who have been trained by it. (12:10–11)

How's that for a sturdy promise?

My dad was a strict disciplinarian. I remember as a teenager going to my mother and complaining that he was too hard on me. Her gentle answer was one I will never forget . . . even though at the time as a rebellious boy it was hard to swallow.

"Your dad is tough on you because he loves you," she told me. "He really believes that this loving discipline is for your good." Then she added with a gentle smile, "And so do I."

> For the LORD reproves him whom he loves,
>   as a father the son in whom he delights. (Prov. 3:12)

Our assignment as dads is to be tender and loving with our kids at the very same pace as we faithfully discipline them.

And what does "discipline" look like? Although there isn't room here to unpack this completely, my counsel would be that your actions with your children are age-appropriate and memorable.

Disciplining your children is not your way to get even with them for the inconvenience their bad behavior cost you.

Taking the car keys away from a three-year-old and spanking an eighteen-year-old would not work in either case. But finding ways to match punishment with infraction is important.

And remember that disciplining your children is not your way to get even with them for the inconvenience their bad behavior cost you. It's most effective when you truly are helping them to learn a lesson from what they've done that could have hurt them, resolving not to do it again.

Fathers, do not provoke your children to anger, but bring them up in the discipline and instruction of the Lord. (Eph. 6:4)

LETTING GO

In God's providence, the morning I was writing this chapter, I received a text from my younger daughter, Julie. Julie and her husband, Christopher, have two teenage daughters of their own now.

Because I was in the process of unpacking this lie, I thanked Julie for being my kid . . . as if she had a choice. And I thanked her for demonstrating a genuine desire to be obedient as she was growing up. Now, let me say that this was a highly spirited child. Even when she was very small, she'd give me "that look" when I disciplined her. "Should I comply or go my own way?" her eyes were saying. Maybe you have one like that.

So this morning when I thanked Julie for her life, for loving her family and faithfully walking with the Lord, she could have said something about what a fantastic dad I was. But she didn't. Bummer. Instead, she credited her heart for the Lord to the instruction and encouragement she'd received from Bobbie and me, and "the restraining power of the Holy Spirit."

I reminded her how often her mother and I prayed for her. These prayers intensified the older she got and the more independent she became. "We can't do anything about Julie's heart," we'd pray. "But You can. Please visit her by way of your Holy Spirit. Speak to her in terms she understands. Help her to fall in love with You and choose to obey Your voice."

WE PRAY FOR OUR CHILDREN

Remember, raising our kids is more like riding a horse than riding a Harley. We cannot control the outcome of their lives or force them to make right choices. Not even with the best parenting techniques. As they grow up, they have the ability to choose to obey. Or not.

So what do we do? We pray.

When I was a little boy, I was often wakened in the darkness of the early morning hours by the sound of my dad praying. His deep voice sent a quiet but audible vibration through our house. My brothers and sisters and I knew that we were being named, one at a time: Ruth, Sam, Ken, Robert, Debbie, Dan.

> *Raising our kids is more like riding a horse than riding a Harley.*

Faithfully, from his knees, he would bring us before his heavenly Father and plead our case. We knew that he prayed for our protection from harm and our obedience to God's voice.

A few months before he died, I sat with my dad in his home. He was suffering from a rare neurological disease that rendered him quiet and withdrawn. He had a hard time talking or listening. His eyes were failing so he couldn't read the newspaper or watch the Cubs or Bulls on television.

"Dad," I said to him. "How does all of this make you feel?"

He looked straight into my eyes. "Useless," he said.

"Dad," I finally said after a few minutes. "Do you remember how you used to pray for us?"

"I still do," he returned with a faint smile.

"Do you know what a difference that makes in our lives?" I said. "Do you know how thankful we are?"

He nodded.

"Even if you were able-bodied and strong," I continued, "there still is nothing more important—more useful—that you could do than to continue to pray."

"Thank you, son," my dad responded.

"No, thank *you*," I said as I walked over to his chair. Kneeling down in front of my dad I put my arms around him and hugged him.

"Thank you," I repeated, kissing him on the cheek. I held him for just a few more moments and kissed him again.[5]

Although you and I will often fail as parents, our duty is to do our best to discipline our children fairly and love them unconditionally. The final result is—and will always be—in the hands of our heavenly Father. And what do we long for that outcome to be? Toward what end do we pray? Why do we hang in there?

Ultimately our prayer is that they have a heart for God, love for Christ, love for righteousness, godly character, and His blessing in their lives, preparing them to be wise, obedient children of God.

THE TRUTH

We must discipline, encourage, and instruct our children, but only God can direct and change their hearts. So that's what we pray for.

THINK ABOUT IT . . . *What do you enjoy most about fathering?*
When is successful fathering not a popularity contest?
How important is it that your children have a father who's not afraid to be the father?

CHAPTER SEVEN

LIES MEN BELIEVE ABOUT

WORK AND WEALTH

His name was C. J. Actually, I never knew what those letters stood for. It didn't matter.

The home where C. J. and his wife lived was like something from *Architectural Digest*. It was nestled in the Carolina mountains but wasn't one of those rustic log-cabin kind of structures you often see in those parts. No, this house was like something from the future. Glass, chrome, granite, and imported hardwoods were everywhere. Interior doors were ten feet high, and the latest high-tech stuff made living in this house wildly convenient.

I had great respect for C. J.'s entrepreneurial courage and business acumen. Somewhere in the tangle of a man with an enormous ego was a guy whose heart I would occasionally see. But C. J.'s work and possessions eventually took him down.

His lovely wife finally grew tired of his blazing pride and passion for more and bigger things, and left him. His grown kids also walked away, wanting nothing to do with their hopelessly strident father. I'm confident that this broke his heart, but soon C. J. was on to the next wild frontier, starting yet another company since the last one went public, adding more zeroes to his already burgeoning net worth.

The last time I heard, C. J. was living in his palace alone. This is a sad story.

The biggest lie about work and wealth is that a prestigious job and lots of money make a man. Surely the proof that this is a lie could come from men you and I know (or know about). Men with killer resumes who we wouldn't want to spend thirty seconds with; fabulously wealthy men whose lives are pure tragedy.

YOU CAN SPOT THESE GUYS

Neighborhood parties are a fact of life. Crowded homes with folks who hardly know each other, standing around, making conversation while scanning the room for more important people to network with. Over the years, I've been to many. I've even hosted lots of them. And, after the men read each other's name tag, here's the way nearly every conversation goes:

"And what do you do?"

"Now, which house is yours?"

If the questioner is observant, he may add, "Is that new black Tahoe I've seen in the neighborhood yours? Nice ride."

Some guy who is clearly in touch with his tender side may even ask about another man's family.

Some guy who is clearly in touch with his tender side may even ask about another man's family. This guy will oblige by pulling out his smartphone and sliding through recent photos of his wife and kids. The man who started the conversation will glance at the phone and act interested.

Then there's the man at these parties who has little time or interest in anyone but himself. He doesn't ask any questions because he really doesn't care. He moves from person to person, making certain that each one knows how terrific, important, or wealthy he is.

Ever since I first heard about him, I've thought that the man named

Nabal must have been like this. His story is in the Old Testament book of 1 Samuel.

> And there was a man in Maon whose business was in Carmel. The man was very rich; he had three thousand sheep and a thousand goats. He was shearing his sheep in Carmel. Now the name of the man was Nabal. (25:2–3)

Nabal's name means "folly." Exactly.

The man lived in the rural town of Maon and owned a business in a larger city, Carmel. This was an important place—the city where Elijah called down fire from heaven that consumed the altar of the prophets of Baal (1 Kings 18). Nothing is said about what kind of business Nabal owned in Carmel, but given his holdings in land and livestock in Maon, it's clear that he was prosperous.

Good job, plenty of wealth. And that's not all. There was more.

> . . . and the name of his wife Abigail. The woman was discerning and beautiful . . . (25:3)

So Nabal had meaningful work, lots of money, and a wife who exercised good judgment and was physically attractive. The guy must have been in hog heaven. *"But"* . . . as this verse goes on to say, there was a downside:

> . . . but the man was harsh and badly behaved. (25:3)

Seriously? With all that going for him, it turns out that Nabal was a selfish, surly scoundrel. And as the story unfolds, we discover that he was also an ingrate. David (who had been anointed by God to be the next king of Israel, but was on the run from Saul, the current monarch on the throne, who was trying to kill him) had protected Nabal's land and Nabal refused to prepare a meal for the Israelite soldiers.

Having been on the receiving end of fits of anger previously, when David received this news, he ordered four hundred of his men to join him in arming themselves and preparing for battle. Next stop? Maon. Brace yourself, Nabal. It's going to be a very bad day.

Fortunately for Nabal, his remarkable wife caught wind of David's plan to terminate her husband.

> Then Abigail hurriedly took two hundred loaves of bread, two barrels of wine, five dressed sheep, two bushels of roasted grain, one hundred raisin cakes, and two hundred fig cakes, and packed them onto donkeys. (25:18 TLB)

> **Have you ever wondered why the text of the Bible includes stories like the one about Nabal?**

Abigail's plan was to try to placate David's rage by catering a sumptuous dinner for his troops. David relented. Nabal was spared. Mission accomplished.

But when she returned home, Abigail found her husband drunk, hosting a raucous bender. The next morning, when she explained to Nabal what she had done to save his bacon, he blew a gasket, suffering a severe stroke. Ten days later he was dead.

EXHIBIT A

Have you ever wondered why the text of the Bible includes stories like the one about Nabal—a prominent, wealthy man with a beautiful wife, dropping dead with a hangover and a really bad attitude? Could it be that God wants us to know that a good job, a hefty balance in our bank account, and an attractive wife aren't enough?

Jesus summed it up when He said:

> "For what does it benefit someone to gain the whole world and yet lose his life?" (Mark 8:36 CSB)

The footnote to this statement could have said, "see Nabal."

Recorded in Luke's gospel, Jesus told a short story about another man much like Nabal. And C. J. Since I was born with an entrepreneurial bent myself, this one is impossible for me to ignore.

> And [Jesus] told them a parable, saying, "The land of a rich man
> produced plentifully, and he thought to himself, 'What shall I do, for
> I have nowhere to store my crops?' And he said, 'I will do this: I will
> tear down my barns and build larger ones, and there I will store all
> my grain and my goods. And I will say to my soul, "Soul, you have
> ample goods laid up for many years; relax, eat, drink, be merry."'
> But God said to him, "Fool! This night your soul is required of you,
> and the things you have prepared, whose will they be?" So is the
> one who lays up treasure for himself and is not rich toward God.
> (Luke 12:16–21)

WORSHIPING STUPID THINGS

So why does God's Word warn us so frequently and earnestly about the
dangers associated with the pursuit of worldly status and financial gain?
What's wrong with these things?

Actually, nothing—in and of themselves, there's nothing wrong with
them. But when wealth and prestige are achieved, our hearts are sometimes captured as well. It's not money that Scripture warns us about, it's
the *love* of money that's the problem. When this happens, we've turned a
good thing into an idol.

When the Israelites were migrating from
Egypt to the promised land—a 250-mile trip
that took them forty years to make—God
schooled them in what it meant to love and
obey Him with all their hearts. On one occasion, Moses went to the top of Mt. Sinai to
speak with God. He was gone for forty days
and forty nights.

*When wealth
and prestige are
achieved, our hearts
are sometimes
captured as well.*

The people grew impatient and grumbled, making a whining appeal
to Aaron, Moses's brother. "Up, make us gods who shall go before us. As

for this Moses, the man who brought us up out of the land of Egypt, we do not know what has become of him" (Ex. 32:1).

So Aaron asked the people to gather their gold and bring it to him. Today, he might have told them to bring their watches, computers, jewelry, cash, stock certificates, summer homes, and foreign imports. Those things we own that make us feel secure.

All the gold was melted down and shaped into an image (or idol) shaped like a calf. You may remember this story, but in case you don't, what happens when the people see this heifer-shaped chunk of gold is stunning. Unthinkable. The people knelt down and worshiped it. After all the miracles their God had done for them in plain view, they foolishly prayed to this inanimate chunk of metal as though it could hear. And answer them.

Their valuables, their jewelry, their stuff had been smelted into an idol. And they worshiped it.

> If you forget the LORD your God and go after other gods and serve them and worship them, I solemnly warn you today that you shall surely perish. (Deut. 8:19)

Reminds us of Nabal, doesn't it? Maybe C. J. too?

THE REAL ISSUE

Before I am tempted to crawl up on a "high horse" and issue judgment on men who are tempted to let their hearts be drawn to status and money and the things that can be purchased with a lot of it, I confess to the temptation to be that guy myself.

I need to continually remind myself of what I know to be true about money and the things it can buy. I need God's perspective on these things. Maybe you do, too?

So let's look at it again . . .

Is a good job a bad thing? No.

Is having money a bad thing? No

Is living in a lovely home and driving a nice car a bad thing? No.

But is loving these good things too much a bad thing? Is it dangerous to experience them without understanding that they truly do not make us who we are?

Yes. Absolutely, yes.

Maybe the apostle Paul knew something about my temptations here or perhaps he had a friend in mind like C. J. when he wrote:

> **The love of money is the root of all kinds of evil. And some people, craving money, have wandered from the true faith and pierced themselves with many sorrows. (1 Tim. 6:10 NLT)**

So there we have it. The lies we're about to unpack have to do with our work and our wealth. You and I are never immune to falling prey to these lies. So as the guy says to his opponent in a sword fight . . . this is a good time to be "on guard."

26 *"Making more money will make me happier."*

You don't really believe this lie, do you? You and I might not ever publicly admit it. We might not believe we believe this. But the devil's subtlety is such that he encourages us to believe things we'd never admit to ourselves or others.

We say we're not this shallow, that money can't buy love, that you can't take it with you, that more money means more problems. But if we look at our lives, if we look at what we make a priority, we see what we actually believe, down deep. The Bible puts it this way: "For as he thinks in his heart, so is he" (Prov. 23:7 NKJV).

JUST A LITTLE BIT MORE

John D. Rockefeller at least was honest with himself. The founder of Standard Oil was the first American billionaire, and was for a time the

> *The poverty we feel isn't the gap between what we have and what we need, but the gap between what we have and what we want.*

richest man in the world. One day a reporter is said to have asked him, "How much money is enough?" Rockefeller responded, "Just a little bit more."[1]

Seems silly, doesn't it? For a man who had so much, he still wasn't satisfied.

Until we consider this: you and I are likely in the "one percent." That is, it's highly likely that we are wealthier than 99 percent of all the people who have ever lived. If you own a car—no matter how battered—if you have hot running water, indoor plumbing, and electric lights, if you have artificial heat in your home, you are enjoying blessings even kings had to do without less than two hundred years ago.

And yet, like Rockefeller, it's not enough. The poverty we feel isn't the gap between what we have and what we need, but the gap between what we have and what we want. By this absurd standard, even Rockefeller was poor.

The thing is, things aren't the thing. It's easy to think that a better car, a nicer home, a bigger, higher-definition, larger TV will feed the hunger inside. But they will not and they cannot. You and I can only find satisfaction in the Giver of blessings. In the fourth century AD, the north African bishop Augustine expressed this truth in a way that has proved to be timeless:

> You have made us for yourself, and our heart is restless until it rests in you.[2]

When we give ourselves over to pursuing wealth and the things that it can buy, we are like a parched man seeking to slake his thirst by drinking from the ocean. The more he drinks the salty water, the thirstier he will become.

ALL I REALLY NEED IS MORE GRATITUDE

Money will not make us happy. Gratitude will. In Romans 1, the apostle Paul presses in with the truth that all men stand guilty before God. We know He exists. We know we do not measure up to His standard. What we also know, however, is that we pretend we don't know. We suppress the truth, trying desperately to push it out of our minds. Paul concludes this way:

> Although they knew God, they did not honor him as God or give thanks to him, but they became futile in their thinking, and their foolish hearts were darkened. (Rom. 1:21)

Money will not make us happy. Gratitude will.

Look at this again. Please don't miss the power. The apostle says that in spite of what we know about God, we don't glorify Him as He deserves. And, he says, we do not give Him thanks for what we have. As a result, our thinking becomes "worthless" (CSB).

Whoever you are, whatever your bank balance, wherever you work and live and drive, compared to most other men on planet Earth, you and I are enormously wealthy. A grateful heart acknowledges that our heavenly Father is the source from which all good and perfect gifts flow (James 1:21), that everything we have belongs to Him, that we are merely stewards of this wealth . . . His wealth. He is the one who determines what, and how much, we will have. We will not get more by wanting more, but by handling well what He has already given us and trusting that if He knows we truly need more to meet our needs, He will provide more.

Not long ago, I was in a conversation with a young man who works for my company. I was expressing to him how thankful I am for the good work he is doing so faithfully, day after day.

We were at a place where we could increase his salary just a bit. I told him that we could give him a small raise.

"I'm okay," he said. "Give it to someone else." And then he added, "My wife and I have enough. And we're grateful."

> **Gratitude is a pathway to deep, unshakable peace.**

My colleague's response was stunning then. It still is.

Gratitude is a pathway to deep, unshakable peace. Please hear this: we can't be grateful and resentful at the same time. We can't be thankful and discontent. Or grateful and fearful. We choose one or the other.

You and I can learn from David. He began Psalm 23 this way: "The LORD is my shepherd; I shall not want" (23:1). He goes on to celebrate that his Shepherd leads him to green pastures and still waters. But even before he is given those gifts, he has all that he needs, as long as he has the Lord for his shepherd. He is good to go. This very Shepherd is actually enough.

THE TRUTH

If Jesus is all we want, He will be all we really need. If a man were to trade everything he owns for Him, this would be a wise exchange.

THINK ABOUT IT . . . *It's only natural to believe that making more money is your ultimate goal. Does this describe you? Do you believe that having more money will make you happier? Why is this fallacious thinking?*

 27   *"How I spend my time is my business."*

The other day I saw a time management chart online.[3] From this I summarized the way I imagined how the average man spends his hours each week. Here are the assumptions I made for the 168 hours you and I have. See how this squares with how you spend your time:

- 40 — Working (the average work week)
- 7.5 — Commuting to and from work (1.5 hours per day)

- • 14 — Eating or preparing meals (2 hours per day)
- • 56 — Sleeping (assuming 8 hours per night)
- • 7 — Various other activities (one hour per day housekeeping, other jobs to be done, taking children to school, etc.)
- • 124.5 — Total

This leaves 43.5 hours per week, unspoken for.

So let's add 7 hours for showers and getting dressed, 7 hours of personal Bible study and prayer, 3 hours for church (worshiping, coming and going), 4 hours for reading, 4 hours for conversation with my wife and kids, and 2 hours for lovemaking.

That totals 27 hours, which still leaves 16.5 hours unspoken for. In other words, I have about a full day per week of "free time."

So what do I do with this spare day each week? And why does it matter?

The French impressionist painter Paul Gauguin (1848–1903) was known as a renegade within the artist community of his day. Among his most famous oil paintings was a treatment depicting man's journey from birth to the grave. Instead of just signing this painting as was his usual practice, Gaugin wrote three short questions in French: "Where do we come from? What are we? Where are we going?"

The painter died in his fifties as a result of living a life of excess. It appears that he went to his own grave with these questions unanswered.[4]

In contrast, here's what God's Word says about living and dying:

> **None of us lives to himself, and none of us dies to himself. For if we live, we live to the Lord, and if we die, we die to the Lord. So then, whether we live or whether we die, we are the Lord's. (Rom. 14:7–8)**

The New City Catechism asks: "What is our only hope in life and death?" The answer follows:

> *That we are not our own but belong, body and soul, both in life and death, to God and to our Savior Jesus Christ.*[5]

One of the things that marks men like you and me, men who hold to a Christian worldview, is the way we view the passing of time and ordering of the events of life. To think "Christianly" is to affirm, "my times, O God, are in your hands."[6]

STEWARDS OF TIME

So back to the way you and I spend our 168 hours, also known as "our times," I have a question for us to consider. Ready? Which of these hours belong to God? The answer should be clear.

They are *all* His; we are stewards of each and every one.

> My times are in your hand;
>> rescue me from the hand of my enemies and from my persecutors!
>> (Ps. 31:15)

The psalmist could have written, "My hours—all 168 per week—are in your hands, O Lord. These hours are a gift from You. And how I spend each one is my gift back to you."

Some might reason that perhaps the quick and obvious answer of what time belongs to God would be the ten hours we spend in church and personal devotions. That's good; but it's not the whole answer.

Each of our activities and assignments is a stewardship from our Creator. Or as the apostle Paul summarized in his first letter to the Corinthian church: "So, whether you eat or drink, or whatever you do, do all to the glory of God" (10:31).

For many years people wore little elastic wristbands with the letters: WWJD printed on them. "What would Jesus do?" As it relates to the way we spend our time—including our "spare" time—my question would be, WDJD: "What *did* Jesus do?" How did He spend His 168 hours?

As He was escaping from the city of Jerusalem, where His enemies had threatened to kill Him, Jesus passed a blind man. His disciples asked a question about why the man was in this condition. Jesus' answer sounds like a change of the subject, but it's not.

"We must work the works of him who sent me while it is day; night is coming, when no one can work." (John 9:4)

He was saying, "When the sun is shining and there is work to do, work."

He was also saying that, no matter what, sunset is on its way. The day will end. That's when what we do in the sunlight will be finished. No more chances to do anything else.

There was a blind man to be attended to, and Jesus healed him. But following this miracle and a dreadful encounter with religious leaders in the temple, the Bible tells us what Jesus did next with His spare time:

> *What you and I do with our "spare time" may say more about us than what we do with our "productive time."*

He went away again across the Jordan to the place where John had been baptizing at first, and there he remained. (John 10:40)

What you and I do with our "spare time" may say more about us than what we do with our "productive time." This is a huge challenge, isn't it? Our time . . . all of it . . . belongs to God.

THE TRUTH

If we belong to God, all of our hours, including those when we have nothing planned, belong to Him.

THINK ABOUT IT . . . *What are some time wasters in your life? What are some practical steps you could take to honor God with your time?*

28   *"I'm not responsible to be the provider for my wife and family."*

Given the heavy pressures that are part and parcel of "bellying up" to their responsibilities at home, let's call what many men are facing today at home the temptation to abdicate. It's real. If not for you, for many of your friends. Just look around.

According to Dictionary.com, in 1975 a brand-new noun entered the English lexicon. This new word is defined as "a father who neglects his responsibilities as a parent."[7]

The word is "deadbeat," and more often than not, it's used with a dad who abdicates his God-given role as the provider for his family.

Could this describe you and me?

Of course, you will wince at this notion since "deadbeat" is often used to describe men who refuse to pay child support following a divorce from the children's mother. But actually, according to my internet dictionary, that's the second definition. The first is simply a dad who decides not to be . . . the dad.

> *Sounds pretty serious to neglect the needs of your family. It is.*

Again, is it possible this describes you and me?

Here's what the apostle Paul says about a man and his role as the provider:

> If anyone does not provide for his relatives, and especially for members of his household, he has denied the faith and is worse than an unbeliever. (1 Tim. 5:8)

Sounds pretty serious to neglect the needs of your family. It is.

Now, this responsibility for provision doesn't mean you and I do all the work required to care for our home and family. And it doesn't necessarily mean that we are the only one who brings income into the family coffers. Wives and moms can and should contribute to the well-being of the family in various ways.

But you and I uniquely bear the ultimate responsibility under God for making sure that our family's needs are being met and for overseeing that realm. Your wife may have a bigger paycheck than you do, but you are responsible. You and I have an innate sense that this is good and right.

In some situations, it may not be possible for a man to fulfill this responsibility. He may be disabled in some way or there may be other extenuating circumstances. In those cases, God will provide through other means. But a man of God will feel the weight of this responsibility and will look to God for wisdom and grace to fulfill it.

So what does this look like? Good question.

ARE YOU A CYCLE BREAKER?

You may have been fortunate enough to have a dad who provided for your family, a man who cherished your mother, a man who was a godly example for you and whose discipline was fair and consistent. This is a special blessing since you have a good example to follow. This is the best way to learn. You know what good husbanding and fathering look like.

And you want to be like your dad.

Or maybe your dad was a "deadbeat." He provided little or nothing in the way of an example. He was anything but a provider for the needs of your family. You've never heard yourself say anything about wanting to be like him. (Maybe your dad was totally absent from your life.) This is a hard way to learn.

You're saying to yourself, "I don't want to be like my dad." Your great challenge is to be a "cycle breaker."

I had the privilege of having a dad who consistently modeled what it was like to be a faithful provider . . . making certain his family's needs were met. Many times throughout my years, I have reminded

His deep familiarity with the Proverbs gave him the tools he needed to be a more-than-capable provider in business and at home.

myself of the many good things Samuel Wolgemuth did in this role.

My wife, Nancy, had the same privilege. In fact, in order to get his marching orders as the family's provider, each day her dad, Art DeMoss, read his Bible, and this included a chapter from the Proverbs.[8] There are thirty-one of them, so the book lasted a month. When he reached the end of his reading and a new month began, he would go back and read them again.

Although I never met Art DeMoss, his legacy of faithfulness is known around the world. In fact, his deep familiarity with the Proverbs gave him the tools he needed to be a more-than-capable provider in business and at home.

Our responsibility to provide for our families cannot be relinquished.

A PIZZA DELIVERY BOY SHOWED ME HOW

If Jon Schrader weren't my son-in-law, I would still be blown away by the story I'm about to tell you. But the fact that Jon is married to my daughter Missy, and is the father of three of my grandchildren, makes the following account even more powerful to me.

Jon received his undergraduate degree in information technology (IT). He earned this from Taylor University, my alma mater and a school that has a great reputation for the high quality of this degree. After graduating from Taylor, Jon moved to Charlotte, North Carolina, found a wonderful church, landed a terrific job, fell in love with Missy, married her, and settled down.

Thanks to his generous employer that picked up the tab for his tuition, Jon enrolled in Queens University, finding time to study on top of his full-time job, and earned his MBA in two years.

In the meantime, children began coming along and Jon became painfully aware that, with daily living expenses rising, he and Missy needed more income.

As bright as Jon was—and is—there was one thing he knew for sure: providing for his family was not negotiable. This was his responsibility and it could not be dodged.

So he took an evening job as a pizza-delivery boy. The hours were flexible enough that he could have dinner with his family before dashing out to the pizza store to receive his orders and drive the bounty to their waiting and hungry buyers.

The accounts Jon would tell us of the generosity of some of his customers when they met this remarkably bright young man standing on their front porch holding a fresh, hot pizza are terrific. (A few were not so terrific.)

If you were to ask Missy what it meant to her that her professionally trained, graduate-schooled husband took his job as his family's provider this seriously, she'd tell you in no uncertain terms.

And as Jon's children grew, he became aware that providing for the family was something that could be managed . . . and shared. Part of the secret of capably providing was the joy of giving his children a "piece of the action."

This is the way providers help teach their children to someday be the providers for their own families.

So Jon and Missy helped their children take part in the running of their household. You know . . . you've heard of these . . . chores. This is the way providers help teach their children to someday be the providers for their own families.

A CENTURY AGO

My ancestors were farmers. And farmers' children were free labor. Farm hands. Parents really didn't care if milking cows or tossing hay bales onto a large wagon were part of their offspring's skill set. It didn't really matter if their child would rather be playing the piano or painting at an easel than scooping out the gutters in the barn. There was work to be done on the farm, and so everyone worked.

If I may step back to that century or so and pose a suggestion to you that I believe is still true: every member of your family should have

> *Our homes can be a dress rehearsal to prepare our kids to succeed in the future.*

a chance to work around the house, to contribute to the well-being of the family.

Yes, you bear ultimate responsibility for provision for your family. But you can spread the joy of "ownership" around and among your children. This may take some creativity and extra effort, but it will teach them valuable lessons about the importance of work and will equip them to be responsible, hard-working adults who will love and serve their families well. Our homes can be a dress rehearsal to prepare our kids to succeed in the future.

OTHER KINDS OF PROVISION

Before leaving this idea of your role as a provider for your family, let me quickly mention that provision encompasses more than just financial support and things relating to your family's creature comforts. Provision comes in different shapes and sizes.

One spring I found a small plot of land and decided to take a shot at a vegetable garden. I had admired little private gardens and it looked interesting, and pretty simple to do. The land was adjacent to my office, and I got permission from the owner to tackle about two hundred square feet of luscious Illinois soil.

You should have seen it. Squash, beans, tomatoes, cucumbers, even some corn.

That year the first few weeks of the season provided just the right amount of rain and sun. My garden flourished.

But alas, the rain stopped falling and the heat became almost unbearable. I had to carry water to my garden in heavy buckets. Sweat seeped through my good office clothes as I tried to sustain the plants. As the days wore on, my enthusiasm wore down. Then it ended. My once strong-looking plants began to wilt. Then turn brown. Then die.

So it was back to the grocery store for me.

But can you imagine a speech I'd make to my dying garden? "So, look at you. What's the matter with you, all withered and brown? What an embarrassment you are."

Of course, that's silly. Why, because this garden was my responsibility. It was mine to tend and care for.

Here's the way the apostle Paul addressed our responsibility for providing.

> **Fathers, provoke not your children to wrath: but bring them up in the nurture and admonition of the Lord. (Eph. 6:4 KJV)**

The word that describes our provision for our families is "nurture." Other translations use *rear, raise, discipline,* or *instruction.* I like the word from the old King James Version. "Nurture."

So this provision means watering, weeding, fertilizing . . . as in providing spiritual, emotional, and relational nurture. It means being alert and attentive to the needs of our wives and children, and asking the Lord to show us how those needs can best be met. This is our call. Our privilege. We nurture our family—body, soul, and spirit . . . not just food, shelter, and clothing.

THE TRUTH	It is our God-given job to serve our families as providers. Through our example, we can show them that they have a heavenly Father who can be trusted to meet their needs.

THINK ABOUT IT . . . *Being your family's primary provider can be good news and bad news. When is it good news? Bad news? How can you do a better job of being your family's provider?*

"*My faith and my work are unrelated.*"

Sometimes the songs we sang in children's church forever consigned Bible men as caricatures. Like this one:

Zacchaeus was a wee little man.
A wee little man was he.
He climbed up in a sycamore tree
For the Lord he wanted to see.

So we forever think of Zacchaeus as a troll. A dwarf. A hobbit. But do you know the whole of his story? It's anything but a silly rhyme wrapped in a catchy tune.

The gospel of Luke tells us that as Jesus entered Jerusalem, Zacchaeus climbed a tree for a better look. While he may have been short of stature, Zacchaeus was not short of standing. He was a chief tax collector, Luke tells us, and very rich. Jesus, seeing him in the tree, told him to come down quickly because He would like to spend the night at his house. Can you imagine?

> While he may have been short of stature, Zacchaeus was not short of standing.

That, however, is not the end of the story. After being with Jesus, his thinking having returned to solid ground, Zacchaeus told Jesus, "Behold, Lord, the half of my goods I give to the poor. And if I have defrauded anyone of anything, I restore it fourfold" (Luke 19:8).

Zacchaeus—this wee little man—is the poster child for the disturbing fact that Jesus was known to hang out with notorious sinners. The people grumbled against the Savior when He announced His lodging plans with Zacchaeus.

Zacchaeus, however, wasn't merely a notorious sinner. As it turned out, he was—and showed himself to be—a *repentant* notorious sinner. And he did so right away by showing that his devotion to Christ would shape every area of his life, including his pocketbook and his job. He understood that Jesus wasn't merely asking to be an invisible Lord of a tiny fraction of his life but that He would be Lord over all that he was and all that he did.

In our increasingly secularized culture, you and I feel the pressure to isolate our faith, to keep it on the backburner. Out of sight. The broader culture doesn't much care what we believe in the privacy of our own hearts, but it is increasingly resistant to us bringing our faith out in public.

Of course, Jesus had a different spin on this. In fact, He bookended His most famous spoken message—the Sermon on the Mount—when He lifted this challenge to us about bringing our love for Him and our faith into the open:

> *The broader culture doesn't much care what we believe in the privacy of our own hearts, but it is increasingly resistant to us bringing our faith out in public.*

"You are the light of the world. A city set on a hill cannot be hidden. Nor do people light a lamp and put it under a basket, but on a stand, and it gives light to all in the house. In the same way, let your light shine before others, so that they may see your good works and give glory to your Father who is in heaven." (Matt. 5:14–16)

In his classic apologetic, *The Weight of Glory*, C. S. Lewis got to the heart of how this works out:

When the modern world says to us aloud, "You may be religious when you are alone," it adds under its breath, "and I will see to it that you never are alone."[9]

The truth is, we are never alone. As I mentioned earlier, we live *coram Deo*—before the face of God. Whether we recognize it or not, the sovereign God is our constant companion.

That said, integrating our faith and our work doesn't mean we make a show of our prayers or shower our coworkers with gospel literature.

Martin Luther said that a Christian shoemaker is not one who etches little crosses on shoes, but one who makes excellent shoes and deals honestly with his customers.[10] Don't you love that?

The apostle Paul made much the same point:

> Whatever you do, work heartily, as for the Lord and not for men, knowing that from the Lord you will receive the inheritance as your reward. You are serving the Lord Christ. (Col. 3:23–24)

WORK . . . FROM THE BEGINNING

When you and I think about Adam living in the garden of Eden, it's easy to picture him chilling out 24/7. We picture a hammock suspended between two trees and history's first man spending his days and nights there. But this isn't the picture Scripture gives us. Consider the following:

> The LORD God took the man and put him in the garden of Eden to *work* it and *keep* it. (Gen. 2:15)

We don't know exactly what this "work" looked like, but it's clear that God's plan was not for Adam to be a naked lummox eating fruit and taking naps. No, his job was to "work" and "keep" this garden.

This was Adam's job description: to cultivate or tend the garden and to watch over it, pointing to his roles as provider and protector. Of course, this was before the fall, so his work was not drudgery; it was a means to glorify the Creator.

After Adam and Eve sinned, God imposed gender-specific consequences on them. The consequence for the woman was in the realm of her responsibility as a mother and caregiver—there would be pain associated with childbearing (Gen. 3:16)

The consequence for the man was

> *We don't know exactly what this "work" looked like, but it's clear that God's plan was not for Adam to be a naked lummox eating fruit and taking naps.*

in the realm of his responsibility to provide—there would be pain, thorns, thistles, and sweaty labor associated with his efforts to work the ground (Gen. 3:17–19).

In other words, Adam's sin transformed his vocation from a flower arranger into a farmer. His primary work wasn't simply to clip blooms for the dining room table but to wrestle food from the stubborn ground for that same table.

But either way . . . florist or plow horse, our work is blessed. It is good. And it is for the pleasure of our God, who is redeeming this broken world and making all things new.

> *But either way . . . florist or plow horse, our work is blessed. It is good.*

In fact, there's a redeeming quality to our work. During the summer, we "redeem" our unkempt lawn by mowing and trimming it. We "redeem" our wayward boxwoods back into shape. We cull the weeds from our flowerbeds.[11]

We fix broken things. We build new things. We change the oil in our car. We make deliveries. We see patients. We manage subordinates. We create marketing plans to turn skids of product into revenues so our family can survive.

Our work is good. It matters. And *how* we work matters as well. We cannot leave our faith at the shop door or office elevator. If we're able to "quarantine" our relationship with God from what we do 9–5 each day, it's a good sign that we may not really have a relationship with Him at all. Honesty, integrity, diligence, these are the marks our Master calls us to bring to our labors. They are the fruit of His work in us; they are His work through us.

The apostle Paul summed the purpose, the goal of all our activities like this:

> So, whether you eat or drink, or whatever you do, do all to the glory of God. (1 Cor. 10:31)

In fact, I believe you and I could paraphrase this priceless text without distorting its meaning. We could say: "So, whether you eat or drink or deliver packages or manage a corporation or pastor a church or treat patients at the hospital . . . do all to the glory of God."

ROAD RAGE TURNED RIGHT-SIDE UP

I have spent most of my professional career in the book publishing business. Over the years I have had the pleasure of meeting some wonderful men and women who lived this Zacchaeus principle of "do all to the glory of God." The late Lloyd Johnson was, for me, one of the most special ones. He told me this story just a few months after it happened.

Lloyd and his son Tim owned one of the premier Christian bookstores in America, The Better Book Room in Wichita, Kansas. Early one morning, Lloyd was tasked with picking up the donuts for his team. So on his way to work he pulled his car into his favorite bakery. After securing the sugar fix for his associates, Lloyd pulled his car back onto the street.

Apparently, a car passing by didn't like Lloyd's potentially treacherous maneuver and laid on his horn at Lloyd. Not just a little friendly toot, it was one of those hard and angry horn blasts.

This both alarmed and infuriated Lloyd who raised his fist and shouted at the offensive driver. They both drove on. No harm, no foul. Or was it?

When he arrived at the bookstore to begin his work, Lloyd couldn't shake his anguish over what he had done.

When he arrived at the bookstore to begin his work, Lloyd couldn't shake his anguish over what he had done. He told me that the Lord was working on his heart.

So he spent the rest of the day trying to remember the make, model, color of the car, and the face of the driver and researched every possible avenue to locate the man.

Incredibly, Lloyd found him. Living his adult life in this smallish town helped. Lloyd called the man, identified himself as the person who had cut him off in traffic that morning and had screamed at him in anger.

"Would it be okay if I'd pay you a short visit?" Lloyd asked the surprised man.

And this is what he did. An hour or so later, Lloyd Johnson was sitting in the office of a local businessman confessing his angry outburst aimed at the man and asking for his forgiveness.

Then Lloyd told the man about Jesus and how it was His love and grace that had saved him and given him a new heart . . . a heart new enough to make things right.

"Can I know this Jesus, too?" the businessman asked. And so Lloyd led his new friend in prayer to the throne of grace. In that moment, his sins were forgiven and the question of the man's eternal home was settled.

When I consider the implications of living my life at work that's consistent with my faith, I always think of this story. And this example. Thank you, Lloyd.

Zacchaeus did not just do the right thing; like Lloyd Johnson, his faith impacted his life and family and his work. And as far as we know, Zacchaeus didn't quit his tax-collecting job. But don't you know he went to work the next morning with a whole new perspective on what he was doing? Same job, different man.

> Therefore, if anyone is in Christ, he is a new creation. The old has passed away; behold, the new has come. (2 Cor. 5:17)

THE TRUTH | Our faith and our work cannot be compartmentalized; we should faithfully serve Him and others in everything we do.

THINK ABOUT IT . . . *What are some ways you can honor God in your vocation?*

"I can't afford to give more money away."

Let me cut straight to the chase on this one and then backpedal a bit. This lie is about a lack of generosity. If you're naturally a stingy person, if you have "miserly" stapled to your DNA, the next few pages have your name on them.

And if you don't think you're miserly (actually, you'd grade yourself pretty decently on generosity), the next few pages are also for you. Sometimes we're blind to our own shortcomings.

Either way, you may want to fasten your seatbelt.

If you're not living as a man with an open hand, you're going to eventually get sick of your hoarding self. But when you learn the absolute joy of giving, you're going to find a new level of happiness you never thought possible.

I know this sounds crazy, but over the years I've learned how to spot wealthy people. Of course, there are the usual trinkets—the latest foreign import parked in the garage, Rolex watches, summer homes, a big boat on the lake—that rich folks sometimes lavish on themselves. Those are easy to see. But there's another way to spot a rich person: he often says "yes" to opportunities to lavish gifts on others, though to be sure, many people with lesser means are also generous with their resources.

There was one such "rich" man I will never forget. I was a young teenager and traveling with my dad, who was involved in a youth ministry and spent time on the road visiting with "friends of the ministry." Donors. These were folks who made their resources available for "the Lord's work."

We had traveled to western Michigan to meet a larger-than-life second-generation Italian guy named Billy Zeoli. I remember how this man treated me . . . just a quiet teenager in his world of fast-moving men. I could have been no more exciting to Billy than wallpaper. But he spoke to me as though I were his equal. I'll never forget how good this felt.

But as wonderful as that was, it wasn't my favorite thing about this particular remarkable man. I recall being impressed with how rich Billy was. Of course, I had no access to his personal balance sheet, but my hunch was confirmed when we got to the Grand Rapids airport.

Our car pulled up in front of the baggage drop area and Billy hopped out to help the skycap with the luggage. Reaching into his pocket, Billy handed the guy a $5 bill—a big tip back in those days—especially since Billy was also helping him wrestle the bags from the trunk. I'll never forget the grateful look on the man's face and the joy that seemed to radiate from Billy as he pressed the money into the guy's hand.

I remember thinking, *Billy Zeoli must be a wealthy man!*

Now that I'm no longer a teenager, I have thought many times about how this moment made an indelible impression on me. In truth, this could have been Billy's last $5 bill. His checking-account balance could have been paltry. But because he was generous, lavishing this baggage-handler guy with this kind of gift, I knew for sure that here was a rich man.

As I have gotten older and embraced the reality and certainty of my own death, I have often replayed an admonition I first heard from world-renowned financial guru Ron Blue: "Do your givin' while you're livin', so you're knowin' where it's goin'."

Does this mean I don't have any long-term financial reserves? No, it doesn't mean that. But when my wife and children see in their husband and dad a man who does not grip tightly to his resources, I hope they will be inspired to do the same. And this gift you give them will bring them joy. They, too, will be rich.

When my wife and children see in their husband and dad a man who does not grip tightly to his resources, I hope they will be inspired to do the same.

Again, let's visit with the apostle Paul on this one. As he was getting ready to move on to the next city, he paid a final visit to his elder-friends in Ephesus. He reminded them of the gift of generosity and a sacrificial lifestyle:

"In all things I have shown you that by working hard in this way we must help the weak and remember the words of the Lord Jesus, how he himself said, 'It is more blessed to give than to receive.'" (Acts 20:35)

You probably have stories like this from your own life where you were generous and, because of that, received this "blessing."

Like Billy Zeoli, bestselling author and counselor, the late Dr. Gary Smalley, was also a generous giver. Compared to truly wealthy men, Gary would not have been considered in the top echelon of country-club-rich folks in his town, but from Gary's perspective, he had more than he needed.

Without the person looking, Gary would slip up to the cashier and hand her his credit card.

One of his favorite activities was to visit the local Walmart and wander the aisles looking for someone to bless. When he'd spot a shopper pushing a full cart who appeared as though he or she might also have been pushing the edges of their financial capability to pay for it, Gary would wait until the person selected a checkout lane.

Then, without the person looking, Gary would slip up to the cashier and hand her his credit card. "When you've finished ringing up that person's purchase," Gary whispered to the clerk nodding to the person he had selected, "please tell them that an unidentified someone has paid their bill in full. Also tell them that God loves them."

Then Gary would find a spot where no one could see him watch from a distance as the joy unfolded. Gary Smalley was truly a wealthy man.

So there you have it. Learning how to be generous brings blessing and joy—not only to the recipient of the gift, but even more to the giver. This is something you and I can do.

THE TRUTH | We can never *not* afford to be generous to others. This blesses them. And us.

THINK ABOUT IT . . . *Are you a generous man? Where does this show up? Like, are you a big tipper? If not, why not? If so, how satisfying is this kind of generosity? Why should you be generous? How generous are you with your expressions of gratitude? To your wife? Your children? Your boss? Your colleagues? Your friends?*

CHAPTER EIGHT

LIES MEN BELIEVE ABOUT
CIRCUMSTANCES

H aving grown up in the Chicago area most of my childhood, I've been a fan of every professional team hailing from the Windy City. Most of this has been a study in patience and longsuffering, although there have been exceptions . . . like the Bears in the mid-'80s, the Bulls in the '90s, the Blackhawks in 2010 and 2015, and of course, the Cubs in 2016.

As a small boy, my personal prayer life grew by leaps and bounds anytime one of these aforementioned teams was in a playoff game against a major rival. I wasn't mature enough to pray that God would be glorified or that no one would be seriously injured. Nope. I asked God to see to it that my team won.

Then it began to dawn on me. What if there were a little boy, just like me, who loved the other guys the way I loved my team? What if he were asking God the same thing I was asking? How would God handle that?

My confusion lifted when I remembered one obvious part of the equation I'd left out. Surely only a heathen little boy could root for our dastardly rivals!

As a grown man, I still care too much about the outcome of a football game. But when my team loses, I try to remember that somewhere in another city there's a man just like me, very happy his team has won. And I've tried to not tie my own personal joy too tightly to the outcome of a game.

A MORE SERIOUS CONTEST

"Of course Job is a good man," Satan seemed to say. "He knows which side his bread is buttered on."

What if, instead of rivals on the field of play, the tug-of-war was between God and Satan? The book of Job tells us of a day when Satan appeared before God, and they began to talk. In what sounds initially like a conversation you and I might strike up with an old friend in the Target parking lot, God asked Satan what he had been up to. Satan replied that he had been walking to and fro across the earth.

"Have you considered my servant Job," God said, "that there is none like him on the earth, a blameless and upright man, who fears God and turns away from evil?" (Job 1:8).

Satan was quick to point out the obvious. Job was a pious man. God had showered him with great blessings. It appeared that this man—and the team he cheered for—won every game. Job was healthy and had great wealth. He sported a large and loving family. "Of course Job is a good man," Satan seemed to say. "He knows which side his bread is buttered on."

What followed next was a test. Suddenly and without warning, poor Job stood in the crosshairs of the argument between God and His archrival. God gave Satan leave to take away many of Job's blessings. Job lost his cattle, his children, and the support of his friends who wrongly assumed Job must be a terrible sinner to be going through such suffering. Job mourned but remained faithful.

And then, with God's permission, Satan upped the ante and attacked

Job's health. His wife excoriated him and eventually Job cracked. And who can blame him? Scripture records his complaint before God (see Job 31:13–40).

And God, who isn't one to be trifled with, swiftly put Job in his place.

> Then the LORD answered Job out of the whirlwind and said:
> "Who is this that darkens counsel by words without knowledge?
> Dress for action like a man;
>   I will question you, and you make it known to me.
>
> "Where were you when I laid the foundation of the earth?
>   Tell me, if you have understanding.
> Who determined its measurements—surely you know!
>   Or who stretched the line upon it?
> On what were its bases sunk,
>   or who laid its cornerstone,
> when the morning stars sang together
>   and all the sons of God shouted for joy?" (38:1–7)

Every time I read this account, my face flushes. Can you imagine having the sovereign God of the universe go after you like this? I can't either.

The reminder of who God is moved Job to deep humility and heartfelt repentance. He realized that his questioning of the Almighty was foolish and vowed never to do so again. The story ends with God restoring to Job what had been taken from him, and we are told, "And the LORD blessed the latter days of Job more than his beginning" (42:12).

THE HAND YOU'RE DEALT

The record of this ancient believer reminds us that God's goodness toward us should not be measured or evaluated by the circumstances in which we find ourselves at any given point. And our joy does not have to ebb and flow on the basis of those circumstances, trying as they may be.

Job's sufferings were historic, so great that his name has become a byword for suffering itself. If we say someone is "suffering like Job," almost everyone knows exactly what we're saying. But, as difficult a road as Job faced, and as pious as he was, there was one man who was *far more* pious, who suffered *far more*.

That would be Jesus.

Jesus was perfect, utterly without sin. He was the spotless Lamb of God, to which all those Old Testament sacrificial lambs pointed. From His birth to His death to His resurrection to His ascension, Jesus never sinned. Not even a little. Not even in private. And yet what He suffered was more severe than anyone on earth has ever been through.

> God's goodness toward us should not be measured or evaluated by the circumstances in which we find ourselves at any given point.

It is common for preachers to highlight the physical agony of Jesus' crucifixion. This barbaric form of execution used in the Roman era was horrific to be sure. But His physical suffering was far from the worst of what Jesus endured for us. He not only suffered the scourging of the Roman government (as did tens of thousands of others, including the thieves crucified on either side of Him), but all the wrath of the Father that rightly should have fallen on sinners, fell on Him. All the suffering in hell that you and I would have received without Christ, He took for us. That is hardship, circumstances to which nothing can be compared.

> All the suffering in hell that you and I would have received without Christ, He took for us.

The cross, which appeared to be a monumental defeat for God, was in fact the greatest moment in history, the victory of the second Adam, our moment of rescue, the triumph of God over evil. Like Job, the disciples mourned when Jesus was crucified; all their hopes dashed to pieces. The devil may have danced as champagne corks popped all over his princedom. Jesus had been executed. But in the end, Satan found out that all was lost, and the disciples discovered that all was found. All this according to God's eternal plan.

The darkest hour gave birth to the brightest moment; the dusk was the dawn.

THE DAYS OF OUR LIVES

So what does all this mean for you and me in the circumstances we face today? The God who created and orders every molecule of the universe has promised us this:

> And we know that for those who love God all things work together for good, for those who are called according to his purpose. (Rom. 8:28)

This is not just a false panacea, an all-too-easy salve to put on our wounds. It is the reality of realities. If we are in Christ, if we love Him, if we have been called according to His purposes, then we can know with certainty that all things work together for our good.

The "good" of our circumstances isn't, of course, a guarantee of temporary happiness or uninterrupted comfort, but is something even better. It is the remaking of us into the image of the Son. Hardships are real, make no mistake. But they have a higher purpose. They purify us. We find fuel for our peace and joy in the face of hardship when we sing the words of this immortal hymn penned in 1787—words that express the heart of our heavenly Father:

> *Hardships are real, make no mistake. But they have a higher purpose. They purify us.*

> *When through fiery trials your pathway shall lie,*
> *my grace all-sufficient shall be your supply;*
> *the flame shall not hurt you; I only design*
> *your dross to consume and your gold to refine.*[1]

If eternal joy is the goal—the transformation of our beings into the image of Christ, the refining of our gold, the perfection of our souls—then we can be assured that whatever is going on around us, whatever path we are being led down, is the pathway to a glorious end.

For example, can you imagine that the apostle Paul sang God's praises while locked up in prison? He did.

And can you picture the second-century martyr Polycarp, looking to heaven and praising God while the flames that would consume his body were licking his bare feet? He did. This is almost unimaginable.

And in like manner, by the end of the book that bears his name, Job lifted up the glory of God in the midst of his loss.

It is true that our circumstances—good and bad—can, and should, determine our joy. We should only have joy in those circumstances in which God is on His throne, in which He is in absolute control of everything that comes to pass, and in which we are His beloved children. That means, if we are in Christ, every circumstance can be an occasion and the backdrop for joy.

> *If we are in Christ, every circumstance can be an occasion and the backdrop for joy.*

The truth is, joy is not the absence of pain or difficult circumstances. Joy is the certain conviction that God is able, and that He is for us. Neither of those two things will ever—can ever—change. All because of the one great "tragedy," the death of the one Man who didn't deserve to die. Our God is able, and He is for us. Therefore, you can rejoice, even if you find yourself in the midst of mourning. Even if the bad guys win the football game.

Take it from a man—the apostle Paul—who repeatedly found himself thrown into painful, humiliating circumstances and could have had great cause for despair:

> So we do not lose heart. Though our outer self is wasting away, our inner self is being renewed day by day. For this light, momentary affliction is preparing for us an eternal weight of glory beyond all

comparison, as we look not to the things that are seen but to the things that are unseen. For the things that are seen are transient, but the things that are unseen are eternal. (2 Cor. 4:16–18)

31 *"I have the right to be angry when things don't go my way."*

Sometimes circumstances are beyond our control and catch us off guard. But sometimes the trouble we find ourselves in is of our own making, as in the case of this bizarre story that was covered by nearly every major news outlet at the time.[2]

A woman made the news in 2002 when she was taken into custody at her local Walmart for trying to purchase $1,675 worth of merchandise . . . with a $1,000,000 bill (there is no such thing!). It was reported that she demanded change from her million dollars. The clerk notified security and the police arrived to arrest the angry woman, charging her with forgery. She was reported to also be very embarrassed. Go figure.

ARE WE FRAUDS?

Like this woman, men can be sensitive creatures. Respect matters a great deal to us. That is as it should be. But the trouble is that we can sometimes be hypersensitive to what we perceive to be affronts to our dignity. We walk around as if we're millionaires and grow irate when our play money isn't taken seriously. Sometimes it's people who fail to treat us as we expect; they wrong, mistreat, or insult us. Sometimes it's circumstances. Someone cuts us off in traffic, the dishwasher refuses to work, we bang our knee into an end table and we get ticked off and sulk or even rage.

Our outrage tends to flow out of an inflated and fraudulent sense of our own character and an unduly harsh assessment of the intentions of others.

Jesus told a parable to help correct our outbursts, our thoughtless responses when we're mistreated. The parable began with a question posed by the disciples: "Lord, how often will my brother sin against me, and I forgive him? As many as seven times?" (Matt. 18:21).

Jesus' answer was not at all what they expected: "I do not say to you seven times, but seventy-seven times" (18:22). He then told of a man who owed his master more money than he could ever possibly pay. The master mercifully forgave the debt. Then the forgiven servant turned around and roughly demanded payment from others who owed him mere pennies. When the master caught wind of this, he rescinded his forgiveness of the servant's massive debt, throwing him and his family into debtors' prison.

> When we grasp that we have been forgiven much, we should find it much easier to forgive others. Properly feeling the weight of our need for grace should enable us to show grace to others.

When we grasp that we have been forgiven much, we should find it much easier to forgive others. Properly feeling the weight of our need for grace should enable us to show grace to others.

But sometimes rather than aiming our anger at others, we direct it heavenward. We can become angry with the God of the universe. We act as though He is unwilling to accept our play money, that He somehow owes us change. Feeling a "right" to be angry about our circumstances actually amounts to feeling a "right" to be angry with God, since ultimately He is the one who ordains our circumstances.

So let me ask you this. Does God ever fail to give us what He owes us?

Yes, He does. Every time. Because we are sinners and deserve ultimate punishment. This mercy is good news.

And does He reward us with counterfeit currency? No. Never.

God has never done less for us than what we are owed, but His grace toward us, while we're on earth, is lavish. When we shake our fist at God and demand from Him that He give us justice, He may just do it, and we will be forever sorry. We may be cast into debtors' prison, for we owe Him much.

Our calling is to recognize that we live every day under His grace and then to give thanks because the glorious truth is that Jesus has paid our debt in full.

Okay, let's summarize the facts: we are sinners; God has every right to be angry at us; if you are a believer, God became angry at Jesus for you, a job that Jesus volunteered for. The truth is that we have no right to be angry with God.

You and I are dependent on the grace of God, which calls us in turn to be grateful, not angry, and to show grace toward others.

THE TRUTH	**We who have been forgiven much must forgive much. This truth must color the way we respond when we've been wronged.**

THINK ABOUT IT . . . *Forgiving others releases them from their obligation to you. It evens the score. Maybe even tilts the scale in their direction. Why is this a good idea in all your relationships?*

32 *"Pain and suffering are always bad."*

The other night I was in the kitchen, helping to clean up after dinner. Wiping the smooth glass top of our stove with a wet paper towel, I had no idea that the surface was still hot. I whooped and pulled my hand back in a hurry, extremely thankful for this thing we call pain. If it weren't for pain, I'd still be in the kitchen, my sizzling hand stuck to the cooktop.

And when it comes to our bodies and exercise, we get the old expression: no pain, no gain. Whether we are building muscles by lifting weights or turning down strawberry cheesecake twice in the same day, we know that it costs us to get into shape. It's painful. And good.

The same is true of our souls. Like flashing red lights on our dashboard, pain and suffering are often gauges that tell us something likely needs to be changed, adjusted, fixed.

> Count it all joy, my brothers, when you meet trials of various kinds, for you know that the testing of your faith produces steadfastness. And let steadfastness have its full effect, that you may be perfect and complete, lacking in nothing. (James 1:2–4)

> *You and I lack steadfastness. We are not perfect, complete. But we will be one day, and trials are the trails that lead us there.*

You and I lack steadfastness. We are not perfect, complete. But we will be one day, and trials are the trails that lead us there.

Sanctification is a thousand-dollar theological term describing the process by which we, who are redeemed by the blood of Jesus, grow in holiness. It's God's intent to use pain, suffering, and hardship in our lives for the same end, to purify and remake us into the image of His Son, a man well acquainted with sorrow.

When hard things come our way, we can be confident that God is at work in us and that we will come out on the other side better for it. God disciplines us, not because He is angry with us. No, He disciplines those He loves in order to teach us (Heb. 12:6). His painful discipline is a gift, proof that He is crazy about us and is at work in us.

THIS POISON IS HEALING YOU

When my brother-in-law, Mark DeMoss, was diagnosed with lymphoma in the winter of 2016, his doctor prescribed poison. That's right, the chemo solution that dripped into his bloodstream was poison, aimed at literally killing cells (cancer cells).

Men are fixers, solution seekers. So when we are hurting, we often want to find a painless solution that will extricate us from the problem. But God may send the poison of pain, suffering, and hardships to help us learn to trust Him, to learn patience. The apostle Paul prayed fervently that God would remove what he called his "thorn in the flesh" (KJV). We don't know exactly what the "thorn" was, but we do know God told Paul that He would not remove that hardship because it helped Paul to remember his complete dependence on God.

> **Men are fixers, solution seekers. So when we are hurting, we often want to find a painless solution that will extricate us from the problem.**

GOD KNOWS WHAT HE'S DOING WITH US

Pastor Mark Vroegop and his wife, Sarah, lost a little girl named Sylvia the day she was born. This painful loss drove Mark to the Scripture for perspective and hope. What he found was the value and necessity of *lament* as part of the Christian experience. He wrote:

> *As a follower of Jesus and in my role as a pastor, I discovered that lament gives a candid voice to the struggle of hardship, acknowledging the real and frightening emotions of pain while creating a path for God-centered worship. Trite answers and quick fixes are eclipsed by a message for hurting people:* hard is hard; hard is not bad.[3]

We cannot measure how far we have to go toward becoming like Christ by measuring how much suffering we are going through. We cannot conclude that those who seem to skate through life untouched by deep hardship are especially holy people who need no discipline. Neither should we conclude that those who suffer greatly must have more sin to be dealt with and therefore need tougher discipline from God.

That was the mistake that Job's friends made. Witnessing all he went through, they were certain that Job must have been harboring some great secret sin, that his piety was just a mask. But the book of Job begins with a description of Job as an upright man who shunned evil. He was not

> **We must not be overconfident in our ability to read God's providence. He knows exactly what He's doing with you and me.**

perfect, but he was a godly man. And, as it turns out, godlier than his friends who were so certain Job must have been a great sinner.

And we must not be overconfident in our ability to read God's providence. He knows exactly what He's doing with you and me. Pain or no pain, He owes us no explanations. Our task is to take a deep breath and rest in the great adventure of living by faith.

A DIAMOND OF SPARKLING BEAUTY

When I was a student at Taylor University, the men who played on the football team were, in my mind, almost godlike. First, of course, there was their physical skill. Their toughness. And then there was the mystery. Normal students like me hardly ever saw them. Most football players lived separately from the rest of the student body. Only a few of them lived in dorms; most lived off campus in "The Shacks." Literally, inexpensively constructed domains that housed four men each.[4]

One of the athletes I admired from distance was Michael Sonnenberg. The center on the football team, Michael was a year older than me but when he started dating one of my classmates, Janet Schneider, he began attending some of my class functions. I met Michael and discovered in him a gentle giant. A tender man who loved the Lord and was eager to serve Him.

In the summer of 1968, Michael and I—along with thirty-nine other Taylor men—rode bicycles from coast to coast. It was during this trip that I came to deeply appreciate the heart of this special man.

Mike and Janet were married soon after we graduated and I lost track of them . . . until I heard the news of a horrific, unthinkably tragic accident that nearly snuffed out the life of their twenty-two-month-old son, Joel.

It was September 1979, when an overloaded tractor trailer slammed into the family car at a New Hampshire toll booth. The carnage that ensued literally melted the plastic car seat around the body of little Joel where he was helplessly strapped. A stranger reached into the backseat and pulled the burned child from the flames.

In the years that followed, Michael and Janet gently shepherded their children, including their little boy, through more than forty surgeries.

The accident had burned over 85 percent of Joel's body, taking his ears, his left hand, the fingers on his right hand, and most of the tissue that covered his skull. And yet as Michael and Janet poured the love of Christ into their young, damaged son, along with countless prayers of Christians, he began to blossom. Joel grew up an articulate man of insatiable self-respect and character . . . now a pastor with a deep love for God.

Almost twenty years after the accident, in court Mike met the truck driver whose carelessness had crushed his son's body. In response to the judge's prompting, the man said a perfunctory "I'm sorry" to the Sonnenbergs.

"I came here to hear you say, 'I'm sorry.' When you ask for forgiveness, I will forgive, but I won't forget," Michael Sonnenberg said. "You took a vibrant, bouncing baby and gave me back a smoldering, screaming lump of coal."

"A lump of coal," he added, that turned into a "diamond of sparkling beauty."

Like Job, Michael had faced unspeakable loss, tragedy, and pain. But he was willing to forgive and lifted the scarred body of his son to the God who loved them both, seeing refracted beauty from the facets of his son's brokenness as only a man of God possibly could.

AN IMPORTANT PREPOSITION

I have stood beside my wife's grave, grieving as the earth slowly swallowed her casket. You have surely faced your own hard times. So how should we treat these awful things?

The apostle Paul gives us the answer, but please notice the preposition that opens his admonition:

In everything give thanks; for this is God's will for you in Christ Jesus.
(1 Thess. 5:18 NASB)

Notice that he did not tell us to give thanks "for" everything . . . rather, "in" everything. There's something important to the experience of pain and suffering in the larger context of God's will. I did not celebrate Bobbie's cancer diagnosis. We were not happy for the news. But we, along with our daughters, knew that God was wise and good and we trusted that He would bring good out of this human tragedy.

The journey we walked through as a family broke us, shaped us, and molded us more closely into His image. Many friends, medical professionals, and others we met along the way were brought face-to-face with the gospel. And so, in the midst of these painful circumstances, we bowed our hearts and offered up humble thanksgiving.

THE TRUTH	**Pain and suffering are tools in God's wise, loving hands, doing His good work, helping us become more like His Son. And for that we need to give thanks.**

THINK ABOUT IT . . . *How do you typically respond to life's inevitable problems and frustrations? How might you respond differently if you believed the truth about God's purposes for pain and suffering?*

 33 *"The world is rigged against me."*

As Greek mythology tells it, Sisyphus was the king of Ephyra. He was a proud man who raised the ire of the gods for his self-serving craftiness and deceitfulness. So, as the story goes, he was convicted of his misdeeds and handed a life sentence. But not to spend the remainder of his days working a chain gang or rotting in a prison cell. His punishment was simple. And horrible. He was forced to roll a great boulder up a hill. Once the boulder reached the top, he had to release it, allowing the stone to roll back down to the bottom. Then he had to follow the path of the bolder, retrieve it, push it back to the top of the hill, and again, let it roll down. Forever.

Can you imagine?

Sisyphus was not a good man, but still, given his life sentence, I sort of feel sorry for him. Of course, this is Greek mythology. There actually wasn't a guy named Sisyphus. Never mind.

But how often do you and I feel like this mythic man? Planning our work, working our plan, reaching our pinnacle, only to see the whole thing come rolling

> *Planning our work, working our plan, reaching our pinnacle, only to see the whole thing come rolling down.*

down. We put our shoulder to the plan and try again. It's frustrating. Maddening. Enough to tempt us into thinking the whole world has been rigged against us. We try. We push hard. But soon the problem reappears and we do it again. We can't win.

We stay up late, preparing for a presentation the following day. The next morning, we oversleep; in our hurry we cut ourselves shaving and hit our head on the shower door; the coffee pot decides that it made its last cup yesterday; and our car won't start. Now we're absolutely convinced that the world is tilted in the wrong direction. It's against us.

As with most lies, this one carries with it a kernel of truth. After Adam and Eve ate of the forbidden fruit, God confronted Adam with the life-long, laborious consequences of his choice:

> "Because you have listened to the voice of your wife and have eaten of the tree of which I commanded you, 'You shall not eat of it,' cursed is the ground because of you; in pain you shall eat of it all the days of your life; thorns and thistles it shall bring forth for you; and you shall eat the plants of the field. By the sweat of your face you

shall eat bread, till you return to the ground, for out of it you were taken; for you are dust, and to dust you shall return." (Gen. 3:17–19)

Sounds like our old buddy Sisyphus. If you've ever weeded your flowerbeds only to discover in a matter of days that those little suckers are back again, you get it. Greek mythology meets weeds.

It's true. The world is a battlefield, a place of war. Which reminds us who the world is actually rigged against. In truth, the world is in a desperate, relentless battle with . . . the Lord. The God of the universe.

A SURPRISE VISITOR

Just before Joshua fought the battle of Jericho, as he was walking near the city, he came across an imposing figure, a mighty man of war with his sword drawn. The trembling Joshua approached him and asked, "Are you for us, or for our adversaries?" (Josh. 5:13).

Joshua asked an either/or question. For or against? But the answer defied those boundaries. "No," the man answered, "But I am the commander of the army of the LORD. Now I have come" (5:14). Some theologians believe that the great warrior was a preincarnate appearance of God the Son. It's as if the warrior answered Joshua, "You're asking the wrong question, Joshua. It's not whether I'm on your side, but whether you're on mine."

As I often do with Bible stories, ever since I first read this story of Joshua and the angel, I've identified with Joshua . . . not because I'm any kind of a great military leader, but because I understand, from personal experience, some of the pressures of life.

And I feel sorry for Joshua, facing a massive assignment but wondering about his own capability, his readiness for the task.

The experience of dealing with discouragement reminds me of a situation I faced in business. I answered to the CEO, who had asked for a financial report. I gathered my team and prepared what I thought was an easily absorbed spreadsheet summary and carried it to my boss's office.

He glanced at the two-page spread. His brow furrowed. Not an unfamiliar sight. I braced myself.

"So where did these numbers come from?" he spit out. "I need more than this."

I dutifully trudged back to my office and reassembled my team with a new assignment. "We need more," I told them.

The next day, I returned to my boss's office, armed with plenty of backup information. Confidently standing in front of his desk, I carefully laid the heavy document down. With his thumb, he lifted the corner of the half-inch stack and spun through it.

> *Sin changed everything. The world is rigged against man and vice versa. And we're all rigged against God.*

The brow furrowed again. Oh, great. "You expect me to read all of this?" he snapped.

How well I remember shuffling back to my office, completely deflated and disheartened. I slumped into the chair behind my desk. What was I supposed to do?

If you're like me, there are times when you also find yourself deeply discouraged by circumstances beyond your control. From the daily onslaught of one depressing news report after another to personal health and circumstances we can't control, the knot in our stomachs is real.

The apostle Paul must have dealt with the debilitating emotion of discouragement, too. How's this for a list of things that could conspire to discourage us? Just listen to these words . . .

> For I am sure that neither death nor life, nor angels nor rulers, nor things present nor things to come, nor powers, nor height nor depth, nor anything else in all creation, will be able to separate us from the love of God in Christ Jesus our Lord. (Rom. 8:38–39)

Tucked in there is clearly a capricious boss and uncertain diagnosis from our doctor. And how's this for the perfect answer to all of it?

Ever since man's fall from grace in the garden of Eden, things have not been as they should be (Rom. 8:22). Sin changed everything. The world is rigged against man and vice versa. And we're all rigged against God. But in His amazing mercy, God rigged the world against His beloved Son so that we may find comfort . . . the peace in our hearts that surpasses understanding (see Phil. 4:7).

The story of our lives isn't a rock that rolls to the bottom, a rock that must be pushed back to the top again. Our lives rest on the Rock of our Salvation. This stone can never be moved. We need to lift up our heads. Our Lord knows what He is doing. All is well, and all will be well.

As the old-time hymn writer put it:

This is my Father's world.
Oh, let me ne'er forget
That though the wrong seems oft so strong,
God is the ruler yet.
This is my Father's world,
The battle is not done:
Jesus who died shall be satisfied,
And earth and Heav'n be one.[5]

For I know the plans I have for you, declares the LORD, plans for welfare and not for evil, to give you a future and a hope. (Jer. 29:11)

THE TRUTH | We live and serve in a world that is rigged against Jesus, and if we are with Him, it's rigged against us. But we have the confident hope that one day all that's wrong will be made right and that, in the meantime, He knows what He is doing and will sustain us in the battle.

THINK ABOUT IT . . . *What is your life's purpose?*
What gives your life meaning?

"I can't help how I react to certain people or circumstances."

I was completely out of control. So was Bobbie, my late wife.

We were standing in the kitchen, verbally fighting at the top of our lungs. Even as I write these words, I'm ashamed of how I was acting. Of course, I have no idea today what the argument was over, but with our raised voices, we were letting each other have it.

If you could see a video of this scene, you would say that I was completely out of control. So would I. My emotions had gotten the best of me. How utterly embarrassing it is to remember this hollering match.

And then, above the commotion, the phone rang. (This was back in the day when every home in America had a wall-mounted telephone in the kitchen with a long, coiled cord.) We let it ring a few times; then I walked over and picked it up.

"Hello," I said in a voice no more intense than as if I'd been asking the grocery stock boy where I could find the barbecue sauce.

The person on the other end of the phone was our youth minister. He was asking if I would be available to meet with him sometime over the next few days. We discussed our calendars, and I jotted down the time and place on a piece of paper on the kitchen counter.

"Thanks for calling, Mark," I said warmly, and hung up.

I looked at my wife in disbelief. She looked back at me with the same. What I had just done was such a dramatic change from the out-of-control behavior I had just been exhibiting, I still remember it many years later. Clearly, I *chose* when and with whom to have a hissy fit.

This lie about self-control is a big one.

Can you imagine how many men are sitting in prison because, in a moment of rage, they convinced themselves that they couldn't help what they were about to do? And because they didn't step back and think twice about it, they went ahead. Their emotions, their anger and resentment, won the day. And now they're stuck in a cell. Some for a few years. Others until they're room temperature and finally get to leave the prison inside a pine box. You and I may not end up behind bars for our outbursts, our out-of-control reactions. But for sure we end up putting ourselves and others in emotional and relational prisons of our own making.

> How often I have spoken unwise things "in the moment." Things I have later—sometimes just moments later—deeply regretted.

How often I have spoken unwise things "in the moment." Things I have later—sometimes just moments later—deeply regretted. And how often have I done something foolish that was spontaneous and uncalculated.

CONSIDERING JUDAS AND PETER

Jesus' twelve disciples were not recruited from Monster.com or LinkedIn. These were ordinary men without impressive resumes. In fact, except for what a few were doing to make a living when the Savior invited them to join His band, we know precious little about these men.

Judas Iscariot, the son of Simon Iscariot, was the only disciple not from Galilee. Kerioth, a city in the south of Judea, was his hometown.

> Judas was a man who did things, as my dad used to say, "without thinking."

In spite of being given the responsibility of managing the disciples' finances according to John's gospel, it's likely that Judas would have been treated by the Twelve as an outsider. Because Judas was from another town, he had been a stranger from the beginning.

Judas was a man who did things, as my dad used to say, "without thinking." He was given to boldly and rudely speaking his mind. In chapter 12, the disciple John tells of a dinner party that Judas interrupted as Mary lavishly dripped Jesus' feet with expensive ointment. "Why was this ointment not sold for three hundred denarii and given to the poor?" (John 12:5).

But God wasn't conned. The biblical record—"[Judas] said this, not because he cared about the poor, but because he was a thief" (12:6)—provides an unvarnished portrait of the man.

Judas' true bent was further revealed when he slipped away to make a deal with the high priest who promised him thirty pieces of silver for betraying his friend Jesus (Matt. 26:15). Knowing what Judas knew, this was when history records his life's most egregious, not-stopping-to-think moment.

In the end, as we so often do, Judas deeply regretted what he had done. In his case, taking his own life as his attempt at penance.

The apostle Peter had the same failure-to-think-in-the-moment disease. We read of his jumping from his fishing boat, once to mirror Jesus' ability to walk on the water's surface (Matt. 14:29), and again, to be the first to sit on the shore with the resurrected Savior (John 21:15–19).

We also see Peter swearing an oath that he didn't know Jesus in a coward's response to a young girl's query as Jesus was being tried by a kangaroo court (Matt. 26:69–75).

Both Judas and Peter believed this lie. They could not (did not) control themselves in the moment. Because of his deep regret, Judas *took* his own life. But because of his deep confession, Peter *gave* his life, eventually dying a martyr's crucifixion.

> *Because of his deep regret, Judas took his own life. But because of his deep confession, Peter gave his life, eventually dying a martyr's crucifixion.*

A SELF-CONTROL GAME

As a dad of young children, I knew that one of my most important tasks was to teach self-control. Maybe it was because I knew my own propensity to do or say thoughtless things in the moment, but I suspected that my kids would need to learn this skill . . . even at a young age.

I think this idea came from Bobbie, my late wife. She was so good at making learning fun. "Let's play a game," she announced over dinner one night. "Let's play the 'no' game."

This was a long time ago but I can still see the skeptical looks on my children's faces. On mine, too. *The no game? Oh, boy!* our countenances were saying. But, of course, we didn't say anything.

Pushing past the predictable skepticism, Bobbie went on to explain.

"Between now and dinner tomorrow night, let's all say 'no' to ourselves at least once. And make it stick. Then we'll give each other our reports."

We smiled and nodded at least a thin modicum of agreement to the idea.

> The challenges of self-control were—and are—relentless, not just for kids at dinner but for you and me. Every single day.

Over dinner the next evening we gave our reports. Missy told us that she had been on her phone, talking with a friend. "I have to stop talking in ten minutes so I can finish my homework," she announced.

"And when ten minutes arrived," Missy went on with a big smile, "I told my friend that I had to go and ended the call." She paused. "My friend begged me to stay on the line . . . but I said, 'no.'"

I can remember the celebration. Even as a young lady, Missy had proven to herself that she could be in control, and our whole family let her know that we thought this was terrific.

Each of us gave our reports, and the others in our troupe affirmed their encouragement.

But this was just the result of a one-day game. It was good, but it was only a day. The challenges of self-control were—and are—relentless, not just for kids at dinner but for you and me. Every single day.

Not surprisingly because, like me, he was a sinful man, the apostle Paul also dealt with the challenges of self-control.

> I have the desire to do what is right, but not the ability to carry it out. For I do not do the good I want, but the evil I do not want is what I keep on doing. (Rom 7:18–19)

Can you relate?

What is it that you desire to do but find yourself impotent to carry out? Consistent time in God's Word and prayer? Attentiveness and kindness to your wife and kids?

What is it that you don't want to do but find yourself impotent to resist? Angry outbursts with those you're supposed to love the most? Sneaking glances at pornography on your laptop? The temptation to be dishonest on your tax return?

Perhaps you would echo Paul's sentiments:

> I find it to be a law that when I want to do right, evil lies close at hand. For I delight in the law of God, in my inner being, but I see in my members another law waging war against the law of my mind and making me captive to the law of sin that dwells in my members. (7:21–23)

So what is the answer? Is there hope? Or are we just destined to keep flailing about, endlessly trying, failing, trying again, and . . .

The apostle understood this frustration: "Wretched man that I am!" he cried out. "Who will deliver me from this body of death?" (7:24)

In one sense, this lie about our inability to control ourselves is actually the truth.

And therein lies our only hope. Not a what, but a *Who:* *"Thanks be to God,"* says Paul with great relief, *"through Jesus Christ our Lord!"* (7:25). He continues in the next paragraph:

> For the law of the Spirit of life has set you free in Christ Jesus from the law of sin and death. For God has done what the law, weakened by the flesh, could not do. By sending his own Son in the likeness of sinful flesh and for sin, he condemned sin in the flesh, in order that the righteous requirement of the law might be fulfilled in us, who walk not according to the flesh but according to the Spirit. (8:2–4)

In one sense, this lie about our inability to control ourselves is actually the truth. We struggle to reign in our minds, our cravings and desires, our tongues, our impatient, angry responses, and our inappropriate or addictive behavior.

But as we confess our sin, acknowledge our need for the gospel, fix our eyes on Christ, renew our minds through His Word, and submit to the Spirit's moment-by-moment leadership, He does the controlling in us, for us, and through us.

THE TRUTH	When we hand over control to the indwelling Holy Spirit, He will produce in us the fruit of self-control.

THINK ABOUT IT . . . *Review the "fruit of the Spirit" listed in Galatians 5:22–23—love, joy, peace, patience, kindness, goodness, faithfulness, gentleness, self-control. Why do you think "self-control" is the last on the list? How does self-control impact all the others? How are you doing in this area?*

35   *"I can run away from God."*

My brother was three years old. Something had happened between him and his twin sister and, from his perspective, the only way to deal with it was to not deal with it.

Grace Wolgemuth was standing at the kitchen sink, looking out the window onto our backyard, not far from a very busy four-lane—Roosevelt Road.

Then she saw a slumped-shoulder little boy, slowly walking away from the house. She knew by his deliberate gait and his uncertain steps that something was seriously wrong. The boy's direction was unmistakable; he was leaving home.

Hurrying out the back door, my mother ran to meet the lad. Soon she reached her son and spoke his name.

Little Danny stopped walking. Grace knelt down so they would be face-to-face. This was something my siblings and I saw her do with us, with our children and grandchildren. Countless times.

"Where are you going?" she asked.

Except for a downcast countenance, there was no answer to her question.

"Where are you going?" mother repeated.

Again, no answer.

"Are you running away?"

The boy slowly nodded.

"Well, you haven't packed a suitcase," she gently said. "How can you run away if you haven't taken any of your things along?"

Still no response from her little boy. After a moment of quiet, she continued.

"I have an idea," she said. "Let's go back to the house and I'll help you pack."

Then she added, "And if you'd like me to go with you, I will."

But Danny wasn't the only man who ran away.

HITCHING A RIDE WITH A LARGE FISH

It's one of the most often read and repeated stories in the Old Testament. The one about a runaway man and the big, hungry fish.

The man could have suffered from depression. You and I probably would have if we'd been in his shoes. Jonah lived under a godless monarch who reigned for over four decades—not exactly an easy time to speak for God. His job was to walk around and warn people to repent of their evil ways, lest God judge them. "Here comes that flame-throwing extremist," people must have sneered. This was no fun at all.

I'm guessing the prophet had few (if any) friends and was rarely invited to parties. Who wants to hang out with a guy like this?

But at least his assignment was among his own people. Sinners, of course, but sinners who had a sense of their own history and the faithfulness of Yahweh.

Jonah's assignment, however, was about to change.

One day, he received a message that he hoped was just a bad dream. To his dismay, it wasn't.

> Now the word of the LORD came to Jonah the son of Amittai, saying, "Arise, go to Nineveh, that great city, and call out against it, for their evil has come up before me." (Jonah 1:1)

It's no surprise that Jonah's immediate response to God's directive was an unambiguous "No way!" Nineveh was a "great" city—great in size, great in influence, and great in evil. It was the capital of the arrogant, ruthless, idolatrous nation of Assyria. The Assyrians were bent on world domination and had long been fierce enemies of Israel.

Disobedience to God's Word has a way of draining your energy.

Now God was calling His prophet to go and preach to these dreaded, hated foes. We learn later that from the outset, Jonah, knowing God as He did, was afraid God would be merciful and compassionate to Nineveh (4:2). Jonah didn't want his enemies to repent and be spared. As far as he was concerned, they deserved God's judgment; he wanted them to die!

So, crazy as this sounds about a man who knew God and His ways well, Jonah ran away. Or tried to run away. You remember that, instead of traveling east a few hundred miles, he jumped onto a boat headed for Spain, a thousand miles to the west.

Jonah climbed on board, found his bunk on the lower deck, and collapsed from complete exhaustion. Sinfulness can have a way of draining your energy.

Jonah may have thought his escape had actually worked. His neighbors, his family—or anyone else who might eventually miss him—had no idea where Jonah had gone. He had downright disappeared.

Perhaps Jonah even thought he had been successful running away from himself. The ship, the sea, a new destination. And, if he was lucky, a new life, a new man.

But God.

THE DOG'S TEETH ON YOUR PANT LEG

A few thousand years after Jonah's vain attempt to run away from the Almighty, Francis Thompson penned the classic poem "The Hound of Heaven." Here are a few lines that, if he had read them, could have saved Jonah a harrowing experience at sea and a few nights of the blinding sting of a big fish's gastric juices.

> *I fled Him, down the nights and down the days;*
> *I fled Him, down the arches of the years;*
> *I fled Him, down the labyrinthine ways*
> > *Of my own mind; and in the mist of tears*
> . . . .
> > *Lo, all things fly thee, for thou fliest Me!*
> > *Strange, piteous, futile thing!*
> . . . .
> > *I am He Whom thou seekest!*[6]

To me, the most striking image of Jonah on the run isn't that he was outrunning or outsmarting God on a path of his own making. It's that God was relentlessly pursuing Jonah and, before it was over, the Lord won the race. The Hound of Heaven had His way.

For many years, "Aaron" ran from God. He refused to face the consequences of his actions, all the while serving in a ministry. I know this sounds unlikely . . . even outrageous . . . but it's true.

Living and working on the West Coast, Aaron had had sexual relations with an underage girl. For many years, the woman stayed silent but then went public, turning on her former youth leader.

> God was relentlessly
> pursuing Jonah and,
> before it was over,
> the Lord won the race.

Although Aaron denied the charge initially, he eventually buckled under pressure and confessed to the judge what he had done. The result was eight years in a federal prison in California.

During these years, Aaron and I often corresponded. I watched his heart soften. His anger and rebellion subsided. Eventually, he embraced his situation as a redemptive "belly of the fish." Many times Aaron told me how thankful he was for the Lord's presence with him in prison. Soon he actually found joy as he organized an inmate choir and led Bible studies with his companions. The "Hound" had won the race.

You and I may decide to take a detour on a path we know is pure folly. We can try to run from God. But our Father knows where we are, where we think we're going, and how to woo us home. One way or another.

"Be strong and courageous. Do not fear or be in dread of them, for it is the LORD your God who goes with you. He will not leave you or forsake you." (Deut. 31:6)

THE TRUTH

We cannot run from the presence of God. We may try, but we will not succeed. Our Father never loses sight of us. He will pursue us and woo us home.

THINK ABOUT IT . . . Describe a time when you tried to run from the presence or conviction of God in your life. What consequences did you experience? How did He pursue you? How did you respond?

CHAPTER NINE

LIES MEN BELIEVE ABOUT
THE WORLD

This may sound silly to you. The amusing daily habits from a sometimes-obsessive man. In fact, what I'm about to do could be considered a confession.

I'm a man who defaults to routines. For example, the sequence of my morning activities—rituals—is the same. Nearly every day.

It starts with quietly crawling out of bed at "dark o'thirty," before my wife does. (If she stirs or reaches out her hand to let me know that she's sort-of awake, I'll roll over and put my face next to hers and whisper a short "Good morning, Lord" prayer, kiss her, and tell her "I love you" before she goes back to sleep.)

Walking into the kitchen, I flip on the coffee, already locked and loaded, and then shuffle to my closet where I have laid out my early-morning "soft clothes." (I set these duds out the night before so I won't need to make a decision about what I'm going to wear first thing.)

Coffee is ready and poured, and I head to my study where my favorite recliner is waiting.

My glasses, my Bible, a pen, and an unwrapped protein bar rest on a table next to my chair. (The crinkling sound of undoing the wrapper that early is annoying to me.) I take the Bible and pen and pick up my reading where I left off the day before. Underlining as I read, I look for passages that hit home in a special way. Messages from my Father.

Next I pick up my smartphone.

"Aha," you might be saying. "I caught you checking your email or the news or the score of last night's late game."

Actually, no.

I use my phone to text Nancy the verses I've just underlined so when she wakes up, she finds the same inspiration I found from God's Word.

Then I slip to my knees and pray. I thank Him for His blessings. I bring my family to the throne of grace. I pray for the needs of my friends and ask for wisdom for the day ahead.

Since this is a confession, let me revisit what I just said about not checking email, the news, or scores on my phone.

> *At least for me, the world—and all that's going on in it—can be a huge distraction.*

I have learned that as soon as my brain gets engaged with what's happening in the world, I've virtually left the solitude of my quiet time with the Lord . . . never to return. A political junkie from the time I was a teenager, I know my brain will engage with the latest happenings in Washington, and my heart will have left the sweetness of this quiet conversation with the Lord.

At least for me, the world—and all that's going on in it—can be a huge distraction. I'm often tempted to pull up an app on my phone and quickly get caught up on the latest new highlight or score. But I don't.

So when I'm spending the dark morning hours in the quiet of God's presence, I avoid doing anything else that could elbow its way into my self-imposed quarantine.

But as soon as I have spent this time with the Lord, I dive in. Full on. My work, my news apps, my email correspondence, and proposals waiting for my review. I avoid these things until I'm ready.

Remember, this is a confession. It's neither a boast nor a directive. As

I said, you may think I'm crazy and not a little eccentric. Right on both counts, but I feel better now that it's off my chest. (Someday, you'll have to tell me about your routine.)

IN THE WORLD, NOT OF THE WORLD

One of my favorite passages in the Bible is found in what theologians call Jesus' High Priestly prayer. Here the Savior tells us that we cannot avoid living in the world, but we must not live just like the world. Sounds like my early morning smartphone battle.

> "I do not ask that you take them out of the world, but that you keep them from the evil one. They are not of the world, just as I am not of the world. Sanctify them in the truth; your word is truth. As you sent me into the world, so I have sent them into the world." (John 17:15–18)

The relationship you and I have with the world often feels complicated, doesn't it? Living in two spheres can be a relentless challenge. How do we blend Bible study and prayer with our career? How are we to live in the world but not of the world? What should we do and why should we do it?

Living in two spheres can be a relentless challenge.

PREPARATION FOR THE BATTLE

Bill Bates played for fifteen years with the Dallas Cowboys. He spent most of his career on special teams, an assignment often seen as second-class in the NFL. Not for Bill. His aggressiveness and courage on the field during a kick-off or a punt made him a fan favorite.

He was revered by many who loved the game.

Tom Landry stated, "If we had eleven players on the field who played as hard as Bill Bates does and did their homework like he does, we'd be almost impossible to beat. Bill Bates and Cliff Harris are the greatest hitters I ever saw." In addition, John Madden said, "Every game starts with a kick, but when Bates is on the field, every game begins with a Bang!"[1]

I had the privilege of knowing Bill Bates, helping him publish his book.[2] During the off-season in 1994, Bill took me on a private tour of the new Cowboys training facility in north Dallas. Walking through this amazing, state-of-the-art complex, I was completely taken with it all . . . like a kid in a candy store.

Remember, this was in the off-season, so I expected the place to be empty. It wasn't. Athletes were everywhere, lifting weights and working the cardio machines.

"How often are you here?" I asked Bill.

The Tennessee-born gentleman smiled what could have been a condescending smile. But it wasn't. He was not a proud man, just a focused man.

> "My opponents are in top condition. I have to be better than they are or I'll die."

"Except Sunday," he said, "every day. Sometimes most of the day."

As you would have been, I was stunned. "Every day?" I repeated. "Really? Why?" I naïvely added.

I'll never forget his answer. I expected Bill to tell me that he did this to stay in top condition so he could make another Pro Bowl. Or help the Cowboys win their division. Surely these were the reasons, but that's not what he said.

After a few moments, he answered my question. "Self-defense," Bill said. "If I'm not in great shape, I'll get killed out there." He wasn't finished. "My opponents are in top condition. I have to be better than they are or I'll die."

The ultimate purpose of Bill Bates' training or my quiet time with the Lord is to get ready for the battle. Time in the Word and prayer, or reps with weights and relentless cardio work, aren't ends in themselves. They're activities with a destination. Clicking on my favorite new app before my heart is ready would be like Bill stepping onto the gridiron before he's strong.

My goal is not a monastic life any more than Bill's goal was body-building. Jesus' prayer was a plea to His Father that you and I not cloister ourselves in an abbey on a hilltop or build our rippled bodies for magazine pictures.

These things are meant to make us ready, to "keep us from the evil one."

Jesus' prayer inspires men like you and me not to avoid the world but to be strong enough to live—even to flourish for God—while living in the world.

> *Jesus' prayer inspires men like you and me not to avoid the world but to be strong enough to live— even to flourish for God—while living in the world.*

The great athlete Eric Liddell embraced this idea and powerfully lived it out. Liddell is remembered most of all for his principled stand that led him to refuse to compete in the 1924 Paris Olympic Games on the Lord's Day. The film *Chariots of Fire* chronicled that moment, and in 1982 the film scored seven Oscars, including best picture.

After his competitive career came to a close, Liddell went on to serve for decades on the mission field in China. If ever there was a man who sought to honor God in both the secular and the sacred spheres, it was Eric Liddell, moving seamlessly from Olympic glory to humble mission service.

Liddell's physical training and success were not the point. Preparing himself—body, mind, and spirit—for God's call on his life was the ultimate reason for his rigorous training. In fact, both the preparation and the performance were absolutely essential. As believers in Jesus Christ, we could go so far as to say that both our quiet time and time in the gym are holy. Set apart. Acts of worship.

> *You and I do not need to build a wall between practice and performance. Preparation and real life.*

You and I do not need to build a wall between practice and performance. Preparation and real life. These are both necessary and important.

Don't you just love this? The wall that some would erect between getting ready and then actually doing "important things" is no longer separated. Rehearsals and battle are both sacred.

God placed Adam in the garden and gave him his job description—to tend and keep the garden (Gen. 2:15 NKJV). He was to glorify his Creator through worship and work. His preparation and his job assignment were both sacred.

A SACRED FIXER-UPPER

In the spring of 1999, my Julie picked out a man named Christopher Tassy to be her husband. Fortunately, about the same time, he picked her out, too. So, according to our original plan, Julie and I decided that this would be a good time to finish remodeling her house.

She had been living in the place that she and I had completely face-lifted a few years before, with the exception of one room we had left unfinished . . . just in case she fell in love with a guy who could finish the project with me. So she decided that since they were going to get married in a few months, this would be a good time to have Christopher help with this final remodeling work. This way, after their wedding in July, he'd not be moving into *her* house . . . rather he'd be moving into *their* house.

A college all-American and former professional athlete, "Tass" had spent most of his growing-up hours on the soccer field.

Home Depot? Not so much.

> We prayed that both the building of this room and eventually living in it would be a sacred adventure.

So for the month of June 1999, Tass and I did our thing. We took what originally had been an attached garage in the little ranch house, turning it into a lovely living area, a laundry room, a full bathroom—complete with black marble floors and a white pedestal sink and claw-foot cast-iron tub. We raised the ceiling and put in a skylight. The finished product was amazing.

Each morning for four weeks, before we fired up the power tools, we would kneel next to a sawhorse and pray. Of course, we prayed for safety from the treacherous teeth of the chop saw, but we also prayed that the Lord would bless our time together. We prayed that both the building of this room and eventually living in it would be a sacred adventure.

Looking back, I realize that Tass and I were integrating the "secular" —lumber, electrical wire, pipes, and bathroom fixtures—with the "sacred"— making our day an experience of male bonding, hard work, and worshiping the Lord together.

BUCKLE UP FOR BATTLE

Since Adam first fell, men have shown a propensity for drawing lines. Like Adam, who confidently one day had a heart-to-heart conversation with God and the next turned to a spineless featherweight with his wife, we draw a sharp line between the "religious" part of our lives and everything else. There are spiritual matters—prayer, Bible reading, church, discipleship, worship—and then, well, there's the rest of our lives—education, work, relationships, family, sex, money, hobbies, recreation, and more.

As citizens of two worlds, you and I must intentionally embrace the realities of a dangerous world—renegade power tools and the relentlessly magnetic power of Satan—and the redemptive truth of God's work and world. And we must intentionally embrace the power of God, the joy of living in the light of Christ.

There is no need to compartmentalize. We can fully engage the "preparation" and the "performance."

We honor Him when we take every thought—every activity, every assignment, every kind of getting ready and the work that follows—captive to the obedience of Christ (2 Cor. 10:5).

"*The world is too messed up to bring children into.*"

To be honest, when my late wife, Bobbie, and I got married in our early twenties, we hadn't given a lot of thought to God's perspective on childbearing. As well as I can remember, we decided to wait until a few years after we were married and had a chance to get settled.

BAM!

I fell into this fathering thing unexpectedly. I know how it happened; I just wasn't prepared.

It was February 1971, just eleven months after our wedding. Bobbie and I were driving to Minneapolis from our home in Chicago to attend a business convention.

I battled high winds and slippery highways. This was long before mandatory seatbelt laws, and Bobbie spent most of the trip stretched out on the backseat, only occasionally waking to make sure I was okay. I scanned the radio dial, unsuccessfully trying to find something more interesting than hog futures.

> We had been married for less than a year and were poor as church mice. What were we going to do?

I listened to Bobbie's irregular breathing. I could tell this was more than just being extra tired. My wife wasn't feeling well.

I sure hope it's not the flu, I worried.

The day after we arrived in the Twin Cities, still not feeling right, she whispered her own diagnosis to me. Too overwhelmed to say the words above a whisper, she said softly, "Robert, I think I'm pregnant."

The words took my breath away. I couldn't believe it.

"What are we going to do?" she asked repeatedly during the next few days. The swirling reality of this responsibility began to sink in.

We had been married for less than a year and were poor as church mice. What were we going to do?

After our return to Chicago, Bobbie made an appointment with her doctor. She wanted to be sure. I went along for support.

The only man sitting in the waiting room, I remember surveying the women seated in the chairs around the perimeter of the room. They were at varying stages of their pregnancies. Most were chatting openly with their neighbors about intimate and graphic details of physiological changes and surprises. I could feel the blood draining from my face. It was all I could do to hang on.

And then I saw her. My wife of less than one year walked from the hallway through the door and into the waiting room where I sat. Our eyes locked immediately. Hers welled up with tears. So did mine. She nodded ever so slightly. She reminded me of an angel.

PREGNANT ON PURPOSE

Most of our friends were married couples three or four years older than we were.

It seemed that they all had determined they were going to wait until they could "afford" children. And I guess that's where we were headed too.

We suspected that these friends, once they learned we were expecting a baby, would be shocked. "You're pregnant? What happened? Surely this must be a big surprise!"

So before any of those comments came our way, Bobbie and I sat down to talk it over.

"You know," I remember saying, "even though this really is a total shock, let's tell everyone this pregnancy was planned. We can't imagine how things are going to work out, but God has obviously blessed us with this baby, so between you and me, let's just rest in the fact that *it was God's plan*. It was exactly what we wanted."

Bobbie agreed. What else would we say about God's sovereign plan? So that's what we decided to do.

> *Even more surprising than the pregnancy itself was our confident response. I can still see them shaking their heads in disbelief.*

And sure enough, friends asked. Some were diplomatic. Subtle. "Hmmm, what an interesting time in your lives to start a family." Others were more direct: "You're what?"

Even more surprising than the pregnancy itself was our confident response. I can still see them shaking their heads in disbelief.[3]

A GOOD GIFT FROM GOD

From many quarters these days, we're being told that children are a burden, an inconvenience, a drain on our time, our bank account, our energy, and our freedom. But the Bible gives us an entirely different perspective:

Behold, children are a heritage from the LORD,
   the fruit of the womb a reward.
Like arrows in the hand of a warrior
   are the children of one's youth.
Blessed is the man
   who fills his quiver with them! (Ps. 127:3–5)

That's right. Not only are children *not* a burden, they are a *blessing*.

CHANGING THE WORLD, ONE CHILD AT A TIME

As with many other lies, there's a kernel of truth to this one. First, the world *is* messed up. Seriously messed up. The reason it's messed up is because it's filled with sinners. And we are not merely the victims of the sinners—we are the sinners. And so are our children. In fact, if we were truly concerned about how messed up the world is, we might be tempted not to have children at all, not because they'd be too good for the world, but because, as fellow sinners, they would be bad for it.

The world, like the believer, however, is not made to stay messed up. But by the power of the Holy Spirit, God is in the process of redeeming this world and making His people holy. We are moving from grace to grace, becoming more and more like the Son whose image we bear. And as we "bring [our children] up in the discipline and instruction of the Lord" (Eph. 6:4), we trust that the same will be true for them.

As sinful men, we are clearly part of the problem with the world. But, thanks to the power of the gospel, we and our children can also be a part of the solution. In the last book of the Old Testament, the prophet reveals God's plan to His people: "And what was the one God seeking? *Godly offspring*" (Mal. 2:15). God is still seeking godly offspring. He is still seeking to bless us with them and to use them to glorify Him in this messed-up world.

> *But by the power of the Holy Spirit, God is in the process of redeeming this world and making His people holy.*

Clearly, raising children is difficult work. They are a blessing, but a blessing that takes a lot out of us. No one who has ever been a parent would say that raising children is easy, free from dangers or pitfalls. Which is why we may be tempted to take a pass on this blessing—to tell the Lord, "No thanks," when it comes to the gift of kids.

There's a proverb that speaks to this temptation:

> Where there are no oxen, the manger is clean,
>> but abundant crops come by the strength of the ox. (Prov. 14:4)

We can be free of the unpleasant work of changing diapers, the expense of feeding and clothing children, and the emotional energy required to care for them, but we will also miss out on the blessings and increased fruitfulness they might have brought to us. And we will find ourselves going into battle with an empty quiver.

Caring for children is a burden that the body of Christ—including those who may not have children of their own—can carry together. Every night before we pillow our heads, my wife Nancy and I pray by name for our daughters and their children, as well as our siblings and their children. We also pray for more than a dozen young men we know or know of, who are at a critical juncture in their lives. We know they each need daily, tailor-made grace to walk with God in this broken world. And we believe He wants to use them to shine the light of Christ into the darkness.

So we are called to receive the children God entrusts to us and to those around us—to welcome them, give thanks for them, and love them. Because they are exactly what He says they are—a blessing.

> *When God wants to give you a gift, and you don't think you want it, think again.*

When God wants to give you a gift, and you don't think you want it, think again. All God's gifts are good, especially those that will last forever. He is always right. Don't let fear keep you from the battle, but trust in our Commander. Don't settle for a clean stable and an unfurrowed field if He wants to give you an abundant harvest. Remember that, because of our children, we are changing the world, one child—one diaper—at a time.

THE TRUTH

Children are a gift from the Lord; He wants to use them to spread the gospel in our messed-up world. When we embrace children as a gift, we partner with God in changing that world.

THINK ABOUT IT . . . *Jesus loved children.*
He welcomed them (Matt. 19:13–15; Mark 10:13–16).
How do you treat children—whether your own or others'?
This can be a window into your soul.

37   *"I'm measured by how I compare with other men."*

"Men compare and compete."

I spoke these words to Nancy when she and I were first married. As the brand-new husband of this fifty-seven-year-old woman who had never been married, I was doing my best to help her understand how men think and act . . . at least from my perspective as a sixty-seven-year-old man.

PERFORMANCE-ENHANCED SIBLING RIVALRY

The conversation with Nancy about men comparing and competing reminds me of the twelve sons of Jacob described in the Old Testament book of Genesis. To say that this family was dysfunctional doesn't come close.

Because the practice of polygamy was common, the twelve brothers all shared the same father, but there were four different mothers involved. Take a moment and let that sink in.

Very little is written about this family until son number eleven comes along. His name is Joseph, and he's the first son of Jacob's favorite wife, Rachel. Did I say "favorite wife"? Yes. Again, let that sink in.

> *A serious conspiracy was born to get rid of the kid.*

And Jacob makes no apology about displaying raw favoritism to the boy. Compare. Compete. Hate. A serious conspiracy was born to get rid of the kid.

So let's look at the unfolding drama from Joseph's perspective. After all, he was the focus of this turmoil. And much of the problem belonged to him. He was also comparing and competing.

GRADUATE WORK IN THE SCHOOL OF HUMILITY

In the Broadway musical *Annie Get Your Gun*, the proud and somewhat defiant Annie Oakley made sure that everyone knew that anything anyone else could do, she could do better. She could outsmart, out ride, out shoot . . . out everything . . . anyone.

Although that show was not performed until more than three thousand years after the seventeen-year-old Joseph made his preposterous claims to his brothers, it's an idea about which he could have written.

It started with his father, Jacob, singling him out. Loving him more than his brothers and proving it by giving him a loud, colorful robe, a graphic symbol of the brothers' reason to hate Joseph. Buoyed by this special recognition, Joseph had visions of personal greatness and reported these dreams to his family.

> *To remind him that this isn't about him and that everything he is and everything he has, is a gift from his heavenly Father's hand.*

Some of Joseph's panache can be chalked off to naïveté. But not all of it can be rightly excused.

So, if you were God and you had a grand plan for this boy, what would be the first thing on your agenda? That's right, you'd need to find a way to teach him humility. Knock him down a few pegs. To remind him that this isn't about him and that everything he is and everything he has is a gift from his heavenly Father's hand.

So for the next thirteen years, without actually knowing it, Joseph enrolled in graduate school, working toward his advanced degree in renouncing his bent to compare and compete. His master's degree in humility. His coursework included: being hated by his brothers, thrown into a pit to die, sold to strangers as a common slave, lied about by his boss's wife who tried to seduce him, thrown in prison on a false charge, and promised by a paroled prisoner that he would be remembered (but wasn't).

The twists and turns of these years for Joseph are the stuff of legend. But it also has a message for us as men, who are tempted to compare and compete. Here it is:

There's no competition for your place in the will of God.

This principle is affirmed in the New Testament:

We do not dare to classify or compare ourselves with some who commend themselves. When they measure themselves by themselves and compare themselves with themselves, they are not wise. (2 Cor. 10:12 NIV)

God's love and leadership in your life has your name on it. He does not compare you to anyone else. His affection for you is singular.

Once we embrace this truth, our tendency to measure our lives by the false standard of the successes of others mercifully subsides. Our hearts are filled with gratitude for who we are before our Good Shepherd and what we have been given by His gracious hand.

Jesus' disciples also had to learn this Joseph-inspired lesson. Traveling with the Messiah must have been quite the heady experience. And it seems they found themselves comparing and competing with each other for status and acclaim. One day, like boys playing sandlot baseball, they boldly asked Jesus to pick them first. This question exposed their hearts, didn't it?

> *Once we embrace this truth, our tendency to measure our lives by the false standard of the successes of others mercifully subsides. Our hearts are filled with gratitude for who we are before our Good Shepherd and what we have been given by His gracious hand.*

"Who is the greatest in the kingdom of heaven?" (Matt. 18:1)

As He did so often, Jesus responded not just by *telling* them the truth (this time, about the danger of comparing and competing); He *showed* them the truth as well. This answer was something they could see.

Then Jesus called a little child to Him, set him in the midst of them, and said,

"Assuredly, I say to you, unless you are converted and become as little children, you will by no means enter the kingdom of heaven. Therefore whoever humbles himself as this little child is the greatest in the kingdom of heaven." (Matt 18:2-4 NKJV)

> *Even though Joseph had to endure trials and hardship brought on by his jealous brothers, he eventually learned the fine art of childlike humility.*

Even though Joseph had to endure trials and hardship brought on by his jealous brothers, he eventually learned the fine art of childlike humility. His brothers learned the same. As did Jesus' disciples.

And this is a lesson you and I need to learn.

Here's a silly example, but I think it works.

NICE RIDE!

The fact that I've been a "car guy" since I was a little boy isn't something I'm ashamed of nor do I try to hide it. With my father before me (who owned four NAPA stores) and his father before him, whose black Chevy was never (I mean *never*) dirty, I came by this thing honestly.

When I'm on the road, it's impossible to not see other cars out there. And sometimes I compare my car to those cars. And in a glance, I see who wins, based on the quality—or coolness—of the vehicles.[4] This is especially true in Southern California when the scale usually tilts away from whatever rental car I'm driving. If you've driven on one of those freeways (or if you live there) you know what I mean . . . lots of expensive foreign imports, and always spotless.

Sometimes the guy driving the car I'm checking out—especially when I'm ogling over a really great car—catches my eye. And if we're next to each other at a stoplight (or in a stop-and-go on one of the aforementioned freeways) and have a few seconds, here's what I try to do every time.

I roll my window down and shout, "Nice ride!" Or "What a beautiful car!" Or "Man, I like your car!"

The guy—who may be a compare and compete guy himself—is almost always surprised and his response is usually a nod, a big smile, or a thumbs up.

So what does this do for my tendency to compare and compete? Simple. Suddenly it becomes a celebration of his stuff rather than an opportunity to strut mine. And if you're not particularly a car guy, this mindset in lots of situations is a powerful antidote to comparing and competing.

> *Suddenly it becomes a celebration of his stuff rather than an opportunity to strut mine.*

Be generous with your kindness and affirmation of people in your life. Your pastor after a sermon, the clerk at the grocery store who zips through your stuff with deftness and skill, the serviceman who works on your furnace and cleans up after himself, your coworkers who are faithful at what they do with a good attitude. When you start looking for chances to do this, you'll discover there are plenty of them.

And your words are not empty flattery. Not, "You're the best plumber in the universe." Rather, "Thank you for your good work. I so appreciate how quickly you came to the house and appreciate your willingness to help."

Or, "Thank you for your faithfulness here at the office. Day after day you do your work well and with a terrific attitude."

This is a habit you and I can pick up. It's simple. And true. It will curb our temptation to compare and compete. Celebrating others rather than dwelling on ourselves.

If we live by the Spirit, let us also keep in step with the Spirit. Let us not become conceited, provoking one another, envying one another. (Gal. 5:25–26)

THE TRUTH | When we receive God's gifts to us with sincere wonder, gratitude, and humility, we are freed from the need to compare and compete.

THINK ABOUT IT . . . *Does your need to win ever get out of hand?*
God loves you and calls you to love your enemies . . .
and the visiting team on the field. How good are you at this?
In what areas could you turn some of your competitive
attitude over to the Lord?

 ## "With everything going on in my life, it's really not possible to live with integrity."

Except for cleaning up after a meal—and I'm very good at that—I'm not worth much in the kitchen.

Actually, I do a passable job as a *sous chef.* Chopping veggies, washing and peeling fruit, or stirring a pot on the stove are within my skill-set reach.

My daughters, on the other hand, are wizards in the kitchen. Hosting an army of guests or baking tens of dozens of cookies is routine for them both. They take it all in stride.

So back to that *sous chef* thing . . . and let's talk about cookies again. Yes, let's. When asked by a legitimate baker like one of the above women, I can man up to a large mixing bowl of disparate ingredients and, with the help of a large wooden spoon, turn eggs, milk, oats, flour, butter, raisins, baking soda, and sugar—white and brown—into a seamless mix of dough, ready for the cookie sheet . . . and the oven.

Take a moment and consider that mixing bowl and the things we've put into it. Some of this and some of that. The things the recipe calls for. This is a metaphor of our lives. The ingredients are as varied as the stuff we put in to make oatmeal raisin cookies. And the way we can tell if we've done a good job at mixing—and we ought to be very good—is that every single spoonful of the mixture will look exactly like every other spoonful of the mixture. They will all look—and be—the same. Perfect consistency.

Here's what I mean. The things you and I are expected to do and be can be as unlike eggs and butter, milk and oats. As different as raisins and baking soda. It's what you and I are called to be—the makings of our daily routines:

Man, husband (if you're married), conversationalist, provider, lover, daddy (if you have kids), negotiator (if you have more than one), counselor, employee (or employer), colleague, friend, mentor, lawn boy, mechanic, churchman, neighbor, sportsman, reader, partier, fixer of broken things . . .

And our most important assignment is that in each of these roles, we live with per-

> *Our most important assignment is that in each of these roles, we live with perfect symmetry. We are the same man in every situation.*

fect symmetry. We are the same man in every situation. Our colleagues don't see a different man at the office or the shop than our fellow deacons see at church. Our children aren't asked to deal with a man who is gentle and tender with his dog and an overly sensitive and impatient boor with them. Our wives aren't asked to reconcile Giovanni Casanova in the bedroom with the Gladiator when he's under pressure.

What I've just described is a man who lives with integrity. It's hard work, but it is possible. It's a man who refuses to draw lines distinguishing the man he is over here from the guy he is over there.

THE LAND BETWEEN

The Korean War began on June 25, 1950. When did it end? The truth is, as of this writing all these years later, it technically still hasn't ended. A ceasefire was agreed to in July 1953, but there was no peace treaty. The negotiations over the ceasefire created a "demilitarized zone," or DMZ. This strip of land runs 160 miles across the Korean peninsula and is roughly 2.5 miles wide. The irony is that there's nothing "demilitarized" about the DMZ. It's one of the most heavily armed places on the planet. Both North and South Korea have troops massed on their own sides of the DMZ, fully equipped for war.

We act as though there's a neutral zone between the kingdom of God and the kingdom of man, where both sides can live in safety, with and from each other. As with the DMZ, however, there is always a fight brewing, either visibly or under the surface. And more often than we would like, war breaks out.

The Bible calls this the battle between our flesh and the Spirit (Gal. 5:17). One side of the DMZ calls for us to live for our selfish passions, the other side to do what pleases and honors Christ.

> **The Bible calls this the battle between our flesh and the Spirit.**

Abraham Kuyper saw through this lie of "successfully" living with duplicity. One guy one place, another guy elsewhere.

Kuyper was an extraordinary man. In his native Netherlands, he created and published two newspapers. He founded the Free University of Amsterdam. He also managed to find time to serve as his country's prime minister. He was a true Renaissance man, equipped with a wide variety of talents. And he traveled the world teaching others about Jesus. What he may be most remembered for is a short aphorism, spoken at the founding of the Free University:

> *There is not a square inch in the whole domain of our human existence over which Christ, who is Sovereign over all, does not cry, Mine!*[5]

YOURS? MINE? HIS. INTEGRATING THE WHOLE.

We have already considered the truth that our work is part of God's first command to man, that we were to exercise dominion over the creation. But there's more to it than that.

We are called to exercise dominion not for our own glory, but for His. This applies to our work, our play, our families, our rest, and anything and everything we put our hand to. We were made to reflect His glory, not to produce our own. When we seek our own apart from God, we find only shame.

There is no "safe" territory between pleasing God and living for ourselves. There is no place for self-justifying complacence amid sinful activities and attitudes. Our Father wants to take all sides of life—every ingredient, activity, and assignment—and eliminate the "safety" of the DMZ.

Put that in your bowl, grab the wooden spoon, and "mix thoroughly until fully blended." With God's help, you and I really can live with integrity.

When Joseph was sold like a piece of something on Craigslist by his jealous brothers and soon found himself in a faraway land where no one knew him—or his family's good name—he had a chance to walk away from the man of character he had been. After all, his former life of obedience to Yahweh God might not fit well in this new Egyptian culture.

But when his boss's wife tried to seduce him, "he refused" (Gen. 39:8). And when she persisted, propositioning him again and again, day after day, "he would not listen to her" (v. 10). And one day when she found herself alone with him in the house and grabbed at his clothes and insisted he make love to her, "he left his garment in her hand and fled and got out of the house" (v. 12).

How did he do it? Joseph had passions, just as you and I do. He was not immune to the offer of an illicit thrill. But there was something that mattered more to him than any short-lived ecstasy.

"How then can I do this great wickedness and sin against God?" (v. 9), Joseph said to his seducer.

The fear of the Lord enabled him to refuse to surrender his foundational core for the sake of immediate pleasure. Again and again.

This is integrity.

THE TRUTH	God sees every piece and part and ingredient of our lives and declares, "Mine!" Our wholehearted, joyful response should be, "I'm Yours!"

THINK ABOUT IT . . . *Would your closest friends say that you're a man of integrity? Take an informal poll and find out what they think. Are you willing to identify and address any areas where you lack integrity?*

39 *"Being a Christian is supposed to be cool."*

As an Amazon Prime member, I regularly receive "opportunities" to purchase things I don't have and, in most cases, don't need. Or want. Like today.

This morning I was alerted to a special price on "Chocolate Covered Insects." I'm not kidding. And, I'm also not interested. Chocolate coating or not, eating a bug would be, well, eating a bug. No thanks.

If you'll forgive me for using this as a metaphor, no matter how some may candy-coat the gospel, it will never be palatable to those who don't have an appetite for it.

> For the word of the cross is *folly* to those who are perishing, but to us who are being saved it is the power of God. (1 Cor. 1:18)

Other Bible translations use the word "foolishness" instead of "folly." What you and I believe about God, the Bible, the cross of Jesus Christ, and salvation is utterly ridiculous, silly, even disgusting to many. To most.

Some try to entice nonbelievers to embrace the gospel by sugarcoating the truth and tickling people's ears with a diluted message that is not the gospel at all. But the heart of the Christian gospel is offensive to those whose eyes have never been opened by the Spirit to see their own sinfulness, the beauty of Christ, and their great need for a Savior.

THE THIRD BOOK IN MY BOYHOOD HOME

So imagine a television quiz show. The category is "Family Norms" and the question is, what three books were absolutely essential in the Wolgemuth home when Robert was a kid?

Can you guess?

Of course there was a Bible. More than one. You got that right, didn't you?

Second, there was a hymnal. My parents would have agreed with Martin Luther, who said, "Next to the Word of God, the noble art of music is the greatest treasure in the world. It controls our thoughts, minds, hearts, and spirits."[6] Maybe you guessed that one, too.

But how about the third one. Give up? This essential book in my boyhood home was . . . *Foxe's Book of Martyrs*.

Actually, it wasn't until just a few years ago that I discovered that the presence of this third book in our home was owing to my parents' Lancaster County, Pennsylvania, roots. I was reading a book about Amish families, many of whom also live in that part of the country, and learned that these three books are standard fare in every home. *Foxe's* was a large, hardback volume filled with stories and illustrations of men and women who had, centuries earlier, sacrificed their lives for the sake of their Christian faith. Some were tortured, hanged, some burned at the stake, some thrown to lions and torn to pieces, simply because they refused to recant their love and devotion to Jesus.

> *Some were tortured, hanged, some burned at the stake, some thrown to lions and torn to pieces, simply because they refused to recant their love and devotion to Jesus.*

How well I remember as a young boy sitting on the living room floor, tucked behind a large, plaid overstuffed chair, carefully thumbing through the pages of this book. My heart raced with thoughts of what this must have been like for those people.

So why would my mother and dad choose to have a book like this in our home? A book that included graphic descriptions and line drawings of Christians being persecuted or executed for their faith.

Although I never had a chance to ask my parents about this, I suspect that they kept this book in our home so their children would never be tempted to believe that following Christ was a popular thing to do. Surrounded by a secular culture that seemed to subtly—or openly—mock men and women who were devoted to Jesus, they wanted their children to be ready for the same.

> My mom and dad knew that a devout commitment to Jesus would never be the path of least resistance.

In other words, my mom and dad knew that a devout commitment to Jesus would never be the path of least resistance. It would never be celebrated by the world. It had no chance to be considered "cool." They were eager that their children would be ready. For anything.

As you know, even Jesus Christ Himself faced this kind of opposition.

TWO KINGDOMS

From all appearances, it was a private conversation two thousand years ago, but its implications are still being felt today.

The morning after Jesus' mock trial that had lasted all night, the Son of God, fully exhausted from the ordeal, was brought to the personal quarters of Pilate, the governor of the region. The occupying Romans had given Pilate jurisdiction over Judea. Given the uneasy relationship between Rome and Judea, and his fear of losing his position, Pilate would not have been thrilled to hear that some rabble-rouser was claiming a right to rule over the Jews.

Pilate didn't beat around the bush with the prisoner: "Are you the king of the Jews?"

"My kingdom is not an earthly kingdom," Jesus replied evenly. "If it were, my followers would fight to keep me from being handed over to the Jewish leaders. But my kingdom is not of this world" (John 18:36 NLT).

Can you imagine how Pilate's head must have been in a whirl? *Your kingdom? You're nothing but a lowly prophet. And a failed one at that. What are you talking about?*

> **Can you imagine how Pilate's head must have been in a whirl? Your kingdom? You're nothing but a lowly prophet.**

NOT COOL AT ALL

This lie is about the challenge of loving God and others well while living on planet Earth with its prevailing anti-God worldview.

It's safe to say that our unbelieving friends and neighbors understand and, for the most part, respect civil authority over them (the earthly kingdom). But when it comes to understanding God's kingdom, the kingdom to which we pledge our highest allegiance, well, not so much. In fact, they may have strong opinions about the claims of Christ and the demands of following Him: "Believe that the Bible is the inspired, inerrant Word of God and that Jesus is the only way to God? Repent of my sin, give up my right to run my own life, and join a church? I don't think so."

And so the message is foolishness—a repulsive insect. However, even if our message may be hard to swallow, our lives—the packaging for the message—must be winsome rather than offensive. We may never face the kind of opposition that those heroes I read about in *Foxe's* endured, but loving lost people well means that we must be willing to be hated by them in spite of how they see (or treat) us.

THIS IS LOVE

Jesus, who is God and pure love, became a man; He came to this broken world to die for sinners and save them from the wrath of God. That's you. That's me. That could be the guy down the street. That's the UPS guy and the lady at the DMV.

The gospel may be repulsive, offensive—insects shrouded in chocolate—to those who do not know God. They may hate us for what we believe, but our assignment is to live as those who belong to God—as undeserving, grateful recipients of His grace—and to lovingly point sinners to the Savior who loves them, praying that their hearts will be drawn to Him.

THE TRUTH	Following Jesus will never be easy or popular. Our greatest goal is not to be cool or relevant, but to be loyal followers of Christ, faithful subjects of His kingdom, regardless of the cost.

THINK ABOUT IT . . . *Are you aware that you may be the only "Jesus" folks may ever meet? The "Bible" that lost people will read? This is not an obligation; it's a privilege.*

 ## "*My death will be the end of my story.*"

One day you and I are going to die. Our demise may come at the close of a protracted illness or it may come suddenly. A struggle with cancer or a fatal car accident. A slow and awful experience with Alzheimer's or a sudden heart attack. Regardless of the journey, the destination will always be death.

So when this happens to you and me, what will it be like? Have you wondered about this?

I have.

And what will you say moments before you breathe your last? Will it be as Sir Winston Churchill said, "I'm bored with it all"? Or perhaps like John Wayne, whose daughter asked him moments before he breathed his last whether he knew who she was, to which he responded, "Of course, I know who you are. You're my girl. I love you."[7] Or maybe like Leonardo da Vinci who sighed, "I have offended God and mankind because my work did not reach the quality it should have."

In 2014, I heard the final words of my wife of almost forty-five years. Lying on her hospital bed in the middle of our family room, she took me by my shirt, pulled my face close to hers and said in a voice clear and strong, "I love you so much." Then she closed her eyes and died. You may not have seen death this close.

I have.

We are not alone in our wondering about death. Throughout history, people have gone to amazing lengths to prepare for their own death. Egypt's pyramids were built by the pharaohs as the final resting place for their bodies and a safe place from which to ascend to the afterlife. Some even ordered the execution of their slaves at their own passing, so they could be as lavishly served in death as they were in life. (Note: Always read the fine print in your employment contract.)

Over the years, men and women have had "near-death experiences." They've expired but been resuscitated. The reports they give are varied— long tunnels, twinkling lights, strange musical instruments, images of glowing beings. But every one of these people who has had a trial run at death will . . . die. No coming back. This time for real. For sure.

It would come as no surprise to you that the Bible has much to say about death.

AND AFTER THAT . . .

In fact, God's Word says two inarguable things. First, it's going to happen. You will die. I will die.

But the second thing is even more important than the first. This is encapsulated in these three words: "and after that."

> And just as it is appointed for man to die once, *and after that* comes judgment." (Heb. 9:27)

After our eyelids close for the last time, family members and friends will say their "goodbyes." Folks will weep. People will recount for each other memories of the friendship they shared with us. Some may describe their experience standing next to our gray, cooling body and what it was like at our end.

But, for us, this will not be the end. Like the infomercials on late-night television or on our computers, "That's not all. There's more."

The writer of the Bible book of Hebrews inserts those three words . . . "and after that."

So what, exactly is, "and after that"? What will happen to us?

In a word, judgment.

CAN I PLEASE SEE YOUR LICENSE AND REGISTRATION?

Not long ago, Nancy and I were driving through a residential area in Atlanta. We were happily chatting about the meeting where we were headed. I was not paying any attention to my speed. Unfortunately for me, someone else was.

Suddenly, a policeman stepped on to the road ahead of me. Literally, on the street right in front of me. He did not look happy. Even though he was wearing dark sunglasses, I knew he was looking directly at me. His finger pointing in my direction further punctuated his displeasure. My heart sank. You've been here, haven't you?

Our "and after that" will be far more sobering than my experience that day in Atlanta. You and I will not be in the presence of a mortal policeman. We will be standing before the God of the universe. His "radar gun" will actually be a record book of everything we have done.

> And I saw the dead, great and small, standing before the throne, and books were opened. Then another book was opened, which is the book of life. And the dead were judged by what was written in the books, according to what they had done. (Rev. 20:12)

Our hearing before this Judge might go something like this: His righteous finger will scan the list until he finds your name. If you have confessed your sin, if Jesus is your Lord and Savior, He will find an asterisk. A footnote. The reference has next to it a familiar symbol. A cross. Because you have received the forgiveness Jesus provided through His death and resurrection, your "and after that" will be access into heaven.

If you have confessed your sin, if Jesus is your Lord and Savior, He will find an asterisk. A footnote.

Here's what He promised about our "and after that."

> "Let not your hearts be troubled. Believe in God; believe also in me. In my Father's house are many rooms. If it were not so, would I have told you that I go to prepare a place for you?" (John 14:1–2)

So, yes . . . you and I will die. This is a certainty. But this will not be the end of your story or mine. And because we know Jesus, the next story will be a good one. He has promised that.

THE TRUTH

Through His death and resurrection, Jesus conquered sin and the grave. Your "end" and mine will not be *the* end. And it will be wonderful.

THINK ABOUT IT . . . *What will happen to you when you die? Where will your spirit go? What have you done in this life to get ready for this? What do you need to do?*

WALKING IN TRUTH

CHAPTER TEN

COUNTERING THE LIES WITH

THE TRUTH

See if you can picture this. It's 1952; I'm the youngest of Sam and Grace Wolgemuth's (then) four children.[1] My dad is the pastor of the Fairview Avenue Brethren in Christ Church in Waynesboro, Pennsylvania, a denominational recovery project that turned a small, dwindling congregation into a vibrant one, still serving its community today.

Our mother, Grace, was a woman of tenderness, elegance, and . . . grace.

Our home—it wasn't a manse, as there was neither a house nor a salary associated with this ministerial assignment—was at the top of Frick Avenue, a gradually sloping three-block street that teed at the bottom of the hill into Main Street, just a mile northwest of downtown.

In my memory, bedtime at our home rarely included our dad. I think he must have been reading or preparing sermons. But it always featured our mother, Grace. We'd gather, post-nighttime baths, wearing our flannel footie pajamas

> *That was a lot of years ago, but in my memory, there's only one book, in addition to the Bible, that I can recall Grace reading to us.*

with drop seats, on one of the upstairs beds and listen to our mother read. "Chippie," our sable-colored Pomeranian, was there, too.

So Ruth, Sam, Ken, and Robert cuddled together as our mother read to us. That was a lot of years ago, but in my memory, there's only one book, in addition to the Bible, that I can recall Grace reading to us.

MAKING PROGRESS

In the summer of 2017, during the months of hunkering down to draft the manuscript for this book, a dear friend sent Nancy and me a beautiful gift collection of eight classic books—fine leather covers, printed end sheets, gilded pages, and ribbon markers. The shipment also included a lovely wooden stand.

That evening, Nancy brought one of the books to the dinner table and suggested that we read it together after we'd finished our meal. I told her that I thought this was a lovely idea.

The book she had selected was the very volume my mother had read out loud to my PJ-clad siblings and me more than sixty-five years before. I hadn't read it since.

Dinner was finished, a beautiful Michigan evening having afforded us the chance to enjoy our meal on the deck. With songbirds providing musical reverie, Nancy opened the book and began to read.

> *As I walked through the wilderness of this world, I came to a certain place where there was a den, and I laid down to sleep there. As I slept, I dreamed a dream. I dreamed, and saw a man clothed in rags, standing there, faced away from his own house, a Book in his hand, and a great burden upon his back. I looked, and saw him open the Book, and read. And as he read, he wept and trembled. Not being able longer to contain, he broke out with a lamentable cry, saying, "What shall I do?"[2]*

This scene had captured our young wondering hearts as my mother read, as the often-archaic words of the text transported us to another land. Another time. Shivers made their way across my small body.

These rich words had the same rapturing effect on me so many years later as I sat with my wife on the deck behind our home.

The book was, of course, John Bunyan's *Pilgrim's Progress*. It's the story of a man named Christian who takes a journey from his home toward the Celestial City, looking for a way to be freed from the heavy burden of sin he was carrying.

As a four-year-old, I cannot imagine what my picture of this burden must have been. A little boy with an acute conscience, I'm sure I envisioned something. Perhaps an unconfessed cross word spoken to my brother or a piece of candy purloined from a box the family had received from a friend at Christmas.

Regardless, as our mother read, I can recall the image of this poor man lugging this burden on his journey and my hope of his finding a way to unload it. I'm sure I wanted the same for mine.

Many decades have passed. As a grown man, I now have a deeper understanding of the meaning of this allegory and the contents of the burden on the man's back. In over seventy years, I've acquired a few things to put in there, in addition to those angry words directed toward a sibling and stolen chocolates.

When my mother reached the end of the story, the reality, the sheer power, of the gospel seared into my soul a wonder, a longing to experience the joy of living burden free. It was around this time that our family went to see a faith-based movie that was being shown in a downtown auditorium.

> *When my mother reached the end of the story, the reality, the sheer power, of the gospel seared into my soul a wonder, a longing to experience the joy of living burden-free.*

We sat toward the back, and as we watched *Mr. Texas*, the life story and testimony of country singer/songwriter Redd Harper, I began to cry. Even at such an early age—with the account of the burden-toting Christian reaching the Celestial City—the Spirit of God was moving in my heart.

Seeing my tears, my mother asked if I would like to invite Jesus into my life.

I said that I would. Slipping to my knees in front of hers, I followed her words as she led me in prayer . . . admission of sin, repentance, acknowledgment of the sacrifice of the Savior, the invitation for Him to enter my life, followed by heartfelt thanks.

For me, the question of eternity was settled, once and for all. It's a stark picture still burned on the hard drive of my soul, my mother, Grace, leading her young son to the throne of God's relentless, amazing grace.

The burden was mercifully lifted from my small shoulders.

ALMOST THE END OF OUR JOURNEY TOGETHER[3]

"So if the Son sets you free, you are truly free." (John 8:36 NLT)

Over the past chapters, you and I have been on a journey, not unlike Christian's trek in *Pilgrim's Progress*. We've surveyed forty alluring lies we might be tempted to believe. But you wouldn't be surprised to learn that Satan doesn't stop at forty deceptions. He has thousands of them. And like a seasoned angler, he opens his tackle box and selects the lure he knows is most likely to attract his intended prey—the one you and I are least likely to consider harmful. He doesn't care which one we believe, as long as we don't believe the truth.

As you've read this book, have you recognized any specific area(s) where you have listened to, believed, and acted on lies?

Have you embraced the sobering reality that believing these lies puts you and me in prison, needlessly shackling our lives?

> **The truth has the power to overcome every lie.**

If so, there may be one or more areas of spiritual bondage in your life—areas where you are not walking in freedom before God. These may be major, deeply rooted issues, or they may be matters that seem relatively insignificant. They may be areas where you have been defeated and struggled for freedom for years. Or they may be issues you are just now recognizing for the first time.

The Truth has the power to overcome every lie. That is what the Enemy doesn't want us to realize. As long as you and I believe his lies, he can keep us in spiritual bondage. But once we know the truth and start believing and acting on it, the prison doors will swing open and we will be set free.

This is right . . . the Truth has the power to set us free and to protect our minds and hearts from deceptive thoughts and feelings. There are moments when I feel besieged with thoughts I know are not of God—angry, irrational, fearful, controlling, selfish, or resentful thoughts. This happens to you, too, doesn't it? That's when we need to run to the truth for safety.

> He will cover you with his pinions,
>> and under his wings you will find refuge;
>>> his faithfulness is a shield and buckler. (Ps. 91:4)

The Truth has the power to sanctify and to make us holy—to purify our minds, our hearts, and our spirits. Just before He went to the cross, Jesus reminded His disciples about the cleansing power of His Word (John 15:3). Two chapters later, He prayed to His Father, "Sanctify them in the truth; your word is truth" (John 17:17).

CHOOSING THE PATHWAY OF TRUTH

When the Enemy bombards me with lies, I often think of one of Nancy's favorite expressions, as she encourages people to "counsel your heart according to the truth."

This means to speak truth to myself, and then to act on the truth, regardless of what my human reason or my feelings may be telling me.

> *This means to speak truth to myself, and then to act on the truth, regardless of what my human reason or my feelings may be telling me.*

"I'M CALLING YOUR NOTE"

On my forty-fourth birthday, I received the phone call every self-employed entrepreneur hopes to never receive, but knows he could.

The person on the other end of the call was (and still is) one of my closest buddies. He was the CEO of the company with whom I had an exclusive distribution arrangement. Because he held my inventory and receivables, I had no ability to borrow working capital, so by contract, I had borrowed money from his company.

But the note was a demand note with no requirement of terms or reason. "I'm a man under authority," he began. I braced myself. This would not be good news. "I have no choice but to tell you what I must tell you." He paused. The clicking noise he couldn't hear was my seatbelt.

"My superiors have given me no choice. I'm calling your note."

Emotions welled up inside that I had never felt before. Not like this. My friend had pulled the plug on my business. In this moment, I knew I would need to report the news to my business partner and that our staff would be sent immediately to the unemployment office. Because every bit of my own personal net worth had been leveraged in this enterprise, I would be completely broke.

If you can envision this, I literally crawled under my desk and wept like a little boy.

Over the next hours, Satan whispered in my ear.

- You're a fool, a worthless idiot. You leveraged everything you had and now look at you.
- You had no business starting this business.
- Your wife will read you the riot act. This was her equity, too.
- You're a fool, a worthless idiot. You leveraged everything you had and now look at you.
- You'll need to leave this industry. Staying will be a huge embarrassment.
- You're a terrible businessman and a worse leader.
- You'll never be able to start over.

- You're a fool, a worthless idiot. You leveraged everything you had and now look at you.

These were the most challenging of Satan's lies. They were a strange mix of reality and fantasy. Yes, I had leveraged everything—and then some. There was no escaping it. But what about the ominous and repeated refrain that I was a fool, a worthless idiot?

That part was the lie. True, I was a fallible and sinful man. A sometimes gullible believer of large promises. But I was a child of God. It was His decision to love me and die for me. It was His righteousness that covered me like a warm blanket on a cold night, rendering me righteous. And in His righteousness, worthy.

Now I had a choice. Would I continue to believe the lies, or would I embrace the truth? My emotions wanted to hold on to the offense. I wanted to nurse the grudge; I wanted to stay angry; I wanted somehow to hurt the people who had hurt me. But in my heart I knew that choice would lead to spiritual bondage.

So, armed with God's grace and with the remarkable support of my wife and children, I shunned the lies Satan had whispered. I embraced the truth and my freedom. Forgave my friends. And started over.

THE GOSPEL

Freedom from lies requires us to consider the gospel. Since the garden, sin has left an ugly mark on your heart and mine. Our natural, sinful tendency is to respond to hurt with anger and bitterness, and to deflect blame at all costs. But because of the gospel—the good news of Jesus—we are compelled to respond differently.

I couldn't drum up forgiveness or talk myself into a holy response to this hurt, but I could lift my eyes from my own "suffering" and toward the One who has "borne our griefs" and "carried our sorrows" (Isa. 53:4). I could surrender my emotions to the Father's will, because Jesus did the same. I could forgive the men who had made this decision forcing my business to close, because Christ forgave my offenses against Him. I

> In essence,
> I said to the Lord,
> "You win."

could lay down my desire to see the other person punished because Christ went to the cross to take on my punishment and extend grace toward me.

I knew I could not wait until I felt like forgiving—that I had to choose to obey God, and that my emotions would follow sooner or later. In essence, I said to the Lord, "You win." I yielded myself and the entire matter to the Lord and agreed, as an act of my will, to forgive the one who had hurt me. Hard as it was, I agreed to "let it go."

In the weeks that followed, my emotions gradually followed my will. The truth had countered the lies; my spirit was free.

THE TRANSFORMING POWER OF TRUTH

Freedom from spiritual bondage is the result of knowing, believing, and acting on the truth. And how can we know the truth? The truth is not merely an idea or a philosophy. The truth is a person—the Lord Jesus Christ. He said of Himself, "I am the way, and *the truth*, and the life" (John 14:6). Jesus did not point men to a religious system; He drew them to Himself. He spoke to those who claimed to be His followers:

> "If you abide in my word, you are truly my disciples, and you will know the truth, and the truth will set you free." (John 8:31–32)

> "So if the Son sets you free, you will be free indeed." (8:36)

> The cross stands
> as a monument
> to freedom
> throughout all
> of history.

Abandoning lies and walking in the Truth is not a formulaic, self-help process. We cannot simply change our minds, chant a few words, and find ourselves walking in freedom. Because of the pervasive and destructive nature of the Enemy's lies, we are all deeply broken by sin and desperately dependent on God and His Word to transform our thinking.

Christ went to the cross to set us free from the chains that sin has wrapped around every man's heart and life. The cross stands as a monument to freedom throughout all of history. Yes, it was painful; the cost of freedom always is, but Jesus hung on the cross so that we could be reconciled to our heavenly Father and declared truly free.

> For freedom Christ has set us free; stand firm therefore, and do not submit again to a yoke of slavery. (Gal. 5:1)

It may sound elementary at first, but it's a revolutionary thought that because Christ set us free, we can *live* free. He did the heavy lifting to raise the yoke of sin off our shoulders. Because of the cross, freedom really is possible!

You and I will have to admit that to truly walk in freedom does require effort on our part. Watch for these action verbs. We must *renew* our minds daily (Rom. 12:2) and *"fight* the good fight of the faith," by *"tak[ing] hold* of the eternal life to which [we] were called" (1 Tim. 6:12).

Even our effort is God-initiated, dependent on His power, energized by His Spirit and released in us by the power of the cross. Walking in freedom is not a matter of simply reshaping our will, but of choosing to depend on Christ and to respond to the work of the Holy Spirit in our lives.

HOW DO YOU SPELL BIBLE? T.I.M.E.

True freedom is only found in a vital, growing relationship with the Lord Jesus. He (the living Word of God) has revealed Himself in the Scripture (the written Word of God). If we want to know Him, if we want to know the Truth, we must devote ourselves to the reading, study, and meditation of His Word. There is no substitute and there are no shortcuts.

Because I have spent my adult

> *If we want to know Him, if we want to know the Truth, we must devote ourselves to the reading, study, and meditation of His Word.*

life as a lay Bible teacher and have written books taken from and about the Bible, I would have told you that I spent plenty of time in the Bible. It's true. I did.

Actually, my late wife, Bobbie, showed me a different way . . . although it took her death for me to really own this. We were both early risers and I'd go straight to my study at 4-ish.

I was a Bible *teacher*. My early morning hours were spent writing or researching. Sure, I'd begin my day with prayer on my knees, but then it was time to get to work—outlining lessons for Sunday school or crafting sentences and searching for the perfect verb for my books. Because Bobbie was a voracious student of the Bible, she went straight to her chair and her Bible during her pre-dawn time. The purpose of this time for her was purely for the joy of unpacking the truth of God's Word and cultivating a relationship with the Author of the Book. No other reason.

When Bobbie stepped into heaven in 2014, I put together a memorial program that I hoped would honor the Lord. The service was also a tribute to this remarkable woman. At the close of the funeral, we showed a video of Bobbie walking on the street in front of our home. I shot this video on my iPhone without her knowledge.

Bobbie was singing an old, favorite hymn.

Trust and obey,
For there's no other way
To be happy in Jesus,
But to trust and obey.[4]

We projected this video on the large screens mounted at the front of the sanctuary. At the end, this verse appeared in white letters on a black background.

"Unless a grain of wheat falls into the earth and dies, it remains alone; but if it dies, it bears much fruit." (John 12:24)

In the days that followed, I believe the Lord spoke to me. Not in an audible voice, but as clearly as if He had. Early one morning, I was sitting in Bobbie's red chair. I took out her *One-Year Bible* and looked up the reading on the current date. As I read the text along with Bobbie's marginal notes, the Holy Spirit nudged me. Again, not with a voice I could hear, but so clearly:

> *It's time you pick up Bobbie's mantle, Robert. You've watched her read her Bible faithfully for many years. Not as preparation for teaching or writing or anything else. Just because she wanted to. Now it's time for this "seed" to be planted in your heart. And this seed needs to produce many "seeds."*

Okay, Lord, I'm in, I silently responded.

So now, even though I still do some teaching and still write books that stand on God's Word, since Bobbie's death I have started each day by spending an hour or so in Scripture reading and prayer. The difference this has made in my learning to walk in the truth has been remarkable. Measurable.

I truly regret taking so long to "get it." But instead of groveling in that regret, I have loved this new experience of beginning each day soaking in the truth of God's Word.

And why is this a good thing? I'm glad you asked.

The Enemy is constantly confronting us with his lies. In order to combat his deception, our minds and hearts must be filled with the Lord Jesus and saturated with His Word.

> *In order to combat his deception, our minds and hearts must be filled with the Lord Jesus and saturated with His Word.*

THE WHITE FLAG IS OUT

But it's not enough to know the truth. You and I must also surrender to the truth. That means we must be willing to change our thinking or our lifestyle in any areas where they do not square with the Word of God. You and I know that millions of professing Christians are being misled; they are walking in ways that simply are not sound. Their values, their responses, their relationships, their choices, and their priorities reveal that they have bought into the lie of the Enemy and embraced the world's way of thinking.

We cannot assume a particular viewpoint is true just because everyone else thinks that way—or because it is what we have always believed, or because a well-known Christian author promotes that position, or because a well-meaning friend or counselor says it is right. Everything we believe and everything we do must be evaluated in the light of God's Word. This is our only absolute authority.

Living according to truth requires a conscious choice to reject deception and to embrace the truth. That's why the psalmist prayed, "Remove from me the way of lying. . . . I have chosen the way of truth" (Ps. 119:29–30 NKJV).

Every time you and I open the Scripture or hear the Word taught, it ought to be with the prayer that God will open our eyes to see any areas where we have been deceived and with a heart attitude that says, "Lord, Your Word is truth; I will submit to whatever You say. I reject Satan's lies. Whether I like it or not, whether I feel like it or not, whether I think I agree with it or not, whether it makes sense or not, I choose to place my life under the authority of Your Word—I will obey."

AND I WILL SURRENDER

Once we know the truth and are walking according to the truth that we know, God wants to make us instruments to draw others to the truth.

> So that we may no longer be children, tossed to and fro by the waves and carried about by every wind of doctrine, by human cunning, by craftiness in deceitful schemes. Rather, speaking the truth in love, we are to grow up in every way into him who is the head, into Christ. . . .
>
> Therefore, having put away falsehood, let each one of you speak the truth with his neighbor, for we are members one of another. (Eph. 4:14–15, 25)

The burden that gave birth to this book was the same as the burden that drew my wife, Nancy, to write *Lies Women Believe* many years ago. But my longing was to see men, not just women, set free through the truth. That vision is expressed in the last verses of the book of James.

> If anyone among you wanders from the truth and someone brings him back, let him know that whoever brings back a sinner from his wandering will save his soul from death and will cover a multitude of sins. (James 5:19–20)

The idea of "bring[ing] back a sinner from his wandering" is largely foreign in our day. The mantra of our postmodern culture is "tolerance," which means: "You can live however you want to live and I will not stand in your way. And don't try to tell me what's right for me—it's none of your business how I choose to live my life."

As deception has inundated our culture, many believers have become hesitant to stand for the truth, for fear of being labeled as intolerant or narrow-minded.

Many Christians display a live-and-let-live attitude, not only toward the world but also in relation to other believers who are not walking in the truth. They don't want to "rock the boat" or to be considered judgmental. It just seems easier to let things go.

> *We must remember that in Christ and in His Word, we have the truth that sets people free.*

We must remember that in Christ and in His Word, we have the truth that sets people free. That is good news! And it's essential news. There is no other way for us or for those we know and love to be delivered from darkness, deception, and death.

You and I must learn the truth, believe it, surrender to it, and live it out—even when it flies in the face of contemporary thinking or culture. Then we must be willing to declare the truth with boldness, conviction, and compassion.

PILGRIM'S PROGRESS . . . A REPRISE

Go back with me for a moment to those pajama-clad kids sitting on the bed with their mother, Grace, as she read from *Pilgrim's Progress*, and hear John Bunyan's description of unloading the burden Christian was carrying. That load I couldn't bear to hear about. As it did in 1952, this still takes my breath away.

> *Now I saw in my dream the highway up which Christian was to go. It was fenced on either side with a Wall and that Wall is called Salvation. Burdened Christian ran this way, but not without great difficulty, because of the load on his back.*
>
> *He ran until he came to a place somewhat ascending and upon that place stood a Cross, and a little below in the bottom, a Sepulchre. I saw in my Dream that just as Christian came up to the Cross, his Burden loosed from his shoulders, and fell off from his back. It began to tumble and continued to tumble until it came to the mouth of the Sepulchre, where it fell in, and I saw it no more.* [5]

This is exactly what "being set free" looks like. When we read about the life of King David in the Old Testament and spend time in the psalms he composed, it's clear that he knew a thing or two about the bondage of sin and the pure joy of being set free.

As far as the east is from the west, so far does he remove our transgressions from us. (Ps. 103:12)

So this is truth. Truth that sets you and me truly free.

We drag our burdens to the cross of Jesus Christ. We may do this reluctantly or enthusiastically. Either way, we bring our stuff to the Savior. And when we do, He takes it. He forgives it. And it's gone.

This is a good reason for some serious celebration, don't you think?

CHAPTER ELEVEN

THE TRUTH THAT SETS US
FREE

Over the years I have had the privilege of teaching God's Word in church. Most of this has been in the context of adult Sunday school classes. At last count, there were about 650 lessons logged. What I love about teaching is looking into the faces of those present and getting immediate feedback. *That makes no sense at all*, they may be saying without actually speaking. So when I see that face, I can step back and take another run at what I just said, trying to say it more clearly.

Then of course every teacher loves the smiles that say *Bingo! I needed that*. My wife, Nancy, calls these *"yes* faces."

A SWEET CONVERSATION,
NOT A BLIND MONOLOGUE

Writing a book is different than speaking to a live group. It's like speaking to a class all right, but this time each person has a brown grocery bag over his or her head with little holes cut out for their eyes.

As I'm writing, I have no idea whether what I've said is making any sense, whether people are hanging on every word, or trying to fight a short night of sleep. Dozing off.

This can make book writing a disconcerting experience.

Many years ago, the late Dr. Tim LaHaye, the author of myriad books, gave me a clue as to how to effectively communicate this way. "A book is a really long letter to one person," he said . . . me sitting at my laptop, you with your e-reader or turning old-fashioned paper pages.

So my sincere hope is that this book has been just that. A quiet, uninterrupted conversation. Maybe over a cup of coffee at your favorite hangout.

The other challenging part of being an author is that I'm chiseling my thoughts and, in some cases, my life into stone. The false assumption could be made that I'm writing as someone who has arrived and has all this down. In truth, though, I'm a sinner. A man who needs instruction and help . . . and a good friend. Maybe you and I have this in common?

So, in this final chapter, I'd love to quickly walk back through the truths we have unpacked together. We've been reminded of the awful lies that plague us. Now we're going to change the focus to the last sentence in each of the short lies chapters.

Doing this reminds me of my mother's favorite admonition to my siblings and me when we needed it. Which was many times.

> Whatever is true, whatever is honorable, whatever is just, whatever is pure, whatever is lovely, whatever is commendable, if there is any excellence, if there is anything worthy of praise, think about these things. (Phil. 4:8)

So, although you're surely tempted to treat this book as finished since you've come this far, I encourage to you take one more look at the truths we've talked about—truths that set (and keep) us free.

Now, here's our walk back through this book . . .

1 *God is holy. His brilliant "otherness" cannot be adequately described. Once I have fully embraced this, nothing is ever the same.* (Pss. 29:2; 99:5)

You could be thinking, "That's nice, Robert. But how 'bout some news I can use?" Sort of like your car breaking down on the freeway, calling AAA, and having them send you a preacher instead of a mechanic. But this truth is fundamental to everything else.

It's like the keel on the bottom of your sailboat. The concrete in your foundation. Without this truth, we are our own god . . . and that's not a pretty sight.

2 *Nothing is too grand or too insignificant for God's care. He made me and is involved in every detail of my life, large and small.* (Pss. 37:23–24; 139:2–3)

Can you imagine fathering a child, standing by your wife's bedside while she delivers, bringing the squirming baby home, and then ignoring it? "You take it from here, kid."

I can't either.

God is love. And just as you and I are eager to be involved in the lives of our offspring, our heavenly Father loves us. He walks with us. He hears our prayers and the longing of our hearts; He cares about the things that concern us.

3 *I cannot earn God's acclamation. I can only receive His favor.* (Eph. 1:4–6; 2:8–9; Titus 3:5)

My spiritual heritage is something for which I am deeply grateful. Nothing I did or could have done would be enough to earn me the benefit of spiritual faithfulness that characterized my parents and their parents and extended family.

But like wayward thistle seeds planted in a vegetable garden, I none-theless grew up believing a lie. It was this: "God's love for me has a con-tingency. I must be a good boy to earn it."

The Old Testament prophet Isaiah understood this well. And so he gave us an unforgettable word picture to describe the street value of our good deeds. He likened our pristine lives—our "righteous deeds"—to filthy rags (Isa. 64:6).

Jesus is the only man who has ever lived a truly righteous life. Though He only ever honored and obeyed His Father, God meted out to His beloved Son the judgment we deserved for our sins. Through faith in Christ, we can receive His righteousness and become beloved children of God, accepted through what Jesus has done for us.

4 *Jesus Christ is the only way to God.*
(John 14:6; Acts 4:12; 1 Tim. 2:5–6)

Living as we do in a pluralistic culture, holding to this truth may not win you points with lost people. But it's what Jesus said, so you're welcome to give Him credit.

And when you do this, love the lost people you're telling about it. They will more warmly welcome this truth if your heart is filled with compassion and not judgment.

5 *For the believer, church is not an option. It's standard equipment.* (Ps. 133; Eph. 2:19–22; 4:15–16; Heb. 10:24–25)

The older I get, the greater the temptation is to skip church.

Actually, it was easier to make Sunday morning worship a standing obligation when my children were living at home. After all, I was the dad and had an example to set. If my kids' dad was a church-slouch, they'd have every reason to be the same.

Now I don't have that same responsibility. I'm no longer setting the standard for my posterity. Nancy and I are empty-nesters and, well,

Sunday mornings sometimes feel like a good time to rest and read and do what I want to do.

And then when I push away these reckless thoughts and head to our church, I am always glad I did. Always. Where else can we sit quietly, or sing lustily, or pray in community, or open our Bibles with the inspiration of our pastor's preaching in the presence of so many people who are opening their Bibles and listening, too?

And then, after the service, we have a chance to connect with the people. And encourage them. And often pray with them. Even though I don't actually discuss my early morning prodigal thoughts about playing hooky, I am wondering to myself, *What was I thinking? Forgive me, Lord, for being such a bum.* We are a family in Christ, being built up together into a dwelling place for the Spirit of God. We cannot survive, thrive, or glorify God as He intends us to do, without staying connected to Him and to each other.

6   *Regardless of what kind of upbringing I may have had, what things that have been done to me, or the difficult or dysfunctional circumstances I may find myself in, I am responsible for my own actions.*
(1 Cor. 13:11; Gal. 6:7–8)

Our circumstances, background, nature, and nurture certainly impact us, but they don't need to have control over us.

We are accountable for our choices, our behavior, and our actions. But by God's grace, our past, our natural and wayward bents can be overcome. In spite of the magnetic draw of our family of origin or the haunting voices of our personal history, you and I can act in a way that pleases our heavenly Father. We really can.

7 *"He is no fool who gives what he cannot keep to gain that which he cannot lose." —Jim Elliot, martyred in cold blood on the mission field at age 29* (Matt. 16:25; John 15:13; Eph. 5:2)

In this age of gathering and hoarding things we don't need, this truth flies in the face of conventional wisdom like few others.

On January 8, 1956, the news broke that five American missionaries had been murdered in Ecuador, South America. The news quickly made its way around the world. I can still see my mother sitting at the kitchen table weeping. A tragic loss of human life? Maybe. Maybe not.

Not long ago, I held the very spear that murdered Jim Elliot. And standing in the home of Jim Elliot's widow, I was struck in a new and graphic way by the power of this story.

Jim Elliot did not lose his life that day; he gained eternity with Christ. His death was not the end, it was the beginning of a work of God in that remote village, many coming to know and trust Christ as their Savior because of the faithful witness of his young widow, Elisabeth, and his fatherless daughter, Valerie, who overlooked the danger and returned to South America.

 8 *The Master is the master of my destiny. Daily submitting myself to Him will bring me joy, purpose, and true riches.* (Pss. 37:5; 40:8; 1 Peter 5:6)

This truth may freak some men out. Like a three-year-old arguing with his mother, these self-starting, self-made, strong-willed men hear themselves saying over and over again, "Me do it."

Other men will find comfort in knowing that, at the end of the day, they are safe.

I choose door number two.

9 *Real men are free to feel and express deep emotions. When I do so, it's actually proof that I am a real man with a heart like God's.* (Ps. 42:3; Eccl. 3:4; Rom. 12:15)

Our emotions can be the window to our soul. We are free to express these emotions as a reflection of God's heart. Our family members and close friends need to see this. We can laugh boisterously. We don't need to hide our tears. These are a gift to us and to those we love.

10 *I need godly, male friends—faithful brothers who love me enough to speak truth. Men whose lives are also open to me so I can speak truth to them.* (Prov. 13:20; 18:24; 27:6, 17; 1 Thess. 5:11)

Men need not just casual buddies, but faithful friends—men who stick closer than a brother. Male friends can relate uniquely to the weaknesses and patterns of rationalization of other men, so they are able, in love, to speak truth. Even hard truth.

A man without these kinds of men in his life is a dangerous man.

11 *God's grace is needed for both the phony everyone sees and the scoundrel inside I know so well.* (Ps. 51:10; Matt. 7:21–23; Rom. 3:23–24; James 4:6)

Can you picture a kid who gets the wind knocked out of him in gym class? Everyone gathers around. The gym teacher steps into the crowd with these orders. "C'mon boys, give him air." Silly, right? But what a strong metaphor for you and me when we're winded from sin or grounded by the pressures of life.

Our loving Father wants direct access to us, lying there on the ground. He sees it all. And He loves us. Exposing your real self to God—giving it air—is a really good idea.

12 *God cares about His rules. I must do the same, for my own good.* (John 14:15, 23; 1 John 5:2–3)

God treats His rules consistently with His perfection. God determines His law. He determines how important it is. He will judge what and who He will judge. And we are not free to stand in judgment over Him. You and I have no right to suggest He is too picky, or that He treats as important what is unimportant.

God's rules are there for our good. He made us. He knows best. The operator's manual for my car was written by the company that made it. They should know. So it is with God's laws.

13 *I cannot look at other, more wicked men to make me feel better. The only comparison that matters is to look at the one righteous Man, the sinless Savior, who alone can make me whole.* (Rom. 14:4; James 4:12)

Like the pace car in a race, you and I must look to Jesus as the One we measure ourselves against. Looking side to side at the others in the race isn't good enough. Even though we may think we're a "nose" ahead of them, that doesn't matter. Jesus said to His disciples, "Follow Me." That's all He requires.

14 *Nothing I have done puts me out of reach of God's complete forgiveness.* (Acts 3:19; Eph. 1:7; 1 John 1:7–9)

Can you imagine this kind of freedom? Nothing you and I have ever done or ever will do is too far from God's healing grace.

Have you ever driven on the German autobahn? No speed limits. No radar guns. No sirens or flashing lights. Crank 'er up and let 'er fly. How does this sound? Pretty cool, right? (As long as you're not driving a 1972 Ford Pinto.)

15 *My secret sins cannot be hidden indefinitely.*
They will one day be brought into the light. I live
in community . . . my marriage, my children, my
neighborhood, my church, my workplace. What I do—
good and not so good—impacts those around me.
(Num. 14:18; Prov. 28:13; Luke 8:17)

Sooner or later, those habits, activities, foolish or sinful choices that you and I think no one knows about will come to light—if not in this life, then in the final judgment.

Unless we live alone in a remote cabin in the deepest woods, everything we do has an impact on others. Achan learned this the hard way. His sin cost him his own life and those of his family. Even his animals had to die.

Is this serious? Yes. Severe? It sure is. What's the lesson? We know, don't we?

16 *Living a holy life, in dependence on the power of the*
Holy Spirit, is a wonderful thing . . . it's my pathway
to happiness and pure joy.
(2 Cor. 7:1; 2 Tim. 1:9; 1 Peter 1:13–16)

Just the notion of holy living—holiness—could sound boring, restrictive, cloistering. It's not. It's actually first-row-of-the-roller-coaster wonderful.

This may be a hard one to sell in a contemporary culture that celebrates standard-free conduct and immediate pleasure. But because God has placed in our minds a conscience and the "gift" of sleepless nights when we get off track, holiness can be a wonderful thing.

17 *Pornography is deadly. As a married man, it's virtual adultery. Intimacy with Christ and shared sexual expression in the context of monogamous marriage offer far greater satisfaction.*
(Ps. 119:37; Matt. 5:28; 1 John 2:16)

Because of the proliferation of the internet, no man can avoid the temptation of pornography. But because of the power of God's Holy Spirit, every man who willingly submits to that power can say "no, thanks."

This discipline will be a man's gift to himself, his wife, and his family.

18 *An honest, open, and transparent relationship with my wife will be sweet . . . worth whatever it takes to get there.* (Col. 3:12–14; James 5:16)

The only thing more painful than full disclosure in your marriage is holding it inside and letting it eat away at your heart and your relationship with your wife.

Sit down with her and unpack what's on your heart. Assure her that you have taken this up with the Lord. You've repented and He has granted forgiveness. And now you'd like to tell her about it and you're willing to deal with the consequences, whatever they may be.

At this moment, you will be free. Your gut will assure you this is true.

19 *God's created order for men, women, and human sexuality is right and good. When we accept His way, repent of going our own way, and rest in Christ, we find forgiveness and the power to live in accord with His plan.* (Eph. 5:1–9; 1 Cor. 6:9–11, 18–20; 1 Thess. 4:3–7; Heb. 13:4)

If you or someone you love is caught up in the net of any kind of sexual sin or disordered affections, there is hope. We will not be cleansed by denying or justifying our sin but by confessing our sin and turning from it.

20 *Because I love my wife, her sexual fulfillment should be more important to me than my own. And when it's really good for her, it will be really good for me.*
(Prov. 5:15–19; 1 Cor. 7:3–4)

It's the whole principle of giving and receiving, isn't it? If the answer to, "Was that as good for you as it was for me?" isn't "yes," then you have some work to do.

Patience. Tenderness. Patience. Tenderness.

And make sure that your intimate time is undistracted and not hurried. Make it as special as you can. Every time. This will bring you a great deal of satisfaction.

21 *In addition to doing good things for my wife, she needs to hear me say kind things . . . including those three magic words: "I love you."*
(Prov. 25:11; Eph. 4:29; Col. 3:19)

It's true. And if you really want to fill her heart, add her name to the end of the sentence . . . or use your favorite nickname. Mine are darling, sweetheart, and precious girl.

I know, for some men, this stuff feels cheesy. And maybe your wife will agree. But my bets are in favor of using them.

22 *God alone can give me ultimate happiness and fulfillment. As I seek Him, I will find the truest joy.*
(Pss. 16:11; 40:16; 119:2; Matt. 6:33)

If you're not a happy (satisfied, purpose-filled, complete in Christ) man, marriage will not make you a happy (satisfied, purpose-filled, complete in Christ) man. If you are a happy (satisfied, purpose-filled, complete in Christ) man and you find a woman who is a happy (satisfied, purpose-filled, complete in Christ) woman, you will have a good marriage.

It's as simple—or complicated—as this.

23 *God has called me to provide godly leadership for my family. I don't have what it takes to do that perfectly; but when I ask Him, He will give me all I need to do it well.* (Jer. 33:3; 1 Cor. 11:3; James 1:5)

We don't have any other truth like this one . . . because the lie it's connected to really isn't a lie. It's true. We don't have what it takes to be the CEO of our family. But there's an important P.S. to this lie. God gives us the wisdom and strength to lead at home.[1]

Here's an analogy. You and I don't need to have a zillion phone numbers memorized. We just know how to access them on our smartphones. We don't have the skill to lead, but the Holy Spirit does. Ask Him. He's on speed dial!

24 *God calls me to become a man who loves, serves, protects, and provides for myself and for my family, by His grace and for His glory.*
(Luke 2:52; 1 Cor. 16:13; 1 Tim. 5:8)

I would never use an expression that included the phrase, "big-boy pants," but if I did, this is where I'd put it.

So, if you'd be open to a strong and encouraging admonition from a friend and you're one of the millions of grown men still living at home with no legitimate reason or if playing video games is taking more of your time than it should . . . please get a grip. It's time to grow up.

25 *I must discipline, encourage, and instruct my children, but only God can direct or change their hearts. So that's what I pray for.*
(Deut. 6:7–8; Prov. 22:6; 29:17; Eph. 6:4)

The battery in your car provides a good metaphor for this. If you disconnect either one of the cables, it will not work. Even if it's brand new and fully charged. As a dad, be lovingly strict . . . and unceasingly kind.

The Bible has lots to say about parents disciplining their children. It also has much to say about unconditional love. Your children have a will of their own, but providing discipline and love in a Christ-centered, Word-based, grace-filled manner will create an environment that is conducive to them choosing Christ.

And then pray like crazy . . . pray as though their lives depend on it. Because they do.

26 *If Jesus is all I want, He will be all I really need. If I were to trade everything I own for Him, this would be a wise exchange.*
(Ps. 16:5–9; Rom. 8:31–32; Col. 2:9–10)

A close acquaintance, an eminently successful attorney, and a man whose driveway includes a brand-new Mercedes every year once said to me, "Money is way overrated." He should know. There are plenty of folks out there with lots of cash on hand whose hearts are impoverished, and lots of folks who live "paycheck to paycheck" whose souls are wealthy beyond measure.

Your true happiness has nothing to do with your balance sheet.

27 *If I belong to God, all my hours, including those where I have nothing planned, belong to Him.* (Ps. 90:12; Eph. 5:15–17)

For many years, people wore little elastic wristbands with the letters WWJD printed on them. "What would Jesus do?" Now, as it relates to the way we actually spend our time—our "spare" time—my question would be, "What Did Jesus Do?" How did He spend his 168 hours?

As we read the Gospels, we see that Jesus was intentional about His time. He worked, He healed, He taught, He traveled . . . and He rested. His life provides a model for how we should spend our time—fulfilling the will of our Father.

28 *It's my God-given job to serve my family as a provider. Through my example, I can show them that they have a heavenly Father who can be trusted to meet their needs.* (Pss. 107:9; 145:15–16; 1 Tim. 5:8)

You and I uniquely bear the ultimate responsibility under God to ensure that our family's needs are being met and for overseeing that realm. This includes not only their material needs but also discerning and caring for their spiritual needs.

29 *My faith and my work cannot be compartmentalized; I should faithfully serve God and others in everything I do.* (Col. 3:23–24; James 2:26)

Our work matters. And *how* we work matters as well. We cannot leave our faith at the shop door or office elevator. If we could walk away from our love for God, we may never have truly loved Him to begin with. Honesty, integrity, diligence—these are the marks our Master calls us to bring to our labors. They are the fruit of His work in us; they are His work through us.

Martin Luther said that a Christian shoemaker is not one who etches little crosses on shoes but one who makes excellent shoes and deals honestly with his customers. He understood that all of our work, if it is legitimate work, is important. Holy. Service to God. The plumber is as much a servant in God's economy as is a pastor.

30 *I can never not afford to be generous to others. This blesses them. And me.*
(Prov. 11:24–25; Luke 6:38; Acts 20:35; 1 Cor. 9:6–8)

Do you know how to get wealthy instantly? I'm serious. Ready?

Start acting like it. Don't show off about this, but be on a constant lookout for ways you can bless others with your help, your smile, kind words, and a generous tip. And if you really want to live in the lap of God's luxury, ask people, "How can I pray for you?" And then when they answer your question, do it. Pray for them. Right there . . . on the sidewalk, the parking lot, the rental car shuttle bus.

Bestselling author H. Jackson Browne says it this way: "Remember that the happiest people are not those getting more, but those who give more."[2]

31 *I have been forgiven much, so I must forgive much. This truth must color the way I respond when I've been wronged.* (Luke 7:47; Eph. 4:31–32; Col. 3:13)

God has never done less for us than what we are owed; rather, He "daily loads us with benefits" (Ps. 68:19 NKJV). His grace toward us is lavish. Jesus has paid in full the debt we owed for our sin, and we live every day under the downpour of His grace.

This calls for us to be grateful, not angry, resentful, or vengeful, and to extend grace and forgiveness to others.

32 *Pain and suffering are tools in God's wise, loving hands, doing His good work, helping me become more like His Son. And for that I need to give thanks.* (Rom. 5:3–4; 8:18; 2 Cor. 4:7–11; Heb. 2:10; 1 Peter 5:10)

Men are fixers, solution seekers. So when we're hurting, we often want to find a quick solution to eliminate the problem. But God may send the "poison" of pain, suffering, and hardships—chemo—to help us learn to trust Him, to learn patience.

The apostle Paul prayed fervently that God would remove what he called his "thorn in the flesh" (KJV). We don't know exactly what the "thorn" was, but we do know God told Paul that He would not remove that hardship because it helped Paul to remember his complete dependence on God.

33 *We live and serve in a world that is rigged against Jesus, and if I am with Him, it's rigged against me. But I have the confident hope that one day all that's wrong will be made right and that, in the meantime, He knows what He is doing and will sustain me in the battle.* (2 Chron. 20:6; Prov. 16:3–4; Isa. 46:8–11; 1 Peter 5:10)

The world is a battlefield, a place of war. Which reminds us who the world is rigged against. In truth, the world is in a desperate, relentless battle with . . . the Lord. The God of the universe.

Unlike Sisyphus in Greek mythology, the story of our lives isn't a rock that rolls to the bottom, a rock that must be pushed back to the top again. Our lives rest on the Rock of our Salvation. This Stone can never be moved. We need to lift up our heads. Because of Jesus, you and I have purpose. All is well, and all will be well.

34 *When the Holy Spirit lives in me, He will produce . . . self-control.* (Gal. 5:22–23; 2 Tim. 1:7; Titus 2:11–12)

Both Judas and Peter believed the lie that they could not control themselves in the moment. Because of his deep regret, Judas took his life. But because of his deep confession, Peter gave his life, eventually dying a martyr's crucifixion.

We will sometimes find ourselves in situations where we cannot—on our own—exercise self-control in the moment. But when we submit to the Savior's leadership, He does the controlling in us . . . for us . . . through us.

35 *I cannot run from the presence of God. I may try, but I will not succeed. My Father never loses sight of me. He will pursue me and woo me home.*
(Ps. 139:7–12; Prov. 15:3; Isa. 57:15)

You and I may decide to take a restless jag on a path we know is pure folly. But our Father knows where we are, where we think we're going, and how to draw us back home. One way or another.

36 *Children are a gift from the Lord; He wants to use them to spread the gospel in our messed-up world. When I embrace children as a gift, I partner with God in changing that world.* (Gen. 18:19; Ps. 127:3–5; 3 John 4)

As sinful men, we are clearly part of the problem with the world. But we, and our children, can be a part of the solution.

In Malachi, the prophet rebukes God's people because they did not honor their wives. "Did he not make them one, with a portion of the Spirit in their union? And what was the one God seeking? Godly offspring" (2:15). God is still seeking godly offspring. The willingness to embrace the gift of children is an opportunity to be blessed and to be a blessing to our world.

When I receive God's gifts to me with sincere wonder, gratitude, and humility, I am freed from the need to compare and compete. (Gal. 1:10; 2 Cor. 10:12)

There's no competition for your place in the will of God.

God's love and leadership in your life has your name on it. He does not compare you to anyone else. His affection for you is singular.

Once we embrace this truth, our propensity to measure our lives by the false standard of the successes of others mercifully subsides. Our hearts fill with gratitude for who we are before our Good Shepherd and what we have been given by His gracious hand.

 God sees every piece and part and ingredient of my life and declares, "Mine!" My wholehearted, joyful response should be, "I'm Yours!"
(Ps. 40:8; John 17:6, 10; Rom. 14:8)

In each of our roles and assignments, we are called to live with perfect symmetry. Integrity.

We are the same man in every situation. Our colleagues don't see a different man at the office or the shop than our fellow deacons see at church. Our children aren't asked to deal with a man who is gentle and tender with his dog and an overly sensitive and impatient boor with them. Our wives aren't asked to reconcile Giovanni Casanova in the bedroom with the Gladiator when he's under pressure.

39 *Following Jesus will never be easy or popular. My greatest goal is not to be cool or relevant, but to be a loyal follower of Christ, regardless of the cost.*
(Matt. 10:38–39; Phil. 1:20–21; Col. 3:1–4)

The gospel we believe and proclaim is incomprehensible, even repulsive and offensive—insects shrouded in chocolate—to those whose eyes have never been opened to see its beauty and truth.

At times, eagerly following Christ may land us in trouble. We could lose friends or find ourselves the brunt of cruel jokes. We may be hated or rejected for what we believe.

But our assignment is still to live out and share our faith as humble, undeserving, grateful recipients of His grace—and to lovingly point sinners to the Savior who loves them, praying that their hearts will be drawn to Him.

40 *Through His death and resurrection, Jesus conquered sin and the grave. My "end" will not be the end. And it will be wonderful.*
(Eph. 1:3; Phil. 3:20–21; 2 Peter 1:4; 1 John 3:2)

Because you have received the forgiveness Jesus provided through His death and resurrection, your "and after that" will be access into heaven.

So, yes . . . you and I will die. This is a certainty. But this will not be the end of your story or mine. And because we know Jesus, the next story will be a good one. He has promised that.

PRACTICE MAKES PERFECT . . . WELL, SORT OF

The old adage, "practice makes perfect," can be applied to many pursuits. Of course, absolute perfection isn't actually achievable. Not this side of heaven.

But as with everything important to us, hard work toward a cherished goal will never be a waste of time.

If you review this list of forty truths periodically, you'll be reminded of God's faithfulness in revealing them to you and you'll be encouraged to continue embracing the truth and allowing it to transform your life.

THAT CARD IN

THE SEATBACK POCKET

IN FRONT OF YOU

Over thirty years ago I flew on an L-1011. This airplane was one of the first "jumbo jets," with two aisles and three columns of seats, a plane that could hold four hundred passengers. I remember being overwhelmed by the experience of climbing aboard this behemoth and contemplating how it would actually get off the ground with all these people on board—including me.

In the seatback pocket in front of me was one of those folded laminated cards that tells about the safety features of the plane. On the back of the card was a paragraph with the heading, "About this Plane." It itemized the weight of the aircraft and the amount of sheet aluminum and number of rivets needed to build it. I read every word.

The opening sentence of that paragraph said: "If you're taking the time to read this, you're obviously a curious person. Most people would never take the time to read it."

The same could be said of you.

If you've read this far, you're clearly serious about this lies and truth thing.

So please know how grateful I am that you've gone the whole way to the finish line. It's been a privilege to share this journey with you.

A WORK IN PROGRESS

As I was writing this book—just in case you mistakenly think I live in an ivory tower—there were times when I found myself believing and being tempted by the very lies I was addressing.

"My wife is supposed to make me happy."

"I can afford to shortcut my time with the Lord this morning."

"Who will notice if I click on this salacious photograph on my laptop?"

"I'm acting this way because I've got so much on my plate."

"My worth comes from what I own."

> **The longer I walk with God, the more I am in awe of the power of the Truth!**

Thankfully, again and again, in hectic, hassled, or frustrating moments, God has directed my heart back to the Truth. As I read about the Truth, meditate on it, believe it, and surrender to it, the Spirit of God sets me free—my mind and emotions are stabilized and I am able to look at my circumstances from God's perspective. The longer I walk with God, the more I am in awe of the power of the Truth!

Of course, there are many more lies that we've not addressed. I encourage you to ask God to help you discern when you are tempted to believe things that are not true. Then search the Scriptures and solicit counsel from godly friends to discover the truth that counters and overcomes each lie.

In the days ahead, anytime you realize you are believing lies, go back and review the truths summarized in the last chapter. Continually renew your mind with God's Word and learn to counsel your heart according to the Truth (Ps. 86:11).

And don't forget that you're a work in progress. An unfinished masterpiece. God's work in you is real and it's not finished. But one day it will be.

I am sure of this, that he who began a good work in you will bring it to completion at the day of Jesus Christ. (Phil. 1:6)

This is the Truth. And it promises amazing freedom. It truly does.

This experience started out as a conversation between friends. Let's keep it going. I would love to hear from you. Let me know how the Truth is changing you and setting you free!

God bless you in this adventure.

Robert

www.robertwolgemuth.com

ACKNOWLEDGMENTS

Listing the folks to be thanked for their investment in this book without first expressing my gratitude to the Lord would be foolishness. So this is where I'll begin. When Jesus said, "I am . . . the truth" (John 14:6), He was giving you and me a new way of countering the lies we believe. The answer was . . . Himself. He is the Truth. Where would I be without His love and provision? His grace has been sweet and more than sufficient.

Second, I thank my wife, Nancy DeMoss Wolgemuth. Her love, affection, and encouragement during the relentless process of drafting a manuscript has been relentless. From her own experience, Nancy knows the price a writer pays to pound out the words in a way that makes sense and communicates clearly. On this front and every other I could name, Nancy is God's precious gift to me. She has been a sweet source of kindness and grace for the dark-o-thirty mornings set aside to get this done. She's also a wonderful source of cool verbs.

In 2001, Nancy wrote *Lies Women Believe: And the Truth That Sets Them Free*. The book has sold over a million copies and has become a classic worldwide. Almost every day, Nancy hears from women whose lives have been deeply impacted by this book. Then in 2008, along with her friend Dannah Gresh, Nancy published *Lies Young Women Believe*. Again, this book found its way into the life experience of hundreds of thousands of women—young women—and continues to make a profound impression on them.

The chance to write a companion volume to the "Lies" brand—this one for men—has been a singular privilege. Thank you to Nancy for letting me hitch a ride on this train. And thank you for your companionship, your brilliant content suggestions, and flawless edits throughout the process.

Oh yes, and thank you for authoring the gracious endorsement that appears on the back of this book.

A few months after *Lies Men Believe* was published, *Lies Girls Believe* (by Dannah Gresh) and a companion *Mom's Guide to Lies Girls Believe* (by Nancy and Dannah) will be released. (That's a lot of lies and, thankfully, a boatload of truth to counter them.)

Moody Publishers has been the home for all the "Lies" books. The partnership of these friends has been a gift. Thanks to Greg Thornton, Paul Santhouse, Randall Payleitner, Connor Sterchi, Ashley Torres, Carolyn McDaniel, Erik Peterson, and Richard Knox . . . and all the others on the Moody team.

Third, My children and grandchildren are a constant source of affirmation and cheering. Actually, Missy and Julie were high school cheerleaders, so they're good at this. I'm thankful for Jon and Missy Schrader, Christopher and Julie Tassy, (Mr. and Mrs.) Ben and Abby Schrader Quirin, Luke Schrader, Isaac Schrader, Harper Tassy, and Ella Tassy.

And speaking of family, Nancy's extended clan has been a wonderful source of kindness as they have welcomed me, their late-arriving son, brother, and uncle.

A year and a half before the manuscript for this book was buttoned up, Del Fehsenfeld, Dan Jarvis, Israel Wayne, and Dr. R. C. Sproul Jr. agreed to help with the coalescing of the list of possible "lies" to include. After a few weeks of bouncing emails back and forth, we met face to face for several hours and pounded out the possibilities. Their wisdom and input were incredibly valuable . . . as was their audible inspiration along the way.

In fact, R. C. stayed with it and loaned me his crisp, theological brain and words to match along the way. Thanks to R. C.

My siblings, and especially my brother Dan, who was a big help with Lie #11. Thanks to these brothers, sisters . . . friends.

Mike and Janet Sonnenberg have been a model of faithfulness and tenacity and patience in the face of untold suffering for many years. Their willingness to let me tell a bit of their story in Lie #32 is deeply appreciated.

Rosaria Butterfield and Christopher Yuan gave me wise counsel in relation to Lie #19. I'm so thankful for these faithful friends.

After over three decades of friendship and professional collaboration as his publisher and agent, I mustered the courage to ask Dr. Patrick Morley to write the foreword to this book. His powerful ministry to men around the world, Man in the Mirror, has changed the lives of millions of men and has been a model for tens of thousands of churches who have used Patrick's books and material in bringing men to faith in Christ and growing them in their Christian walk. Patrick's willingness to lend his name and trustworthy reputation to this book is a generous gift.

When it came time to design the cover, our dear friends Bob and Dannah Gresh stepped in along with the ever-amazing Erik Peterson at Moody. The layout of this book's jacket owes much of itself to their creativity. Thank you.

The men who added their good names to endorse this book are pretty special. And very kind: Jack Graham, Tim Challies, Bryan Loritts, George Grant, Paul Santhouse, and Bob Lepine.

Thanks to Nancy's *Revive Our Hearts* family and her ministry's parent, *Life Action Ministries*.

Since my precious kids and grands live many miles away, three families have adopted us as their own, providing us with lots of hugs from children big and small whom we love . . . Nate and Jessica Paulus and their three: Addie, Ellie, and Beckett; Aaron and Victoria Paulus and their five: Jonathan, Annalise, Eliya, Ian, and Karah; Del and Debra Fehsenfeld and their four: Shepard, Kária, Chálissa, and S l. My love and thanks to them.

And to my agents: Andrew Wolgemuth, Erik Wolgemuth, and Austin Wilson. I'm happy you guys know what you're doing.

Finally, and just as important as all the above, thanks to you for taking time to actually read this book. Your time is your most valuable asset and you've invested a bunch of it here. Color me thankful.

Notes

INTRODUCTION

1. Nancy DeMoss Wolgemuth, *Lies Women Believe: And the Truth That Sets Them Free* (Chicago: Moody, 2018), 38.
2. You can keep the dry-walling.

CHAPTER ONE: THE PROBLEM OF PRIDE

1. An updated, expanded version of *Lies Women Believe* was published in 2018.

CHAPTER TWO: LIES MEN BELIEVE ABOUT GOD

1. This saying has come down in many variations over the centuries.
2. Including the ones that wind up in our hair brush or on our shower floor every day.
3. C. S. Lewis, *Mere Christianity* (New York: HarperCollins, 1952), 55–56.
4. Part of God's punishment of Satan after the fall was that he would spend the rest of his existence—and that of all the serpents that would follow—crawling on his belly (Gen. 3:14). So his inaugural appearance may have been a pre-slithering-on-the-ground appearance.

CHAPTER THREE: LIES MEN BELIEVE ABOUT THEMSELVES

1. Darlington Omeh, "Top 10 Richest People of All Time in Human History," wealthresult.com, https://www.wealthresult.com/wealth/richest-people-history.
2. Adapted from Ann Spangler and Robert Wolgemuth, *Men of the Bible* (Grand Rapids: Zondervan, 2010), 160–62.

CHAPTER FOUR: LIES MEN BELIEVE ABOUT SIN

1. https://www.goodreads.com/quotes/407467-i-once-sent-a-dozen-of-my-friends-a-telegram.
2. Paul F. Pavao, "3rd Corinthians," *Christian History for Everyman*, https://www.christian-history.org/3rd-corinthians.html.

3. This Ananias was a different Ananias than the man who laid his hands on Paul, restoring the apostle's sight. Apparently, baby-boy-name books had far fewer entries than they do these days.

4. Bruce Larson, *Living on the Growing Edge* (Grand Rapids: Zondervan, 1969).

5. R. C. Sproul Jr., *Believing God: Twelve Biblical Promises Christians Struggle to Accept* (Lake Mary, FL: Reformation Trust, 2009), 13.

6. Portions of this story are excerpted and adapted from Robert Wolgemuth and Ann Spangler, *Men of the Bible* (Grand Rapids: Zondervan, 2002), 114–15.

7. Bill and Pam Farrel, *Men Are Like Waffles—Women Are Like Spaghetti* (Eugene, OR: Harvest House, 2007).

8. Nancy Leigh DeMoss, *A Revive Our Hearts Trilogy: Holiness: The Heart God Purifies* (Chicago: Moody, 2008), 280.

9. Ibid., 280–81.

10. Kevin DeYoung, *A Hole in Our Holiness* (Wheaton, IL: Crossway, 2014), 74.

CHAPTER FIVE: LIES MEN BELIEVE ABOUT SEXUALITY

1. Mélanie Berliet, "15 Married Men Who Cheated Reveal What It's Like to Have an Affair," *Thought Catalog*, July 8, 2015, https://thoughtcatalog.com/melanie-berliet/2015/07/15-married-men-who-cheated-reveal-what-its-like-to-have-an-affair/.

2. It's more than stereotypical to say that the drive for sex in men is generally stronger than in women. It's true. https://www.webmd.com/sex/features/sex-drive-how-do-men-women-compare#1.

3. Lauryn Chamberlain, "US Mobile Usage In 2017: Stats You Need To Know," GeoMarketing, February 16, 2017, http://www.geomarketing.com/us-mobile-usage-in-2017-stats-you-need-to-know.

4. Levi Lusko, *Swipe Right: The Life-and-Death Power of Sex and Romance* (Nashville: Thomas Nelson, 2017), 96.

5. Nancy R. Pearcey, *Love Thy Body: Answering Hard Questions about Life and Sexuality* (Grand Rapids: Baker, 2018), 11. Her source: "Leonardo Blair, "Nearly Two-Thirds of Christian Men Watch Pornography Monthly: They are Watching at the Same Rate as Secular Men, Says Study," *The Christian Post*, August 27, 2014.

6. If you don't struggle with pornography, it's almost certain that there is a friend in your life who does. This admonition may not be for you, but for this other guy.

7. Stephen Harding, "Take an Insane Plunge on the World's Tallest Roller Coaster in Virtual Reality," *USA Today*, November 10, 2016, https://www.usatoday.com/story/news/nation-now/2016/11/10/take-insane-plunge-worlds-tallest-roller-coaster-virtual-reality/93587402/.

8. I deal with this in greater detail in my book, *Like the Shepherd: Leading Your Marriage with Love and Grace*. Chapter 7 is called "A Shepherd Satisfies His Sheep." This will give you more information about how you can help make your wife's sexual experience as happy as yours.

9. John Piper, "Husband, Lift Up Your Eyes," Desiring God, July 10, 2017, https://www.desiringgod.org/articles/husband-lift-up-your-eyes.

10. Christopher Yuan, *Out of a Far Country: A Gay Son's Journey to God. A Broken Mother's Search for Hope* (Colorado Springs: Waterbrook, 2011), 188–89.

11. Rosaria Champagne Butterfield, *Openness Unhindered* (Pittsburgh, PA: Crown & Covenant Publications, 2015), 26–27.

12. Leon F. Seltzer, "The Triggers of Sexual Desire: Men vs. Women," *Psychology Today*, May 11, 2012, https://www.psychologytoday.com/us/blog/evolution-the-self/201205/the-triggers-sexual-desire-men-vs-women.

13. Robert Wolgemuth, *Like the Shepherd: Leading Your Marriage with Love and Grace* (Washington, D.C.: Regnery, 2017), 47–48.

CHAPTER SIX: LIES MEN BELIEVE ABOUT MARRIAGE AND FAMILY

1. Gary Thomas, *Sacred Marriage* (Grand Rapids: Zondervan, 2000), 236.

2. Gary Chapman, *The 5 Love Languages* (Chicago: Moody, 2015).

3. This admonition to be obedient to parents is repeated throughout Proverbs. See 2:1; 3:1; 4:1, 11, 20.

4. Karol Markowicz, "Why So Many Men Are Living with Their Parents," *New York Post*, May 30, 2016, https://nypost.com/2016/05/30/why-so-many-men-are-living-with-their-parents/. That same year, *Psychology Today* reported that, in the state of New Jersey, 45 percent of men between the ages of 18 and 34 now live with their parents (Hara Estroff Marano, "The 'Failure to Launch' Epidemic," *Psychology Today*, December 5, 2016, https://www.psychologytoday.com/us/blog/nation-wimps/201612/the-failure-launch-epidemic).

5. Robert Wolgemuth, *Prayers from a Dad's Heart* (Grand Rapids: Zondervan, 2003), 12–13.

CHAPTER SEVEN: LIES MEN BELIEVE ABOUT WORK AND WEALTH

1. New World Encyclopedia contributors, "John D. Rockefeller," *New World Encyclopedia*, last modified August 25, 2016, http://www.newworldencyclopedia.org/entry/John_D._Rockefeller.

2. Saint Augustine, *Confessions*, trans. Henry Chadwick (New York: Oxford University Press, 1991), 3.

3. http://stress.lovetoknow.com/time-management-chart.

4. "Paul Gauguin Biography," Biography.com, last updated April 27, 2017, https://www.biography.com/people/paul-gauguin-9307741#artist-in-exile.

5. "The New City Catechism," http://newcitycatechism.com/new-city-catechism/#1.

6. Special thanks to Dr. Alistair Begg for this insight from a private conversation.

7. Dictionary.com, s.v. "deadbeat dad," http://www.dictionary.com/browse/deadbeat-dad.

8. See Lie #23 for some helpful insights on how Proverbs gives us solid parenting direction.

9. C. S. Lewis, *The Weight of Glory* (San Francisco: HarperOne, 1976), 160.

10. https://www.goodreads.com/quotes/924405-the-christian-shoemaker-does-his-duty-not-by-putting-little.

11. Thanks to John MacArthur for this insight in a sermon titled, "The Theology of Work," https://www.gty.org/library/sermons-library/80-362/a-theology-of-work.

CHAPTER EIGHT: LIES MEN BELIEVE ABOUT CIRCUMSTANCES

1. "How Firm a Foundation," J. Rippon's *Selection of Hymns*, 1787, alt., Hymnary.org, https://hymnary.org/hymn/LUYH2013/427. Public domain.

2. Lauren Johnston, "Shopper Busted For Fake $1M Bill," CBS/AP, March 9, 2004, https://www.cbsnews.com/news/shopper-busted-for-fake-1m-bill/.

3. Mark Vroegop, *Dark Clouds, Deep Mercy: Discovering the Grace of Lament* (Wheaton, IL: Crossway, 2019).

4. No college co-ed would have been willing to live this kind of Spartan existence. Other, non-varsity athletes also lived in the Shacks in order to save money.

5. Maltbie D. Babcock, "This is My Father's World," 1901, alt., Timeless Truths, https://library.timelesstruths.org/music/This_Is_My_Fathers_World/.

6. Francis Thompson, "The Hound of Heaven," in D. H. S. Nicholson and A. H. E. Lee, eds., *The Oxford Book of English Mystical Verse* (Oxford: The Clarendon Press, 1917), 409–15.

CHAPTER NINE: LIES MEN BELIEVE ABOUT THE WORLD

1. Bill Bates, *Shoot for the Star* (self-pub., CreateSpace, 2011), 4–5; "Bill Bates," Wikipedia, last edited on May 18, 2018, https://en.wikipedia.org/wiki/Bill_Bates.
2. Bill Bates with Bill Butterworth, *Shoot for the Star* (Brentwood, TN: Wolgemuth & Hyatt, 1996).
3. Robert Wolgemuth, *She Calls Me Daddy* (Wheaton, IL: Tyndale, 1996), 27–29.
4. Ironically, these days some men treat dirty as good. The filthier, the better. This is especially true when we're talking about a truck that's just been off-roading. A mud ball on wheels.
5. https://www.goodreads.com/author/quotes/385896.Abraham_Kuyper.
6. "Luther on Music," http://www.eldrbarry.net/mous/saint/luthmusc.htm.
7. Miss Cellania, "The Final Days of John Wayne," Neatorama, http://www.neatorama.com/2014/03/05/The-Final-Days-of-John-Wayne/.

CHAPTER TEN: COUNTERING THE LIES WITH THE TRUTH

1. In 1955, twins were added to my family. Debbie and Dan missed this particular nighttime ritual.
2. John Bunyan, *The Pilgrim's Progress*, Legacy of Faith Library (Nashville: B&H Publishers, 2017), 151.
3. With the exception of personal illustrations, the essence of the rest of this chapter has been borrowed from chapter 10 of my wife Nancy's book, *Lies Women Believe* (Chicago: Moody, 2018), used with permission.
4. John H. Sammis, "Trust and Obey," 1887, public domain.
5. Bunyan, *The Pilgrim's Progress*, 187.

CHAPTER ELEVEN: THE TRUTH THAT SETS US FREE

1. If I may be a little presumptuous, let me commend to you my book, *Like the Shepherd: Leading Your Marriage with Love and Grace* (Washington, D.C.: Regnery, 2017). This book should help you in cultivating and exercising godly leadership at home.
2. H. Jackson Browne, *Life's Little Instruction Book* (Nashville, TN: Thomas Nelson, 2000), 54.

"If you'd like to
take this terrific book
and turn it into a study
experience for you
or a discussion
experience for you and
your friends, go to

LIESMENBELIEVE.COM/DISCUSSIONGUIDE

and get started. Trust me.
You will be very glad you did.
God bless you, my friend."

BILL ELLIFF

SENIOR TEACHING PASTOR, THE SUMMIT CHURCH,
LITTLE ROCK, ARKANSAS

For the Woman in Your Life.

Revive Our Hearts™

Through its various outreaches and the teaching ministry of
Nancy DeMoss Wolgemuth, *Revive Our Hearts* is calling women
around the world to freedom, fullness, and fruitfulness in Christ.

**Offering sound, biblical teaching and encouragement for
women through . . .**

Books & Resources Nancy's books, True Woman Books,
and a wide range of audio/video

Broadcasting Two daily, nationally syndicated broadcasts
(*Revive Our Hearts* and *Seeking Him*) reaching over one million
listeners a week

Events & Training True Woman Conferences and events
designed to equip women's ministry leaders and pastors' wives

Internet ReviveOurHearts.com, TrueWoman.com, and
LiesYoungWomenBelieve.com; daily blogs, and a large,
searchable collection of electronic resources for women
in every season of life

**Believing God for a grassroots movement of authentic revival and
biblical womanhood . . .**

Encouraging women to:

- Discover and embrace God's design and mission for their lives.
- Reflect the beauty and heart of Jesus Christ to their world.
- Intentionally pass on the baton of truth to the next generation.
- Pray earnestly for an outpouring of God's Spirit in their families,
  churches, nation, and world.

Visit us at **ReviveOurHearts.com.** We'd love to hear from you!

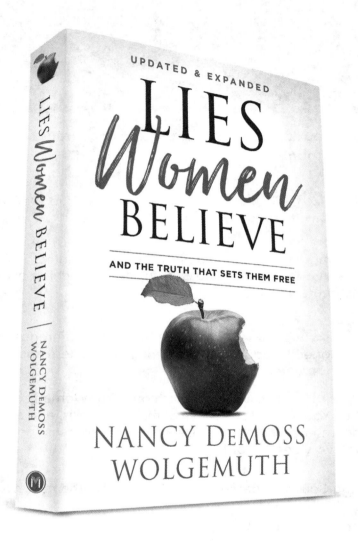

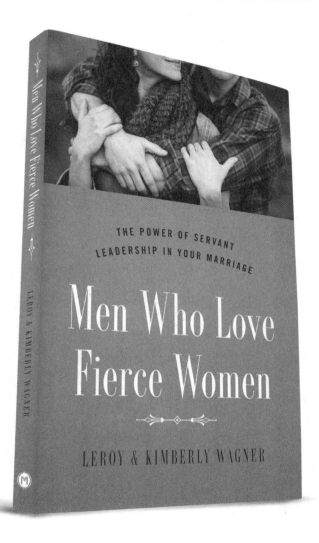